Nine Parts of Desire

NINE PARTS

GERALDINE BROOKS

ANCHOR BOOKS

A DIVISION OF
RANDOM HOUSE, INC.

New York

OF DESIRE

The
Hidden
World
of
Islamic
Women

FIRST ANCHOR BOOKS TRADE PAPERBACK EDITION, JANUARY 1996

Copyright © 1995 by Geraldine Brooks

The Library of Congress has cataloged the Anchor Books hardcover edition as
follows:

Brooks, Geraldine.
Nine parts of desire : the hidden world of Islamic women / Geraldine
Brooks. — 1st ed.
p.   cm.
Includes bibliographical references and index.
1. Muslim women.   2. Muslim women—Social conditions.   I. Title.
HQ1170.B76   1995
305.48'6971—dc20   94-17496   CIP

ISBN 0-385-47577-2

Book design by Susan Yuran
Map by Martie Holmer

www.anchorbooks.com

Printed in the United States of America

20 19 18 17 16 15 14

A NOTE ON SPELLING

Since there is no standard method of transliteration from Arabic to English, I have followed my own whim, which is to select, wherever possible, the simplest spelling of a word or name that conveys an approximation of its sound in Arabic. The exceptions are names of authors who publish in English translation, in which case I have followed their spelling preference, and for the name of the prophet Muhammad, which I have rendered in the spelling preferred by most Islamic sources.

To Gloria, who convinced her daughters
that they could do anything.
And to Tony, of course.

Contents

ACKNOWLEDGMENTS

I would like to thank Lee Lescaze, for his calm voice on the end of so many crackly phone lines; Paul Steiger, for tolerating a leave that lasted too long; Karen House, for having confidence that I could cover the Middle East long before I had; Mary Ellen Barker, John Fitzgerald and Elinor Lander Horwitz for their comments on the manuscript; Melissa Biggs for painstaking fact-checking; Michael Lewis for neighborly advice and inspiration; Deborah Amos, Christiane Amanpour, Nora Boustany, Jacki Lyden and Milton Viorst for good company in war zones; and David Chalfant, agent and champion, without whom this book would not be.

Finally, I would like to thank the many Muslim women who, across so many obstacles, made me welcome in their world.

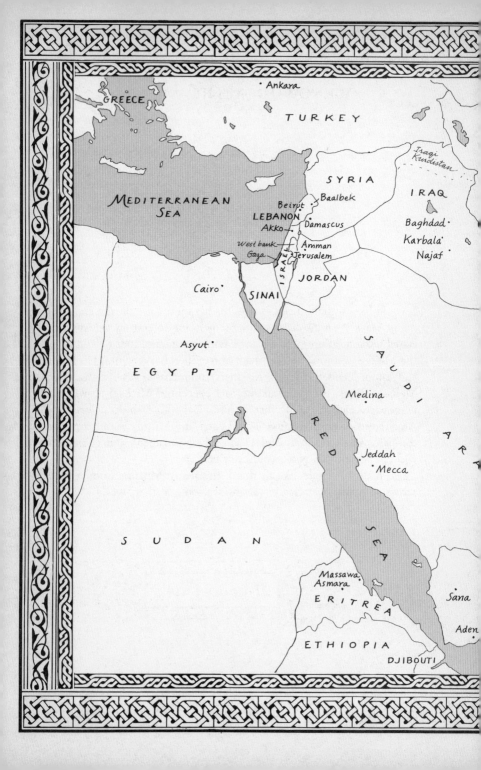

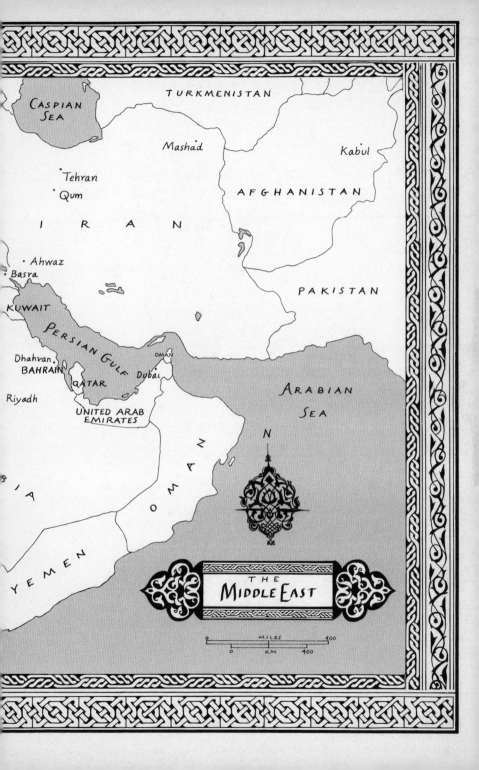

"Almighty God created sexual desire in ten parts;
then he gave nine parts to women and one to men."

—Ali ibn Abu Taleb, husband of Muhammad's
daughter Fatima and founder of the Shiite sect
of Islam

NINE PARTS OF DESIRE

PROLOGUE

"Say, I fly for refuge unto the
Lord of the daybreak, that he may
deliver me from the mischief of
those things which he hath
created."

THE KORAN
THE CHAPTER OF THE DAYBREAK

The hotel receptionist held my reservation card in his hand. "Mr. Geraldine Brooks," he read. "But you are a woman."

Yes, I agreed, that was so.

"I'm sorry, but our reservation clerk has made a mistake."

"That's okay," I said. "Just add an *s* and make it 'Mrs.' "

"No," he said. "You don't understand. I can't give you a room. It's against the law for women."

I glanced around the hotel's gleaming lobby. "What about them?" I said, nodding my head in the direction of two black-cloaked Saudis heading for the elevator.

"They are here with their husband," the receptionist explained. "In Saudi Arabia a lady does not travel alone. There is no reason for it. Unless she is a prostitute."

There was a time—a year, two years earlier—when I would have lost my temper. Now I just sighed and walked away from the desk. It was after 11 P.M. I knew no one in the city of Dhahran. I could take a taxi back to the airport and wait out the night on one of its plastic chairs. But at the hotel entrance there were no taxis. The plush sofas of the empty hotel lobby looked inviting enough. I made myself comfortable behind a potted plant and pulled my black chador out of my bag to use as a blanket. I was closing my eyes when the receptionist coughed behind me.

"You cannot stay here."

I quietly pointed out that I had nowhere else to go.

"Then," he said, "I have to call the police."

The Dhahran police station had the same hard benches and harsh lights as police stations everywhere. The only difference was that the plain-clothes detectives wore long white *thobes*. Whenever I'd been in police stations before, it had been to report on crime. This was my first visit as a criminal.

Behind a desk across the room a young police lieutenant shuffled my identity documents. I had press credentials from Australia, Britain, Egypt, Iran, Iraq, Jordan, the United States and Yemen. I had passes to Arab summit meetings and presidential palaces. I even had a plastic press badge issued by Saudi Arabia's own Information Ministry. The lieutenant peered at them all. First he lined them up vertically, then horizontally. Then he stacked them in a neat pile, as if to evaluate them by height.

Finally he looked up, letting his gaze rest on a patch of wall just above my head. Like most very strict Muslims, he didn't want to risk polluting himself by gazing at a strange woman. When he spoke, he addressed me in the third person. "I think the lady hasn't been in Saudi Arabia very long. She doesn't know our customs." He resumed his tedious perusal of my documents. Plucking one of my passes from the pile, he dangled it between his thumb and forefinger. "This one," he said with a tiny triumphant smile, "expired yesterday."

Sometime in the wee hours of the morning the lieutenant handed back my documents, adding a permit allowing me to spend the next few hours in a hotel. Back at the front desk, the receptionist summoned a bellman, a Filipino, to show me to my room. It was on a completely empty floor. An armed guard hovered by the elevator.

"They must think I'm dangerous," I muttered. The bellman didn't smile.

"They think all women are dangerous," he replied, dropping my bag just inside the door and retreating under the guard's watchful gaze.

I lay on the bed, staring at the decal glued to the mirror, showing Muslims the direction that they should face to pray. Nearly every hotel room I had stayed in during the past three years had had a similar arrow—stuck on the night table, pinned to a curtain, fixed to the ceiling. It was just a few minutes before dawn. I walked to the window and waited. As a pale disc of light crept up over a hazy blue horizon, the stillness shattered, as it did every dawn, and had done for the last thirteen hundred years.

"Come to prayer!" wailed the muezzins of the city's hundreds of mosques. "It is better to pray than sleep!" As the sun edged its way westward, a billion Muslims would do as the citizens of Dhahran were doing at that moment: rise from their beds and bow toward the town of Mecca, about seven hundred miles west of my hotel room.

The reason for my sleepless night lay in that desert town. I couldn't check myself into a Saudi hotel room in the 1990s because thirteen hundred years earlier a Meccan named Muhammad had trouble with his wives.

Islam's prophet loved women. He married his first wife when he was twenty-five years old. Illiterate, orphaned and poor, he hardly expected to receive a proposal from his boss, Khadija, a rich Meccan businesswoman at least ten years his senior who hired him as a manager for her international trading company. While it wasn't typical for women to propose to men in Meccan culture, Khadija was among those with the clout to do so. She gave him money, status and four daughters—his only children to survive infancy. The Ayatollah Ruhollah Khomeini, King Hussein of Jordan and the thousands of sheiks and mullahs who today wear the black turban that signifies descent from the prophet all trace their lineage to one of those daughters.

It was to Khadija that Muhammad crawled, trembling, the first time he heard the voice of the angel Gabriel pronouncing the word of God. Despairing for his sanity, Muhammad found himself repeating the first words of the Koran—which means simply "recitation." Then he made his way to his wife on his hands and knees and flung himself across her lap. "Cover me! Cover me!" he cried, begging her to shield him from the angel. Khadija reassured him that he was sane, encouraged him to trust his vision and became the first convert to the new religion, whose name, Islam, means "the submission."

The message of Islam arrived in seventh-century Arabia where female infants, of limited value in a harsh herding and raiding culture, were exposed on the sands to die. In Mecca's slave market, soldiers sold the women captives they'd won as spoils of war. But a few women, like Khadija, had the money and influence to choose their own husbands and shape their own lives.

For twenty-four years Khadija was Muhammad's only wife. It wasn't until she died, nine years after that first vision, that Muhammad began receiving revelations from God on the status of women. So Khadija, the first Muslim woman, was never required to veil or seclude herself, and never lived to hear the word of God proclaim that "Men are in charge of women, because God has made the one of them to excel the other, and because they spend of their property [to support them]." Such a revelation would have come strangely from Muhammad's lips had Khadija still been alive and paying his bills.

Six years after her death, and after a battle between the Muslims and the ruling tribe of Mecca that had left about sixty-five Muslim women widowed, Muhammad had the revelation that endorsed the taking of up to four wives: "Marry of the women, who seem good to you, two or three or four; and if ye fear that ye cannot do justice [to so many] then one [only]." Needing to make alliances through marriage with defeated enemies, he had a further revelation exempting himself from the four-wife limit. Every time he took a new wife, a room for her was added to his apartments near Islam's first mosque. Gradually the rooms increased until they housed eight or nine women.

Soon there was jealousy, intrigue and scandal. Relatives of lesser wives conspired to discredit the prophet's favorites. Enemies of the new religion harassed the prophet's wives. Any small incident was an occasion for gossip. One wife brushed the hand of a male dinner guest as she handed him a plate of food; another drew a rude comment as she made her way at night to an outdoor latrine; a third caused all kinds of controversy because her first husband had been Muhammad's adopted son Zaid.

Just after these incidents, God sent his prophet a message telling him to seclude his wives. Some of the wives had been battlefield nurses; others had preached the new faith in the mosque. Now they were expected to stay hidden behind a curtain in their rooms, going out only when shrouded from head to foot.

Gradually the rules meant to safeguard the prestige of the prophet's wives came to be applied to other Muslim women. As the Islamic message spread out of Arabia and into neighboring lands, the idea of seclusion found an easy audience. Unlike the Arabians, Persians had long segregated women: in ancient Assyria, wives of the nobles veiled as a sign of status, while lower classes were obliged to go uncovered. A slave caught veiling herself could be punished by having molten pitch poured over her head. These customs easily drifted back to Islam's Arabian heartland and endured there. In Saudi Arabia most women today still live curtained off from the world. A woman can't check herself into a modern Saudi hotel because, like the prophet's wives, she is supposed to be secluded in her home.

But a few miles away, across an invisible desert border, those rules have ceased to apply. In Saudi Arabia's neighboring state, the United Arab Emirates, Muslim women soldiers, their hair tied back in Islamic veils, jump from helicopters and shoulder assault rifles. A little farther, across the Persian Gulf, the strict Muslims of Iran vote women into Parliament and send them abroad as diplomats. Pakistan was the first Islamic country to elect a woman prime minister; Turkey now has a female economist as its prime minister, while Bangladesh has women both as prime minister and as leader of the opposition. Instead of adhering to the rules set down for the prophet's wives, these women cite other role models from the history of early Islam. The soldiers look to Nusaybah, who helped save Muhammad's life in battle, standing her ground at his side when the male soldiers fled. The politicians cite Fatima, Muhammad's shy daughter, who spearheaded a political power struggle after the prophet's death.

Islam did not have to mean oppression of women. So why were so many Muslim women oppressed?

I went to live among the women of Islam on a hot autumn night in 1987. I arrived as a Western reporter, living for each day's news. It took me almost a year to understand that I had arrived at a time when the events of the seventh century had begun to matter much more to the people I lived with than anything they read in the morning paper.

It was a Muslim woman, Sahar, who gave me my first clue.

Sahar had been *The Wall Street Journal*'s bureau assistant in Cairo for two years when I arrived there as its Middle East correspondent. My first year in Egypt was set to the syncopated tattoo of her stilettos, clip-clipping their precarious way across Cairo's broken pavements. She was twenty-five years old, six years my junior, but about a decade ahead of me in poise and sophistication. Her English was formal and precise, and so was her grooming. No matter what story we were covering—a building collapse in a teetering slum, sewage seep at the Pyramids—Sahar always dressed for a soiree. Her makeup was so thick it would have required an archaeological excavation to determine what she really looked like. Her hairdos needed scaffolding. As I shuffled beside her in my sneakers, I felt like a sparrow keeping company with a peacock.

Sahar's father worked for an American car company in Cairo. She had spent a year in America as a high school exchange student and graduated top of her class at the American University in Cairo. She wanted to go to Harvard. Sahar was both reassuringly familiar and depressingly unexotic. I had imagined the Middle East differently. White-robed emirs. Almond-eyed Persians. Camels marking the horizon like squiggles of Arabic calligraphy. An Egyptian yuppie hadn't been part of the picture.

At work, as well, it was hard to find the Middle East I'd imagined. I found myself stuck on the flypaper of Arab officialdom, sitting in the gilded salons of deputy assistant second secretaries to ministers of information, sipping tiny cups of cardamom-scented coffee and listening to lies. These men—urbane, foreign-educated—had no problems talking to a Western woman. But out on the streets, among the ordinary people I really wanted to meet, most men only spoke to women to whom they were related. To them, being approached by a lone woman reporter was either an occasion for embarrassment or an opportunity to test the widely held assumption that all Western women are whores. I hated the kind of reporting I was being forced to do: the head-of-state interviews, the windy think pieces on U.S. Middle East policy. I'd signed on as Middle East correspondent looking for risk and adventure. But it seemed the biggest danger I'd be facing was boring myself to death.

Tony, my husband, who had given up his newspaper job to come with me as a freelancer, wasn't having that problem. A few weeks after our arrival, I looked over Sahar's shoulder as she cut out my latest article—"Iraq-Syria Reconciliation Seems Tenuous"—and placed it in a folder alongside Tony's—"Egypt's Camel Corps Roams the Desert Tracking Smugglers." Tony had talked his way onto a patrol with the last Egyptian camel corps. The army wouldn't give approval for a woman to go. In the mine-strewn waters of the Persian Gulf, Tony crewed on a supply boat and came home with tales of turbaned Omani fishermen, Sindbad-style dhows and Persian carpet smugglers. I couldn't join him: the shipping agent wouldn't send a woman to sea.

For almost a year I fretted and kicked at the Middle East's closed doors. Then, thanks to Sahar, I looked up and noticed the window that was open only to me.

Sahar and I worked side by side in a big bright room of my Nileside apartment. When I wasn't traveling, we sat at desks just feet from each other. As I wrote my articles, Sahar translated items in the Arabic press, scheduled appointments or arranged my visas. After about a year of working alongside her, I felt we'd come to know each other well.

Then, one morning at the beginning of Ramadan, the holy month when Muslims fast from dawn to dusk, I opened the door and faced a stranger. The elaborate curls were gone, wrapped away in a severe blue scarf. The makeup was scrubbed off and her shapely dress had been replaced by a dowdy sack. Sahar had adopted the uniform of a Muslim fundamentalist. It was like watching a nature film run in reverse: she had crumpled her bright wings and folded herself into a dull cocoon.

It had been impossible to live for a year in the Middle East and not feel the rumbling of religious revival. All over the Arabian Peninsula and North Africa, more women were covering their hair, more men growing beards and heading for the mosque. I'd assumed that the turn to Islam was the desperate choice of poor people searching for heavenly solace. But Sahar was neither desperate nor poor. She belonged somewhere near the stratosphere of Egypt's meticulously tiered society.

On that Ramadan morning I stood at the door staring at her, stunned. Egyptian women had been the first in the Middle East to *throw off* the veil. In 1923, on their return from a women's suffrage conference in Rome, the pioneer Arab feminists Huda Sharawi and Saiza Nabarawi threw away their coverings at the Cairo railway station, and many in the crowd of women who had come to greet them followed suit. Sahar's mother, growing up under the influence of Sharawi and her supporters, had never veiled.

The Islamic dress—*hijab*—that Sahar had opted to wear in Egypt's tormenting heat signified her acceptance of a legal code that valued her testimony at half the worth of a man's, an inheritance system that allotted her half the legacy of her brother, a future domestic life in which her husband could beat her if she disobeyed him, make her share his attentions with three more wives, divorce her at whim and get absolute custody of her children.

During those weeks of Ramadan, I spent hours talking to Sahar about her decision. In reply, Sahar mouthed the slogan of Islamic Jihad and the Muslim Brotherhood: "Islam Is the Answer." The question, certainly, was clear enough: how was her desperately poor country going to continue to feed, educate and employ a population that increased by a million every nine months? Flirtations with socialism and capitalism had failed to arrest Egypt's economic decline. The Islamic movement wanted to abandon these recently imported ideologies and follow the system set down so long ago in the Koran. If God had taken the trouble to reveal a complete code of laws, ethics and social organization, Sahar argued, why not follow that code?

Sahar had joined a women's study group at a local mosque and had been influenced by the young, veiled, woman instructor. "I would sit there and read in the holy Koran that women should be covered, and then walk out into the street with bare arms," she said. "It just seemed to me that I was dressing that way because it was Western. Why imitate everything Western? Why not try something of our own?"

That "something" took many forms. Extremists rampaged down

the Pyramids road, torching tourist clubs that served alcohol. In rural Egypt a sheik urged a ban on the sale of zucchini and eggplants, because stuffing the long, fleshy vegetables might give women lewd thoughts. In Cairo a writer mocking that pronouncement was gunned down and killed outside his office. Yet, when an earthquake convulsed the city, fundamentalists set up tent camps and soup kitchens, caring for the afflicted with a speed and compassion that had eluded the government.

As the weeks passed, Sahar drifted deeper into her new identity. I began to adjust my secular life to accommodate her, giving up coffee on Ramadan mornings in case the aroma made it harder for her to get through her fast; treading softly as she made her midday devotions on a prayer mat spread out in our living room. There were minefields everywhere. "What is a maraschino cherry?" she asked, suspiciously eying the contents list on a box of chocolates. "I can't eat anything with alcohol inside." Slowly, I became familiar with the rhythms and taboos of her new life. The evocative names of her festivals started to make their way onto our calendar: the Night of Power; the Feast of Sacrifice, the Hajj.

Sahar seemed comfortable with her new self. "I was up most of the night sewing," she said one morning when she'd arrived for work bleary-eyed. Now that she had adopted hijab, she'd given away most of her bright dresses. But she hadn't wanted to abandon the entire contents of her wardrobe. "Everything had something wrong with it —a slit in the back, a tight waistband—it's really a lot of work to salvage a few outfits."

Hijab, she said, gave her security on Cairo's bustling streets. "You never hear about veiled girls being raped," she said. In fact, it was unusual to hear about anyone being raped in Cairo, where violent crimes of all kinds were rare by the standards of Western cities. But bottom-fondling and suggestive comments were a hazard, especially in crowded quarters, especially for women in Western dress.

Sahar felt hijab also gave her access to an unusual women's network. Prying permits and appointments out of government departments became easier if she sought out other veiled women among the bureaucrats working there. Wanting to see an Islamic sister succeed in her job, they'd give her requests a preferential push. At the same time, she felt easier dealing with men. "They have to deal with my mind, not my body," she said.

Dress was only the beginning, she said. The West's soaring crime rate, one-parent families and neglected elderly proved to Sahar the bankruptcy of our secular ways. At the root of it, to her, was Western feminism's insistence on an equality of the sexes that she felt ignored women's essential nature. "Islam doesn't say women are inferior to men; it says they are different," she argued, trying to explain the ban on women judges in some Islamic courts. "Women are more emotional than men, because God has designed them to care for children. So, in court, a woman might show mercy where logic demands harshness."

Talking to Sahar gave me a feeling of déjà vu. When I was fourteen years old, a convent girl in a Sydney Catholic school, the deputy head nun called us to assembly and read us the riot act. Some of us had been seen in the streets wearing our school sweaters without blazers over them. Sweaters, she said, were indecent, since boys would be able to make out the shape of our breasts. The school uniform included a blazer, and if any of us ventured out of the grounds in a sweater without a blazer over it, she would know what kind of girls we were. That same nun insisted we wear hats in church. Quoting St. Paul, she told us that woman, as the instrument of man's downfall in Eden, wasn't fit to appear bareheaded in the house of the Lord.

I thought the nun was a fossil. I stopped going to church as soon as I understood how Catholicism's ban on birth control and divorce could ruin women's lives. Sahar, a woman of my own generation, had made a choice exactly opposite to mine. Something was going on here, and I determined to try to understand it.

I started with Arabic, the language of the Koran. Only one in five Muslims is an Arab; yet Arabic is the language in which the world's more than one billion Muslims—a fifth of the world's population—talk to God.

The Arabic language is as tribal as the desert culture that created it. Each word trails a host of relatives with the same three-letter cluster of consonants as its root. Use almost any word in Arabic, and a host of uninvited meanings barge into the conversation. I learned that one of the words for woman, *hormah*, comes from the same root as the words for both "holy, sacrosanct," and "sinful, forbidden." The word for mother, *umm*, is the root of the words for "source, nation, mercy, first principle, rich harvest; stupid, illiterate, parasite, weak of character, without opinion." In the beginning was the word, and the word, in Arabic, was magnificently ambiguous.

The nature of the Arabic language meant that a precise translation of the Koran was unobtainable. I found myself referring to two quite different English interpretations—George Sale's for a feel for the poetry of the work, and Mohammed Marmaduke Pickthall's for a clearer sense of what the text actually said about sex and marriage, work and holy war. But even when the language was clear the message was often mixed. "Respect women, who have borne you," the Koran says. But if wives are disobedient, "admonish them, send them to beds apart, and scourge them." To try to reconcile such conflicting instructions, I sat in on classes at the new women's religious schools springing up throughout the region, and learned about the dozens of women who shaped the early history of Islam. Again, ambivalence. Women behind the curtain of seclusion; women at the forefront of Islamic holy war.

Meanwhile, in Afghanistan, Algeria and Sudan, Islamic fundamentalists were struggling into power. In Egypt and Jordan powerful minorities pushed their governments toward *sharia*—literally, the road to the water hole, or the straight path of Islamic law. Muslims migrating to the West also were making demands: ban offensive books, let our daughters wear veils to school, give us sex-segregated classrooms.

Was it possible to reclaim the positive messages in the Koran and Islamic history, and devise some kind of Muslim feminism? Could Muslim fundamentalists live with Western liberals, or would accommodating each other cost both of us our principles?

To find the answers, I did something so obvious I couldn't believe it had taken me a year to get around to it. I started talking to women.

Chapter 1

THE HOLY VEIL

"Tell the believing women to lower their gaze and be modest, and to display of their adornment only that which is apparent, and to draw their veils over their bosoms."

THE KORAN
THE CHAPTER OF THE LIGHT

As the bus full of women inched and squealed its slow way through Tehran traffic toward Khomeini's home, I was the only one aboard who wasn't weeping. We eased to a stop beside a black-bannered alley. The keening gained pitch, like a whistling kettle reaching the boil. At the end of the alley was Khomeini's house and the small adjoining *husseinya* where he'd prayed and preached until just before his death five weeks earlier. Drenched with sweat and trying not to trip on my chador, I filed off the bus and joined the tight black phalanx, making its way down the alley with sobbing chants of "O Khomeini! O Imam!"

Ahead of us, a group of men entered the husseinya. They were factory workers from the city of Mashad, rubbing their tear-stained faces with callused fists. The balcony from which Khomeini used to speak had been hastily glassed in since his death because mourners had been shinnying up over the railing to kiss and fondle his chair. Our group turned aside from the husseinya to a curtained entrance flanked by female Revolutionary Guards. Under their chadors—the big black squares of fabric tossed over the head and falling to the ankles—the guards wore the same olive-drab uniform with its emblem of a rifle, Koran and clenched-fist as their male counterparts. Behind the curtain, Khomeini's widow waited to serve us tea.

In one corner of a cracked concrete courtyard, she sat flanked by her daughter and daughter-in-law. With chadors pulled tight around their squatting figures, they looked like a trio of ninepins waiting for a bowling ball. Khomeini's wife Khadija, at seventy-five, had the crinkly face of a kindly grandmother. She peered through wire-rimmed glasses, smiling as she reached up a gnarled hand to greet me. When she held my hand and patted it gently, her chador slid backward to reveal a half inch of silver roots topped by a tumble of carrot-colored curls. Until her husband's death, Khadija had dyed her hair.

Somehow, I'd never imagined that the stony-faced ayatollah had a wife—certainly not one with vamp-red hair. And I hadn't pictured him with the cute, giggling great-grandchildren who romped around us in the carpet-strewn courtyard. "I know that when you saw him he looked very serious, even angry," said Zahra Mostafavi, Khomeini's forty-seven-year-old daughter. "But he wasn't like that with us. With children he made so many jokes. He used to let us hide under his robes when we were playing hide-and-seek." According to Zahra, Khomeini had been quite the sensitive, New Age man, getting up in the night when his five children were infants to take turns giving them their bottles and never asking his wife to do anything for him— "not even to bring him so much as a glass of water." The family snapshots being passed showed the ayatollah laughing merrily as a plump-fisted toddler tried to aim a spoonful of food at his great-grandfather's mouth.

We squatted alongside the Khomeini womenfolk on red Persian rugs spread over the concrete. "The carpets are all borrowed. The family doesn't own anything this good," explained one of the Revolutionary Guards who had worked as household help as well as bodyguard to Khadija for six years. Handing us plastic plates with pictures of ducks on them, she offered dates and slices of watermelon. "I'm sorry we have received you so simply," Khadija said. "But all through his eighty-seven years of life my husband insisted on simplicity."

Ruhollah, an impoverished clerical student from the dusty village of Khomein, had been twenty-seven when he asked for the hand of fifteen-year-old Khadija Saqafi. Her father, a prominent ayatollah (the word, meaning "reflection of God," is applied to the most learned of the Shiite clergy), didn't think much of the match. But Khadija felt differently. She had glimpsed her suitor when, wrapped in a chador, she brought him a glass of tea. She convinced her father to agree to the match after relating a dream in which the prophets proclaimed Ruhollah from Khomein as destined to become a great religious leader.

She had been his only wife. Her public profile had been so low that most Iranians didn't even know her real name. "Someone made a mistake once and wrote that her name was Batul, which was actually the name of her servant," Zahra explained. "My mother *hates* the name Batul." Still, the name stuck, because the ayatollah would have frowned on calling attention to his wife by asking for a correction. Despite her public anonymity, insiders knew that Khadija's influence counted. Men who wanted Khomeini's ear, even on matters of state policy, would have their wives raise the issue with Khadija.

The Khomeinis' boxy, two-floor house contrasted sharply with the opulent green marble palace of the former shah, now open nearby as the Museum of Reversion and Admonition. In the Khomeinis' house, green paint peeled from the walls and a torn screen dangled from a window. In one bare room, the thin mats that served as beds were rolled up and piled in a corner. In the kitchen, an old-fashioned stove and an electric samovar were the only appliances. "Once, when the imam saw that two pomegranate seeds had fallen in the sink, he reminded me not to waste food," said the Revolutionary Guard who had been waiting on us. "He was always reminding us to turn the lights off when we left a room."

Every small reminiscence brought a new flood of tears from the other guests. One of the loudest weepers, a woman from Lebanon's Hezbollah—the Party of God—rose to her feet and launched into an emotional speech of thanks to the imam's widow for admitting us to the hallowed precincts of the imam's home. "O God, please send us patience," she sobbed. "We have come to this place where the great imam used to breathe. We have all gathered here in this holy place to show our allegiance to his way."

The call to sunset prayer, wafting over the courtyard wall from a nearby mosque, was our signal that the tea party was over. In the corner, Khadija was already on her feet, on her way to wash for prayers. As we filed back into the bus, which nosed back through the traffic, the Hezbollah woman was still declaiming. "We have to divide our lives into two parts—before and after Imam's death," she sobbed. "We haven't yet had time to understand the loss we've suffered."

I, for one, hadn't had time to understand it. After the U. S. Embassy occupation in 1979, Iran had been virtually closed to reporters from the American media. The rarely granted visas had usually allowed no more than thirty-six hours in the country to report on a specific event. Before Khomeini's death, I'd been allowed in only once, in 1988, to cover the funerals of the 290 Iranian civilians killed when the cruiser U.S.S. *Vincennes* shot down an Iranian Airbus on a scheduled flight across the Persian Gulf.

But I needed to understand. What was happening to Muslim women from Algeria to Afghanistan had its roots here, in that austere, boxy house in North Tehran. Somehow, Khomeini had persuaded women that the wearing of a medieval cloak was a revolutionary act. Something in his message had brought thousands of women into the streets to face the shah's army and risk their lives calling for the return of a code of laws that allowed child marriage, polygamy and wife beating.

Khomeini spoke with a voice that drew its authority from the earliest days of Islam. Khomeini was a Shiite, a member of the minority branch of Islam that had broken with the mainstream in the years following the prophet Muhammad's death. The majority of the early Muslims agreed that their leader should be appointed by consensus of the elders, as was the long tradition of the desert. Since the Arabic word for "tradition" is sunnah, they became known as the Sunni Muslims. A minority, however, felt that Muhammad's successor should come from within his own family, and chose his son-in-law and cousin, Ali. They were the Shiat Ali, or Partisans of Ali, known today as Shiites. Because of their origins as dissenters, Shiites hold it an obligation to question those in power, and revolt against them if necessary. And because their origins lay in the defeat of Ali and his sons, Shiites' most profound identification is with the beaten and poor. Khomeini tapped all of those deep convictions when he launched the revolution against the shah in 1978.

When Khomeini died in June 1989, Iran opened its doors to any journalist who showed up. After the frantic funeral, Hashemi Rafsanjani held a rare press conference for foreign reporters. I went, wearing a black chador. Because such events are always televised in Iran, I knew the press conference organizers wouldn't let me near a microphone with so much as a hair showing. But when I finally got to put my question about the shape of the post-Khomeini power structure, Rafsanjani gazed at me, a hint of a smile playing on his moon-shaped face. "I have a question for you," he said. "Why do you wear that heavy veil when a simple scarf would do?"

The huge, old-fashioned cameras of Iranian TV swung in my direction. What was I to say? That the chador was great camouflage for getting into places I wasn't supposed to go? That I found its billowing folds less appallingly hot than the scarf-and-coat alternative? That just a day earlier the same dress had been deemed inadequate by one of the functionaries from the Ministry of Islamic Guidance? (I'd been running to board a helicopter to get to Khomeini's graveside, and the gust from the rotor had momentarily blown the chador aside, revealing my trousers and shirt beneath. "Cover yourself!" the official yelled, his face full of loathing.)

Rafsanjani's question was disingenuous. It took more than a simple scarf to escape the eighty-lash penalty with which Iran threatened women, even foreigners, who flouted the Islamic dress code. Along with hair, all skin except face and hands and all curves of the body had to be concealed. For a second, I wondered if I should do as the Italian journalist Oriana Fallaci had done, in an interview with Khomeini, and rip off the garment she'd dubbed a "filthy medieval rag."

"I'm wearing it," I said, "in a spirit of mutual respect."

Rafsanjani looked taken aback. The two other Western women reporters at the press conference rolled their eyes. Later, I wished I'd spelled out more clearly what I'd meant to convey: that if I were prepared to respect Iranian society's requirements, Iran should be prepared to respect mine. But to most Iranians, watching by the millions at home on TV for a hint about what their lives would be like after Khomeini, what I had said wasn't important. What mattered was that Rafsanjani had sent them a signal of moderation. In the bazaar, the riyal surged against the dollar, as word went round that Rafsanjani had told a woman reporter she could take off her chador. To the traders, any signal of liberalism meant good news for business.

To one or two people, what I had said *did* matter. That night a member of Iran's small Christian community called on me at my hotel, berating me for missing a chance to speak out against hijab on behalf of all the women who hated being forced to wear it. And a few days later Khomeini's daughter Zahra invited me to a conference sponsored by the Women's Society of the Islamic Republic of Iran titled "Aspects of His Highness Imam Khomeini's Personality." I studied the title with bemusement. The only aspects of His Highness Imam Khomeini's personality I was familiar with were his penchants for condemning novelists to death, dispatching young boys to the war front as human minesweepers and permitting little girls to be married off at the age of nine.

The venue for the conference was Tehran's Revolution Hotel. A prerevolutionary glass-walled elevator, designed to give a view of the swimming pool, had been newspapered over for the duration of the conference, so that religious women wouldn't be offended by the sight of glistening male torsos. Since the revolution, only men are allowed to swim in public.

It took about five minutes at the first evening's ice-breaking cocktail party—fruit-juice cocktails only; no un-Islamic alcohol—to realize that I was odd woman out amid a female Who's Who of Iran's exported revolution. The delegates from Lebanon included wives of the men most often named as heads of the hostage takers. The Turkish contingent included a student who had become famous after being expelled from architecture school for insisting on wearing an Islamic scarf to class. There were, as well, Muslim militants from Pakistan, Sudan, Guinea, Tanzania, India and South Africa. It was a group with a lot of enemies, and the hotel was surrounded by a cordon of armed Revolutionary Guards. No one went in or out without permission.

The party dress code was basic black—layers of it. Chadors were only the finishing touch over long pants, socks, calf-length tunics and hoods called *magnehs*—a circle of fabric like a nun's wimple that falls over head and shoulders, leaving just a hole for the face. As the black-cloaked figures milled around me, I began to feel I'd been locked up by mistake in some kind of convent from hell.

The party chat left me a little at a loss. "Of course, Hong Kong people are brainwashed by colonialist-Zionists and don't feel any grief at the passing away of the imam," said a diminutive Chinese woman named Khatima Ma, who introduced herself as a fellow reporter, working for the Hong Kong *Muslim Herald.* "The enemies of Islam, led by the Americans, want to see the Iranian nation without a leader. Everybody expected turmoil here but, thanks be to God, we don't see it. Even though Hong Kong media is completely under the control of the Zionists, they haven't been able to create any story about trouble in Iran."

I asked the Turkish architecture student, now veiled except for her eyes and nose, why a Muslim country like Turkey was so insistent about secular dress. "You know, of course, that there are two kinds of Islam—American Islam and Muhammad's Islam—and in Turkey we have American Islam. In American Islam, religion is separate from politics, because it suits the superpower interests. Our government is very much afraid of Islamic revolution, because it wants to grovel to the West."

I had been assigned an interpreter for the conference, a tall, pale young woman named Hamideh Marefat. When I complimented her on her excellent English, she told me she had perfected it during her time "in the nest."

"Excuse me?"

"In the nest. The nest of spies—the American Embassy," she said. Hamideh had been part of the black-veiled horde that occupied the embassy and held its personnel captive for 444 days. Her job had been to translate the hostages' mail. I asked her if she'd ever felt sympathy for them. "Sometimes," she said, when she read the letters from American schoolchildren, sent to cheer up the hostages. "But I knew they were spies who had tried to ruin this country. I was disappointed when we released them. Personally, I thought they should be executed."

A South African student from the University of Cape Town nodded in wistful agreement. Then she brightened. "At least, we will certainly execute Rushdie." She had helped found a mosque in Cape Town dedicated to teaching "the line of the Imam." But there had been a recent setback when two of the mosque's leading lights were put on trial for treason.

The South African kept glancing uncomfortably at her Islamic sister from Guinea. This tall, stately woman would have stood out in any crowd, but in this one she was particularly eye-catching. Instead of shapeless black, she wore a length of lilac fabric wrapped closely around her sinuous curves. An end of the fabric draped loosely over her head, leaving most of one smooth coppery shoulder bare. Naked toes peeped from under the hem of her lovely robe. Over the next few days I would notice one or another of the Islamic sisters standing on tippy-toe, trying to tug the robe up over that shoulder or to wrap the end piece more closely around her hair. Guineans and Iranians clearly had a different definition of hijab.

The word "hijab" literally means "curtain," and it is used in the Koran as an instruction to believers of Muhammad's day on how they should deal with the prophet's wives: "If you ask his wives for anything, speak to them from behind a curtain. This is purer for your hearts and their hearts." The revelation on hijab came to Muhammad on one of his wedding nights, just as he was about to bed Zeinab, the most controversial of his brides.

Islamic scholars generally agree that the marriage to Zeinab caused the most serious of several scandals surrounding the prophet's ever growing number of wives. Visiting the house of his adopted son, Muhammad had glimpsed the young man's wife only partially dressed. The woman was beautiful, and Muhammad quickly turned away, muttering a prayer against temptation. Believing Muhammad desired his wife, the young man divorced her. Muhammad's subsequent marriage to Zeinab provoked uproar in the community, since it violated the rules of incest already set down in the Koran. The uproar subsided only when Muhammad had a new revelation proclaiming all adoptions invalid, and therefore exempting himself from the rule that barred a father from marrying the wife of his son.

The revelation of hijab put the prophet's wives, including

Zeinab, into seclusion where they would be safer from scandal. The Koran's instructions for women outside the prophet's household weren't as severe: "Tell the believing women to lower their gaze and be modest, and to display of their adornment only that which is apparent, and to draw their veils over their bosoms."

In Cairo, when Sahar began wearing hijab, I dug out this quote and argued with her that it made no reference at all to covering hair. What it seemed to me to be asking was that women conform to conservative norms of dress—in our day, to shun see-through blouses and skimpy miniskirts. But Sahar replied that it was necessary to go beyond the Koran for guidance on such matters. She said that the sunnah, the "trodden path" of Muhammad—those things which he had said, done or permitted to be done in his presence—made it clear that "that which is apparent" meant only a woman's face and hands. The rest of her "adornment"—including ankles, wrists, neck—should be hidden from all men except her husband and a carefully specified list of close male relatives to whom the Koran forbids marriage. That is, her father, brothers, father-in-law, nephews, sons and stepsons. She can also be unveiled, the Koran says, before prepubescent boys and "male attendants who lack vigor," which in Muhammad's era probably meant eunuchs or old slaves.

But Sahar's interpretation wasn't universal. Some Muslim women believed, as I did, that the religion only required them to dress within contemporary limits of modesty. Others insisted on going beyond a covered head to gloved hands and veiled faces, arguing that the corruption of the modern world made more extreme measures necessary now than in the prophet's day.

At Cairo airport, the great crossroads of the Islamic world, it was possible to see almost every interpretation of Islamic dress. Women from Pakistan, on their way to jobs in the Gulf, floated by in their deliciously comfortable *salwar kameez*—silky tunics drifting low over billowing pants with long shawls of matching fabric tossed loosely over their heads. Saudi women trod carefully behind their husbands, peering from behind gauzy face veils and 360-degree black cloaks that made them look, as Guy de Maupassant once wrote, "like death out for a walk." Afghani women also wore 360-degree coverings, called *chadris*—colorful crinkly shrouds with an oblong of embroidered latticework over the eyes. Women from Dubai wore stiff, birdlike masks of black and gold that beaked over the nose but left their luminous, treacle-colored eyes exposed. Some Palestinians and Egyptians wore dull-colored, floor-length button-through coats and white head-scarves; others wore bright calf-length skirts with matching scarves held in place by headbands of seed pearls.

The oddest interpretation of Islamic dress I encountered was in the arid expanse of the Algerian Sahara, where the nomadic tribes known as Tuareg hold to the tradition that it is men who should veil their faces after puberty, while women go barefaced. As soon as they are old enough to shave their beards and keep the Ramadan fast, the men must cover all but their eyes in a veil made of yards of indigo cloth. "We warriors veil our faces so that the enemy may not know what is in our minds, peace or war, but women have nothing to hide," is how one Tuareg man explained the custom. The Tuareg are Mus-lims, but their interpretation of the faith gives women considerable sexual freedom before marriage and allows close platonic friendships with men after they wed. A Tuareg proverb says: "Men and women toward each other are for the eyes, and for the heart, and not only for the bed." Other Muslims find Tuareg customs close to heresy. In fact, the word "Tuareg" comes from the Arabic for "The Abandoned of God."

Where women wore the veil, there was money to be made in Islamic fashion. Cairo had the Salam Shopping Center for Veiled Women, a three-floor clothing emporium that stocked nothing but Islamically correct outfits. Most of the store was devoted to what the management thought of as "training hijab"—color-coordinated long skirts and scarves, long jackets studded with rhinestones and bulging with oversized shoulder pads—that covered the Islamic minimum. Ideally, explained one manager, customers who started wearing such clothes would gradually become more enlightened and graduate to dowdier colors and longer, more shapeless garments, ending up com-pletely swathed in black cloaks, gloves and face veils. But these plain outfits, which cost around ten dollars, were hard to find amid the racks of more profitable "high-fashion" hijab, where the cost for an Islamically correct evening outfit could run to three or four times a civil servant's monthly salary.

In Beirut, in the basement of the Great Prophet Mosque, Hezbollah established an Islamic-fashion factory to cash in on the growing worldwide demand for hijab. "My Islam isn't a bunch of fighters. It's a revolution of culture, of ideas," enthused the factory manager, a rotund woman who introduced herself as Hajjia Zahra. Flipping through a German couture catalog, she showed me how the latest styles in pockets, zips and sleeves could be grafted onto the long, figure-hiding dresses the factory turned out by the hundreds. Around us, bolts of cloth soared to the ceiling. She explained that the bright bales, the reds and yellows, would be used for Hezbollah's hot-selling line of children's clothes. The muted browns, grays and mossy greens were for the women's fashions. "These are calm colors," she explained. "Part of the philosophy of Islamic dress is for a woman to project an aura of calm and tranquillity."

Hijab was the most obvious sign of the Islamic revival that had swept up Sahar and so many other young women. It began in 1967, after Egypt's catastrophic loss to Israel in the Six-Day War. To explain the humiliation, Muslim philosophers pointed to the secularism of Gamal Abdel Nasser's government, and urged Egyptians to return to the Islamic laws they had abandoned. Slowly, the number of veiled women began to increase.

But the real surge came with Iran's theocratic revolution, when donning hijab became a political as well as a religious act. In 1935 the shah's father had banned the chador. Reza Shah wanted his country to look modern and he thought the ancient black cloak didn't. But devout women, especially the elderly, couldn't suddenly make so drastic a change. In her memoir, *Daughter of Persia*, Sattareh Farman Farmaian writes of her mother's desolation. "When my mother had learned that she was to lose the age-old modesty of her veil, she was beside herself. She and all traditional people regarded Reza's order as the worst thing he had yet done—worse than his attacking the rights of the clergy; worse even than his confiscations and murders." Fearing the shah's displeasure, her husband ordered her to go out in public unveiled. "The next day, weeping with rage and humiliation, she sequestered herself in her bedroom. . . . As she wept she struggled futilely to hide her beautiful masses of waist-length black hair under the inadequate protection of a small French cloche."

For others, the so-called liberating edict became a form of imprisonment. Men who had just begun allowing their daughters to attend school revoked their permission when it meant girls walking to class uncovered. Women who disobeyed the shah's order and ventured into the streets veiled risked having their coverings ripped off and scissored by soldiers. Chador-wearing women were forbidden to use public transportation and denied entry to many stores. Rather than risk such humiliation, many women simply stayed inside. Khomeini's wife Khadija, for one, didn't leave her house at all. Such confinement was a particular hardship at a time when most homes didn't have bathrooms and women gathered to bathe and socialize during the women's hours at local bathhouses—*hamams*. The ban was compulsory from 1935 until 1941, when draconian enforcement eased, but unveiling continued to be encouraged and women who wished to veil were derided as backward.

As revolutionary pressure mounted in the late 1970s, wearing the chador became a symbol of protest against the shah and his Western backers. Some clerics advocated it for predictable reasons. If all women wore it, reasoned the Iranian cleric Ibrahim Amini, wives "could rest assured that their husbands, when not at home, would not encounter a lewd woman who might draw his attention away." In Britain, the Muslim scholar Shabbir Akhtar came up with an alternative rationale. The aim of the veil, he wrote, "is to create a truly erotic culture in which one dispenses with the need for the artificial excitement that pornography provides." In both cases, women are expected to sacrifice their comfort and freedom to service the requirements of male sexuality: either to repress or to stimulate the male sex urge.

Neither of these arguments carried much weight with young intellectuals such as my Iranian interpreter, Hamideh Marefat. For her, wearing the chador was, first and foremost, a political act. Growing up in a middle-class home, she had never thought of veiling until she started attending clandestine lectures by a charismatic young intellectual named Ali Shariati. Shariati, Iranian-born and Sorbonne-educated, married his knowledge of Marxism to his own Iranian Shiite Islam, with its roots in rebellion against the status quo after

Muhammad's death—and came up with a revolutionary creed designed to uplift the masses and challenge despots. Western dress, he said, was a form of imperialism, turning women's beauty into a product of capitalism to be bought and sold, at the same time as it made third-world women dependent consumers of fast-obsolete fashions. Muslim women, he urged, should assert their freedom by adopting Islamic dress. To young women such as Hamideh Marefat, the chador served much the same purpose as the denim overalls worn by the militant American feminist Andrea Dworkin. To Hamideh, the chador symbolized liberation. She put it on a year before the Iranian revolution of 1978, and when she occupied the U. S. Embassy, she wore it like a flag.

But by the time I met her, ten years later, the revolutionary thrill had started to wear off. Every time we got out of the sight of men, she'd shrug off the big black cloth with relief. "I wish I'd never put it on," she confided one day. "In the beginning, it was important, to prove your revolutionary views. But now we don't have to prove that. You can be a revolutionary with just a scarf and coat."

When I went to visit her at home, Hamideh looked preppy in pleated skirts, silk blouses and discreet gold jewelry. But when she went out, she donned the full uniform of revolutionary Islam. For me, it was easier to deal with Hamideh in her chador. The things she said somehow seemed less jolting coming out of that anonymous darkness. In her family's tastefully furnished living room, as we chatted about neutral subjects like Persian poetry or the difficulty of meeting eligible men, it was easy to begin to see her as just another smart woman my own age with whom I had a lot in common. Then she would run a hand through her bobbed chestnut hair and deliver an opinion devastating in its extremism. "Israel has to be obliterated," she would say, reaching for her teacup and taking a delicate sip. "I'm looking forward to taking part in the war for its destruction."

While Sunni Muslims assume a direct relationship between believers and God, Shiites believe in the mediation of a highly trained clergy. Usually, each Shiite chooses a high-ranking clerical thinker and follows any religious ruling, or *fatwa*, from that person. Hamideh had chosen Khomeini, which meant that she ordered every detail of her life according to the opinions he set out in his eighteen volumes of religious interpretation. "Some ayatollahs say women must wear gloves," she explained, "but Imam Khomeini says that the lower part of the hand can be uncovered." Other ayatollahs considered the female voice arousing and barred women from speaking in mixed gatherings unless they first put a stone in their mouths to distort the sound. Khomeini, citing the prophet's meetings with mixed groups of men and women, had no problems with the female speaking voice.

I asked Hamideh if Khomeini could ever be wrong in a religious ruling. "For sure," she said. "We don't believe any human being is infallible. But if I follow his fatwa, and it's wrong—say I kill someone he orders me to, and the person is innocent—the person I killed will go to paradise, and the sin of the killing is on the one who issued the fatwa, not on me."

Now that Khomeini was dead, Hamideh felt she couldn't abandon the chador. To suddenly stop wearing it after his death might look as if her commitment to his line had weakened. Articles in newspapers constantly reminded women that the chador was a "trench against Western values." And men in positions of power believed it. One friend had gone to an interview for a government job covering her hair and curves with an Islamically impeccable coat and scarf. "You're naked," the interviewer snarled, and declined to hire her.

At first, I'd naively assumed that hijab would at least free women from the tyranny of the beauty industry. But at the Iranian Women's Conference, locked up day and night with a hotelful of Muslim radicals, I soon learned I'd been mistaken.

I'd asked Hamideh to arrange a meeting for me with the women of Lebanon's Hezbollah. The group's strongholds were the Bekaa Valley and Beirut's southern suburbs—no-go areas for Western journalists since the kidnapping of the Associated Press bureau chief, Terry Anderson. I wanted to ask about Anderson, who was spending his days chained to a radiator in a lightless Beirut basement. To meet the women said to be married to his captors seemed like the best chance I'd ever have to get information for his desperate family.

In the end, I learned nothing about his plight, but meeting the women was instructive in other ways. They invited me to join them that evening for tea in their suite, provided that I promised not to name them in any articles I wrote. When the door opened to my knock, I thought I had the wrong room. The woman in front of me had frosted blond hair streaming to her waist. She wore a silk negligee with a deep plunge neckline. On the bed behind her, another woman lay languidly in a bust-hugging, slit-sided scarlet satin nightgown. Through the filmy fabrics, it was obvious that their bodies were completely hairless, like Barbie dolls. It was, they explained, *sunnat,* or Islamically recommended, for married women to remove all body hair every twenty days. The traditional depilatory was a paste of sugar and lemon that tugged the hairs out by the roots. Muslim men, they said, also should remove their body hair. For men, the recommended time between depilation is forty days.

It took a few minutes to recognize the bleached blonde as the same woman who had wailed the emotional eulogy at the Khomeini house. When I mentioned my surprise at the way she looked, she laughed. "This is how we are at home," she said, striking a seductive pose. "Islam encourages us to be beautiful for our husbands." I suddenly understood why Khadija, Khomeini's widow, had hennaed her hair to carrot-orange, and why an inch of gray had grown in since she stopped doing it on her husband's death.

Her daughter Zahra somehow didn't seem like the carrot-curl type, or the plunge-neck negligee type, for that matter. Under her chador, she wore matronly twin sets and tweedy skirts—donnish clothes for a donnish woman who taught philosophy at the University of Tehran.

It took me three years and many meetings before she relaxed enough to allow me to see her in anything but her chador. Even in a room full of women, she rarely let the chador fall from a clenched-fist grip that kept it pulled down past her brows and up over her lips. The style led to confusing graphics in the Women's Society literature. The Society liked to promote its prominent women—its members of Parliament, artists and authors. But in photographs everyone came out looking exactly the same: a little white triangle, apex down, inside a big black triangle, apex up.

Once, during the Tehran conference, Zahra momentarily let go of her chador, revealing some lip and chin. Someone's flash bulb popped. Consternation. Could whoever had taken the picture please hand over the film? The Women's Society would develop it, excise the offending picture and send back the rest of the shots on the roll, along with an appropriate picture of Mrs. Mostafavi. All eyes in the room turned to me. As a journalist, I was the prime suspect. Flapping my chador to prove there was nothing up my sleeve, I explained that I didn't have a camera with me. A sheepish Khatima Ma confessed to being the culprit. As she handed over the film, she looked a little crestfallen at the Hong Kong *Muslim Herald*'s lost scoop.

Zahra Mostafavi was a heavy-set woman, pallid and jowly, with the same fierce profile and intense expression as her father. Austere wire half-spectacles perched on her nose and an elaborate diamond-encrusted gold ring flashed on her hand. As head of the Women's Society, she was the most politically active of Khomeini's three surviving daughters. Sedigheh, a widow, lived quietly with her seven children. Farideh, a theology scholar, was married to a rug merchant in Qum.

Zahra's position as a philosophy professor was quite an achievement for a woman who had never been to school. Like many religious Iranians before the revolution, Khomeini refused to send any of his children to what he felt was the corrupt state-run education system. Zahra was educated at home by handpicked men of religion. Every day, at her request, her father tutored her himself for half an hour. Zahra found herself drawn toward metaphysics and to Western philosophers such as Bertrand Russell and Immanuel Kant.

Khomeini, she said, was an easygoing parent most of the time, but unyielding on Islamic issues. "If I wanted to play at a house, and he knew there was a boy there, he would say, 'Don't go there, play at home,' " she recalled. "You couldn't say, 'Come on, Dad, let me go,' because what he said was based on Islam, not on his own opinion."

Once she finished her studies, Khomeini began to scrutinize potential husbands. Zahra turned down three suitors he suggested before accepting the fourth. "My father would come to me and say, 'I've chosen one, I think he's not bad, he has this and that characteristic, but it's up to you.' " All were men she had met through the family. "It wasn't as if they were strangers. I knew what they were all like; I waited for the one that I knew would suit me." She chose an academic, who now heads an educational think tank. As a married woman, she stayed behind when the shah ordered her father into exile. But she would visit him each year, returning with revolutionary tracts and tapes hidden in her clothes. Back in Tehran, she would go out at night to distribute them. "I'd take my son and have him scramble up trees and drop copies over people's fences," she recalled.

Her own daughter, coming of age after the Islamic revolution, didn't face the kinds of restrictions that had kept Zahra mostly at home. Once the revolutionaries gained control and purged institutions such as schools, universities, banks and businesses, Khomeini had no objection to the participation of women (correctly veiled) in politics and the economy. So his granddaughter went to law school, married a cardiac surgeon, and wound up living in London while her husband completed his training.

In the winter of 1993, when Khadija needed specialist medical care, Zahra didn't hesitate to bring her to London. I had moved from Cairo to London by then, and was surprised to get a call inviting me to lunch with her at the Iranian consulate. It was the week of the fourth anniversary of her father's death sentence on Salman Rushdie, and to mark British displeasure the foreign secretary had met with Rushdie. The Iranians, miffed, had immediately raised the visa fee for British travelers to Iran to a staggering £504.

But Zahra waved all that off with a flick of her plump wrist. She had never been an easy person to chat with: every conversation I'd ever had with her started with the words *"Bismillah al rahman al rahim* [In the name of God, the compassionate, the merciful]"—always a disincentive to small talk. As well, the combination of growing up in a preacher's home and working as a university lecturer had left her with a tendency to monologue. Once she got going it was hard to interject a question, much less hold anything that resembled a conversation.

But over lunch in London she seemed much more relaxed. Encouraging me to take more rice, more chicken, more kebab, and piling her own plate with healthy portions, she talked merrily about the pleasures of London: the trees, the wide avenues, the polite people. I knew that Khomeini, when he went into exile in France, had averted his eyes on the drive from the airport to his residence, so as not to be contaminated by a Western environment. At his house outside Paris he'd had the pedestal toilet removed and a humbler, oriental-style squat version installed. Zahra smiled when I asked if the un-Islamic atmosphere of London bothered her. "I have no problems here," she said. The only slight unpleasantness had occurred when an Iranian exile who recognized her in the street had shouted an abusive remark about her father. "Of course, I don't like anyone to insult my father, but he was always ready to forgive anything aimed at him personally. It was attacks on Islam that he couldn't forgive."

In her chador, Zahra stood out on the streets of London. Many devout Iranian women didn't wear their chadors in the West for that reason. One of the main objectives of hijab is to make a woman *less* eye-catching. In London, a chador drew many more stares than a scarf and coat would have. But for Zahra the chador was like a second skin that couldn't be discarded.

One reason she had invited me to the consulate was to show off the women diplomats working there. One handled international law, another studied the status of women in Britain. Their presence was something of a triumph for the Women's Society, which had pushed to have women assigned abroad.

These women were an entirely different group from the modern, middle- and upper-class minority who had thrived under the shah's liberalizations, many of whom were destroyed by the revolution. One, Esfand Farrokhrou Parsa, the first woman in the Iranian cabinet, had been wrapped in a sack and machine-gunned for the crimes of "corruption on earth, expansion of prostitution and warring against God." What she had done was direct schoolgirls not to veil and order textbooks revised to present a more modern vision of women. Hundreds of women had been imprisoned for refusing to follow revolutionary dictates; thousands fled into exile.

But others, from poor, conservative, rural families, emerged for the first time from behind the high walls of the *andarun*—the women's quarters of traditional homes where the vast majority of Iranian women used to live their entire lives. Khomeini encouraged these women to come into the streets, where they had never been welcome, to demonstrate for the revolution. He even stated that they didn't need their male guardian's permission to leave the house for such a purpose. His views on the matter weren't, he said, *his* views at all, but the literal laws of Islam. If Muhammad's sunnah was that women could marry at nine, then of course they could marry at nine. If it said they couldn't be judges, then of course they'd be banned from the bench. But if it said they could do other things—run a business, as the prophet Muhammad's first wife had done, or tend the sick, or even ride into battle, as women of the prophet's era had— then of course Iranian women must be permitted to do the same. Suddenly, because the imam had spoken, conservative fathers, husbands and brothers had to listen. To women who would have spent their lives in seclusion, wearing a head covering was a small price to pay in return for the new freedoms.

Still, it intrigued me that, while public pressure and state laws could be brought to bear to force women into hijab, no one seemed to pay much attention to Islam's dress code for men. The Koran urged men, as well as women, to be modest. Muhammad's sunnah was unambiguous on the matter: as women must cover all but hands and face, men were obliged to cover the area of the body from navel to knee. The covering had to be opaque and loose-fitting enough to conceal the bulge of male genitals.

But all over the Islamic world men flouted that code. Crotch-hugging jeans were the fashion among the youths of the Gulf. Soccer players—national heroes—competed in thigh-high shorts. Top-rating televised wrestling matches featured sweaty men in jockstraps. At the Caspian Sea, where Iranian women had to swim in chadors, no one insisted that the men wear swimsuits covering their navels.

The hypocrisy was especially evident at Iranian soccer matches, where chador-wearing women couldn't take their sons to see a game because the male players weren't Islamically dressed. Meanwhile, the same matches were televised nightly on state TV that called itself the Voice and Vision of the Islamic Republic. Whenever I asked Iranians about this, they would simply laugh or shrug. "Women are supposed to leave the room if their husbands want to watch football," one friend said. "Even this government knows there's a limit. You can ask a country to make many sacrifices, but expecting men to give up watching football would be pushing things too far."

The answer, of course, went much deeper. In Muslim societies men's bodies just weren't seen as posing the same kind of threat to social stability as women's. Getting to the truth about hijab was a bit like wearing it: a matter of layers to be stripped away, a piece at a time. In the end, under all the concealing devices—the chador, jalabiya or abaya, the magneh, roosarie or shayla—was the body. And under all the talk about hijab freeing women from commercial or sexual exploitation, all the discussion of hijab's potency as a political and revolutionary symbol of selfhood, was the body: the dangerous female body that somehow, in Muslim society, had been made to carry the heavy burden of male honor.

Chapter 2

WHOM NO MAN SHALL HAVE DEFLOWERED BEFORE THEM

"The whore, and the whoremonger, shall ye scourge with an hundred stripes. And let not compassion towards them prevent you from executing the judgement of God."

THE KORAN
THE CHAPTER OF THE LIGHT

*T*he operating theater was a whitewashed cavern gouged out of an African hillside. In its bleaching light, the patient's flesh looked like a slab of putty. Reaching wrist-deep into an abdominal incision, the surgeon grasped the woman's slippery, glistening uterus as if it were the enemy.

The patient, at forty, was an old woman by the harsh reckoning of this Ethiopian province. She was a survivor of famine, war and the routine violence waged against women by the country's ancient customs. At the age of eight, she had been held down while her clitoris was scraped away with an unclean knife and the raw flesh sealed with inch-long acacia thorns. On her wedding night, her husband had to use his dagger to slice his way into the jagged cicatrix that had become her genitals. That pain had been the prelude to recurring agonies as she delivered four children through a birth canal choking on its own scar tissue. Here, one in five births ends in the mother's death.

That risk, at least, would soon be over. Wrapping her gloved fingers around the woman's diseased uterus, the surgeon hacked with unexpected force at the last shreds of tissue holding it in place, bracing her foot against the operating table as she tugged the organ free.

33

The smell in the small, rock-walled room was a pungent medley of ether, disinfectant and freshly butchered meat.

Wielding clamps the wrong shape for pelvic surgery and aged, bent suturing needles, the doctor paused from time to time to wring blood from the swabs packing the patient's abdomen. "We have a shortage of gauze," she explained.

Abrehet Gebrekidan was used to shortages of almost everything, except patients. In 1977 she left her job at Syracuse Medical Center in New York to join a ragtag secessionist movement waging Africa's longest war. As an obstetrician and gynecologist, she knew her skills would be needed in the mountain hideouts from which her people, the Eritreans, fought Ethiopian annexation from 1962 until the central government fell in 1991.

When I met her, late in 1989, Dr. Abrehet worked in a hospital whose "wards"—thatched shelters with saline drips hanging from tree branches—rambled for almost three miles through a steep-walled mountain valley. Much of her work had nothing to do with the war. Instead, it involved saving women from the worst consequences of genital mutilation. In Eritrea, girls were subjected to both clitoridectomy—the excision of the clitoris—and infibulation—the cutting away of the labia and the sealing of the wound to leave only a tiny opening for urination and menstruation. If the malnourished little girls didn't bleed to death from the procedure itself, they often died from resulting infections or debilitating anemia. In others, scar tissue trapped urine or menstrual fluid, causing pelvic infections. Women with scar-constricted birth canals suffered dangerous and agonizing childbirth. Sometimes the baby's trapped head led to fatal hemorrhage or ruptured the bladder, causing seepage of urine that made the woman smell like a latrine and poisoned her later fetuses.

With antiquated equipment, each procedure took much longer than it should. The hysterectomy, a job of about an hour and a half at Syracuse Medical Center, dragged on into the night. From first incision to final, awkward suture took Dr. Abrehet almost five hours. Outside, the next case, a thirteen-year-old, waited patiently for the operation that would reconstruct her vaginal wall. The girl, a Muslim nomad, had been married at ten. Her husband's rough intercourse had been too much for her immature body, tearing the tissue that divides the vagina from the rectum. The girl had run away from her husband and joined the Eritrean guerrillas. They had enrolled her, for the first time, in school, and brought her to Dr. Abrehet.

Above her green surgical mask, Dr. Abrehet's sweaty brow bore a crudely tattooed cross. Eritrea, an England-sized wedge of land along Ethiopia's coast, has three and a half million people divided almost equally between highland-dwelling Christians and coastal-lowland Muslims. Dr. Abrehet drew her patients from both communities. The practice of mutilating women's genitals in Eritrea predated the arrival of both religions, and for hundreds of years neither faith had questioned it. The Eritreans' guerrilla movement was among the few African organizations trying to wipe it out. The campaign was part of a wider agenda of promoting women's rights that included reforming land distribution to give women a share and pressing for women's representation in politics.

"We can't force them, we can only teach them," said Amina Nurhussein, one of six women elected to the Eritreans' seventy-one-member policy-making body. Infibulation had begun to decline in the highland areas, where the predominantly Christian population saw the custom as a cultural duty rather than a religious command. But in the Muslim lowlands the issue remained extremely sensitive. As a Muslim herself, Amina understood the obstacles. "The women have been told it's written in the Koran that they must do these things," she said. She could tell them it wasn't but, as an outsider and a woman, her word meant little against the word of the village sheik.

Educating the women so that they could read the Koran for themselves was the keystone in the Eritreans' patient campaign against genital mutilation. A year before I met her, Aset Ibrahim would have told anybody who asked that clitoridectomy and infibulation were essential to a woman's beauty and well-being. "My mother, my grandmother and my great-grandmother all told me it was right, that without it a woman wouldn't be able to control herself, that she would end up a prostitute," said Aset, a beautiful twenty-eight-year-old whose own genitals had been mutilated when she was about seven years old. "I even learned to believe that it looked nicer that way. We grow up reciting the saying, 'A house isn't beautiful without a door.'"

As it turned out, infibulation hadn't saved her from prostitution. Because of her beauty, Aset had been forced into servitude by the Ethiopian army, required to work as a domestic servant and sometime prostitute in a soldiers' barracks. When the town fell to the Eritreans, the guerrillas offered Aset a chance to train for four months as a birth attendant, learning nutrition, hygiene, family planning and mid- wifery. Part of the course covered the dangers of genital mutilation, information that Aset now passes on to each of her patients.

Aset's job wasn't easy: she had to talk her patients out of ancient practices such as placing heavy stones on the bodies of laboring women to hasten delivery, or firing off rifles next to their ears to "frighten" the baby out of the womb. Traditionally, infibulated women are restitched after each childbirth, an excruciating procedure that delays recovery and increases the risk of infection.

"Now I know there's no use to it, and as I was convinced I hope I'll convince others. But it's a difficult job," Aset said. Sometimes women demanded the stitches because they feared their husbands' rejection. Others just didn't believe Aset's assertion that the practice was damaging. If a woman insisted, Aset reinfibulated her, hoping at least that the clean instruments she used would do less damage than those of the traditional local midwife, who would almost certainly be called in if she refused.

Because some Christians and animists also practice genital muti- lation, many Muslims resent the way it is linked most closely with their own faith. But one in five Muslim girls lives today in a commu- nity that sanctions some sort of interference with her genitals.

Widespread mutilation seems to have originated in Stone Age central Africa and traveled north, down the Nile, into ancient Egypt. It wasn't until Arab-Muslim armies conquered Egypt in the eighth century that the practices spread out of Africa in a systematic way, parallel to the dissemination of Islam, reaching as far as Pakistan and Indonesia. They drifted back to a few places on the Arabian Peninsula: in the Buraimi Oasis in the United Arab Emirates, it was traditional until a few years ago to remove about an eighth of an inch of the clitoris from all six-year-old girls. Asked the reasons for the practice, the Buraimi women couldn't give any. Well versed in their religion, they knew that no such practice was advocated in the Koran, and they were aware that many neighboring tribes didn't do it. But they knew that what they hoped for from the operation was to safeguard their daughters' chastity, because upon that chastity depended the honor of the girls' fathers and brothers.

While some Muslims protest the linkage of mutilation with their faith, few religious figures speak out against the practice, and numerous Islamic texts still advocate it. In Australia, I once heard an educated and articulate young Muslim express gratitude for the removal of part of her own clitoris: "It reminds me that my marriage is about more important things than pleasure," she said.

In London in 1992, Donu Kogbara, a *Sunday Times* investigative reporter, had no trouble finding a doctor who agreed to remove her clitoris, even though the operation has been banned in Britain since the Prohibition of Female Circumcision Act was passed in 1985. The reporter simply told the Harley Street doctor, Farouk Siddique, that her fiancé was insisting she have the operation before their marriage.

In most Muslim countries women are the custodians of their male relatives' honor. If a wife commits adultery or a daughter has sex before marriage, or is even suspected of having done so, they dishonor their father, their brothers and sometimes the whole family that bears their name. To lessen or destroy sexual pleasure is to lessen temptation; a fallback in case the religious injunctions on veiling and seclusion somehow fail to do the job.

Yet the lessening of women's sexual pleasure directly contradicts the teachings of Muhammad.

To Muslims, every word of the Koran is sacrosanct. "There is no doubt in this book," the Koran says, and every Muslim believes that its 6,000 verses constitute the direct instruction of God. But there *are* debates about Islam's second source of religious instruction: the massive body of *hadith,* or anecdotal traditions about the prophet's life and sayings, compiled by the early Muslims in a formidable research effort in the two centuries following Muhammad's death. Because Muslims feel that emulation of Muhammad is ideal, every detail of his habits, no matter how apparently trivial, has been preserved from the accounts of his survivors. The result is a collection of anecdotes, each with a genealogy that documents the source of the story and exactly how and through whom it was passed on. Each tradition gets a ranking: "true," "good" or "weak." Thus, Muslim scholars can make their own determination about whether the chain of transmission is reliable.

From the study of hadith, various schools of Islamic thought have emerged, and within those schools, particular teachers have developed wide followings. Most agree on what is *haram,* or forbidden, such as eating pork and drinking alcohol, and also on what is *wajib,* or obligatory, such as the content and timing of the five daily prayers. A Muslim sins either by doing a forbidden act or by neglecting an obligatory one. In between, though, are *makruh,* or discouraged and unbecoming acts; and *sunnat* acts, which are desirable but not obligatory.

To most Muslim men, growing a beard is sunnat—a desirable act that expresses humility and emulates the prophet. A man will be rewarded for doing it; he won't be punished for neglecting to do it. In the Muslim communities that practice female genital mutilation, removing the clitoris is on a par with growing a beard—a sunnat act. Some Muslims believe Muhammad's sunnah—tradition or "trodden path"—encouraged the removal of one third of a female child's clitoris. The majority of Muslims say no such sunnah exists. The evidence supports the latter view, for there is an immense body of hadith in which Muhammad and his closest disciples extol women's sexuality and their right to sexual pleasure.

Many hadith reveal that Muhammad loathed the kind of sexual repression required by Christianity's monastic traditions. One night, when a woman came to Muhammad's house to complain that her husband, Othman, was too busy praying to have sex, Muhammad was so irritated that he didn't even wait to put on his shoes. He went straight to Othman's house, his shoes in his hand, and berated him: "O Othman! Allah didn't send me for monasticism, rather he sent me with a simple and straight law. I fast, pray and also have intimate relations with my wife." Compare that with St. Paul to the Corinthians: "It is good for a man not to touch a woman. . . . But if they cannot exercise self-control, let them marry: for it is better to marry than to burn." Muslims see the West's sexual revolution as an inevitable reaction to churches that tried to suppress and make shameful the God-given sexual urge.

To Muhammad, sex within marriage was to be enjoyed by the husband and wife alike. He especially encouraged foreplay: "When any one of you has sex with his wife, then he should not go to them like birds; instead he should be slow and delaying," he said. Once, discussing cruelty, he cited intercourse without foreplay as a form of cruelty to women.

Nor does Islam set limits on the kind of sex married couples can enjoy. "Your wives are your tillage," says the Koran. "Go in therefore unto your tillage in what manner soever ye will." Most Islamic scholars interpret this to mean that all kinds of intercourse, including oral sex, are permissible. As for positions for intercourse, there are few taboos for enthusiastic lovers. It is *makruh,* or discouraged, to make love standing up, or with either the head or the rear end facing Mecca. The few unequivocal *don'ts* in Islamic marital life—don't, for example, make love to your wife after she's dead—reveal the religion's willingness to contemplate the gamut of sexual possibilities.

Islam is one of the few religions to include sex as one of the rewards of the afterlife—although only for male believers. One of the Koran's many descriptions of paradise reads like a brochure for a heavenly whorehouse. In a fertile garden with fountains and shade, male believers will be entertained by gorgeous supernatural beings with "complexions like rubies and pearls," whose eyes will be incapable of noticing another man, and "whom no man will have deflowered before them."

If Muslim women aren't mentioned as partaking in this sexual afterlife, at least they are provided for on earth. In many Muslim countries, one of the few grounds on which a woman can initiate divorce under Islamic law is the failure of her husband to have sex with her at least once in four months. The reason: a sexually frustrated wife is more easily tempted to commit adultery, which leads to *fitna,* or the social chaos of civil war.

"Almighty God created sexual desire in ten parts; then he gave nine parts to women and one to men," said Ali, the husband of

Muhammad's beloved daughter Fatima and the founder of Shiite Islam. At my Catholic school, we were taught the reverse: girls, the less sexually active gender, had to guard their behavior because boys, driven crazy by lust, weren't capable of guarding theirs. In either culture, women somehow managed to get the wrong end of the stick. Women bear the brunt of fending off social disorder in the Catholic tradition because they *aren't* considered sexually active, and in the Muslim tradition because they *are*. It is this notion of women's barely controllable lust that often lies behind justifications for clitoridectomy, seclusion and veiling. "You think we hide our women because we're confused about sex," a Saudi friend named Abdulaziz said to me one day. "On the contrary. We hide them because we're *not* confused."

But it continued to confuse me. In Saudi Arabia, I got to know a couple who had fallen in love over the phone. He edited a magazine; she contributed a poem. He called her to discuss its publication, and the two of them were soon having long, intimate discussions on poetry and politics. They agreed to marry before they ever met.

Like most Saudi homes, theirs had two entrances—one for men, one for women. I arrived at the high-walled villa one night for a party. White-robed men moved to the front door. Their wives, black-veiled and clutching colorfully dressed toddlers, made their way to an entrance at the side.

Each door opened on a large, sofa-lined salon, the women's decorated in floral pink cottons and plush carpet; the men's a more austere and formal room. The two groups didn't mingle. But there was one male guest the hosts particularly wanted me to meet: an academic who had been jailed for political views that pitted him against the Saudi monarchy. To talk with him, I had to break with convention and sit with the men. When I returned to the women's salon, the man's wife winked at me. "You just did me a great favor," she said. "My husband *loves* to talk politics. And talking politics to a *woman* is sure to have made him aroused. Now I can't wait to get him home. I know I'll have great sex with him tonight." I blushed. The woman laughed. "You Westerners are so shy about sex," she said. "Here, we talk about it all the time."

Although Saudi women wanted large families, none of them

would have understood the Catholic notion that sex was purely for procreation. The prophet Muhammad had children only in his first marriage, yet he enjoyed sexual relations with all his later wives, some of whom were beyond childbearing age. He also sanctioned coitus interruptus, the common birth control method of the day.

The issue of contraception arose when Muslim soldiers began to win big victories. Women were part of the booty of war, and the Koran gave men sexual rights over their war-captive slaves. But Muhammad introduced new limits on these rights. First, the Koran encouraged Muslims to free their slaves "if you see any good in them"; a novel and highly unpopular idea in an economy that thrived on the slave trade. The Koran also enjoined Muslims not to force female slaves to have sex, if the women wanted to preserve their chastity.

Contraception became important because any Muslim's slave who bore her owner's child could not be sold and was automatically freed on the man's death. Her child, meanwhile, became the owner's heir. For a soldier who didn't want to lose the marketability of his captives, or see his estate dispersed among slave-born offspring, preventing pregnancy became essential to preserving wealth. Muhammad told a soldier to go ahead and practice withdrawal, for if God really wanted to create something, no human action could prevent it.

Islamic jurisprudence tries to keep up with modern sexual dilemmas by applying ancient reasoning to contemporary circumstances. For instance, Islamic scholars have ruled that artificial insemination is permissible, but only with the sperm of a woman's own husband. Citing the Koranic injunction that believers should "guard their private parts except from their spouses," most Muslims rule out the use of donor sperm. But what if a couple, desperate for a child, transgresses this ruling and conceives a baby through insemination by donor sperm? Whose child is it, for purposes of Islamic custody or inheritance laws?

When the Shiite jurist, Mohamed Jawad al-Mughniyah, was asked to rule on such a case, he referred to an ancient inheritance battle in which a woman had intercourse with her husband, then went straight to her slave girl and had lesbian relations. The semen of the woman's husband supposedly flowed to the vagina of the slave, impregnating her.

After explaining the punishment to be meted out to the two women for having illicit lesbian sex, the imams ruled that the slave's child was the heir of the owner of the semen. Following that judgment, Sheik al-Mughniyah ruled that the child of donor-sperm insemination must always be considered to have been fathered by the sperm donor. It can't be considered as related to, or an heir of, its mother's husband.

The more time I spent in Muslim countries, the more the paradox between sexual license and repression bewildered me. One hot summer day in Iran, I traveled to the religious center of Qum with Nahid Aghtaie, a medical student who had abandoned her studies in London to return and take part in her country's Islamic revolution. A gold-domed mosque dominates Qum's flat desert skyline, and its mirror-tiled interior houses the remains of a saintly Shiite woman, Fatima Massoumah (Fatima the Chaste One). Iranians generally don't let non-Muslims enter important shrines but Nahid, saying the regulation came not from Islam but from narrow-mindedness, had insisted I ignore it.

As Nahid washed for prayer, I wandered through the mosque's vast forecourt, watching families setting out picnics in its blue-tiled enclaves. Eventually I became aware that a turbaned man was following me. He was a youth with a wispy beard, wearing the pale green gown and thin black cloak of an Iranian cleric in training. Qum is full of such young men. As I turned around, he took a step closer and whispered something urgent, in Farsi: *"Honim sigheh mishi?"* I was worried that he'd spotted me as a non-Muslim and was asking me to leave. I pulled my chador tighter across my face and walked briskly away from him with downcast eyes. Finding Nahid, I joined her in the press of bodies surging toward the women's entrance. At the door we handed over our shoes and passed into the shrine's shimmering interior.

Inside, tongues of light from a chandelier danced off the glass mosaics and spilled over intricate enamel medallions set in carved marble. Nahid made her way through the crowd of women and wrapped her hands around the pillars of beaten silver that formed a tall cage around Fatima's tomb. She stood between a toothless crone and a pregnant girl, offering prayers to this female saint who might sympathize with womanly problems.

Months later, describing the beauty of the place to an Iranian friend, I mentioned how glad I was to have seen it, and how I'd very nearly been evicted by a mullah. My friend laughed. "I don't think he doubted you were a Muslim. He was asking you to marry him." What he had asked—"Does the lady want a temporary marriage with me?"—had been an invitation to an exclusively Shiite contract named *sigheh*, or *muta*. "You probably had your chador on the wrong way around," my friend explained. "That's one of the signals women use if they're looking for sigheh."

Sigheh, agreed between a man and woman and sanctioned by a cleric, can last as little as a few minutes or as long as ninety-nine years. Usually the man pays the woman an agreed sum of money in exchange for a temporary marriage. The usual motive is sex, but some temporary marriages are agreed upon for other purposes. When sex is the motive, the transaction differs from prostitution in that the couple have to go before a cleric to record their contract, and in Iran, any children born of the union are legitimate. Otherwise, sigheh is free of the responsibilities of marriage: the couple can make any agreements they like regarding how much time they will spend together, how much money will be involved and what services, sexual or nonsexual, each will provide.

Shiites believe Muhammad approved of sigheh. Sunnis, the majority branch of Islam, don't agree. Even in Shiite Iran, sigheh had fallen from favor until Rafsanjani encouraged it after the Iran-Iraq War which ended in 1988. In a 1990 sermon, he argued that the war had left a lot of young widows, many of them without hope of remarriage. Such women, he said, needed both material support and sexual satisfaction. At the same time, plenty of young men who couldn't afford to set up house for a bride were postponing marriage. Sexual tension needed healthy release, he said, and since sigheh existed for that purpose within Islam, why not use it?

His remarks sparked a heated debate among Iranian women, some of whom bitterly opposed the practice as exploitative. They argued that the state should provide for war widows adequately, so that they didn't have to sell their bodies in sigheh. But others spoke out in its favor. Sigheh, they said, wasn't just a matter of money. Widows and divorcees had sexual needs and a desire for male company, and the sigheh "husband" was a welcome male presence for the children in their homes. Iran's satirical weekly magazine, *Golagha*, ran a cartoon lampooning the likely effects of Rafsanjani's argument. It showed two desks for marriage licenses, one for sigheh and one for permanent wedlock. The clerk at the permanent desk had no customers; the queue for sigheh stretched out the door.

Mostly, it is poorer women who consent to sigheh. A lawyer friend told me about her cleaner, whose husband had died young and left her to support two children. "For a long time, she was a very bitter person," my friend said. "She would come to my house and see me enjoying my life with my husband and daughter, while her life was nothing but work." Then the cleaner contracted a temporary marriage. "Her personality changed overnight. It wasn't just the money. Suddenly, she had a man to spend time with, to take her out. In our culture, a man and a woman can't just go out on a date and enjoy each other's company, but with sigheh they can."

Some Shiites also use sigheh to create a relationship that will allow a woman to appear unveiled in front of a man before whom it would otherwise be forbidden—for instance, a distant relative sharing the same house. These sigheh contracts are written to specify that no sexual relations are involved. In the West, some Shiite families are using sigheh as a way to make it possible for young couples to get to know each other well before marriage. A sigheh contract that bans sexual relations can allow a boy and girl to date each other for the duration of their engagement, without defying religion or tradition.

Sigheh also provides an answer to the kinds of infertility problems that Westerners are now trying to solve with legal contracts for surrogate motherhood. In the Sunni branch of Islam, if a woman is infertile her husband usually divorces her or brings home a second wife. In Iran, a sigheh contract can be drawn up signifying that the object of the temporary marriage is a child that the husband and his permanent wife will raise.

Sigheh is also the only way a Shiite man can marry a non-Muslim woman. Unlike the Sunnis, who allow Muslim men to marry other monotheists, Shiites demand conversion from all non-Muslim women, as well as non-Muslim men, before a permanent marriage is valid.

Rafsanjani's revival of sigheh came as a boon to nonreligious Iranians whose private lives had been disrupted by revolutionary intrusions. Unmarried lovers, for instance, couldn't go away together for a weekend—hotels wouldn't give them a double room without a marriage license, and Revolutionary Guards might catch them at any roadblock. For Lou, a European woman who had fallen in love with Persian culture and adopted Iranian citizenship, this posed problems. Although she had to convert to Islam to remain in Iran, her religious leanings were a mélange of Zen, yoga and spiritualism. A bohemian at heart with no intention of conforming to Islamic sexual rules, she took many lovers, and many risks, until the reevaluation of sigheh. Now, when she takes a lover, she simply signs him up for a few-months sigheh and has a paper to wave at any prying revolutionary zealots. It probably isn't what Rafsanjani had in mind.

Yet, for both Sunnis and Shiites, whatever license their faith allows comes walled around with ghastly penalties for sexual transgression. The limits on sexual freedom in Islam are drawn strictly around the marriage bed, be it temporary or permanent. Extramarital sex and homosexuality are prohibited, and both offenses can draw the most horrific punishments in the Islamic legal code.

While the death penalty, in Islamic law, is optional for murder, it is mandatory for any convicted adulterer who could have satisfied his or her sexual urge lawfully with a spouse. The sentence is commuted to a hundred lashes if the adulterer is unmarried, or if the spouse was ill or far away when the adultery was committed. In Iran, stonings, or, as the Iranians prefer to translate the word, lapidations, are still carried out in cases of adultery. Saudi Arabia also specifies stoning as punishment for married adulterers. Some of the victorious Afghan mujahedin supported so enthusiastically by the U. S. Government during their war with the Soviet Union want to reintroduce stoning in Afghanistan. Yet stoning is never specified as a punishment for adultery in the Koran. The Koran states that adulterous wives should be confined "to their houses until death overtakes them." During Muhammad's years in Medina, however, stonings for adultery were often carried out by the large Jewish community in the town, and several hadith have Muhammad also prescribing this punishment for Muslims. But it was after Muhammad's death, during the rule of the second caliph, Omar, a man notoriously harsh on women, that stoning became codified as the means of an adulterer's execution.

Today, in Iran, men to be stoned are buried up to their waists, women to the chest, and the size of the stones is carefully regulated. Neither boulders nor pebbles may be used, so that death is neither mercifully quick nor endlessly prolonged. In November 1991 a thirty-year-old woman named Zahra, who managed to scramble out of the pit in which she'd been buried, had her death sentence commuted: the judiciary felt that her escape must have been the will of God.

Those who have recently witnessed stonings describe all-male crowds, different from the mixed groups who attend beheadings. The mood is commonly one of rage and bloodlust. Part of the ritual of the Hajj—the holy pilgrimage to Mecca—is the stoning of pillars meant to represent Satan. Witnesses say the woman being executed somehow becomes as dehumanized as those pillars—an outlet, perhaps, for the men's guilt at their own uncontrollable sexuality. Yet the stones in this case hit soft flesh. Because of the way she is buried, each impact snaps her neck backward in a series of excruciating whiplashes. Death often comes when her head is knocked completely off.

It is hard to imagine a worse way to die. Yet the punishments set down for homosexual sodomy are designed to be even more cruel. If the partners are married men, they may be burned to death or thrown to their deaths from a height. If they are unmarried, the sodomized partner, unless he is a minor, is executed, the sodomizer lashed a hundred times. The variation in the penalty reflects the Muslim loathing of the idea of a man taking the feminine role of the penetrated partner. Lesbian sex, if the women are single, draws a hundred lashes. Married lesbians may be stoned.

"Why is Islam so severe in matters of adultery, homosexuality and lesbianism?" asks Mohammed Rizvi, a cleric with the Vancouver Islamic Educational Foundation, who writes on Islam and sex. "If the

Islamic system had not allowed the gratification of sexual urge by lawful means without associating guilt with it, then it would be right to say that Islam is very severe. But since it has allowed the fulfillment of sexual instincts by lawful means, it is not prepared to tolerate any perverted behavior."

But "perverted" behavior went on, even among the most sanctimonious Muslims. In the fall of 1990, when American troops were pouring in to defend Saudi Arabia from Saddam Hussein, I went to report on how the Saudis were reacting. On my first night in the country I interviewed an influential oil company executive. Educated at Georgetown University and the Wharton School, I expected him to give me a Western-influenced, liberal view. Instead, he told me he hoped the Americans would stay sequestered on their bases to prevent "unholy ramifications" from contaminants such as alcohol and women drivers. He said he thought it was "obnoxious" that CNN had sent a woman reporter, the veteran correspondent Christiane Amanpour, to cover the troop deployment. For him, America's obsession with sexual equality was nothing but a front for immorality. "In any corporation, tell me the boss isn't looking at his secretary and figuring out a way to have her. If it doesn't happen, it's only because of self-interest—too much to lose if they get caught."

His glass-walled study looked out on a floodlit swimming pool and a flower-filled courtyard. If the wall were not glass, he explained, he wouldn't be able to sit with me. "If a man and a woman are alone together, the third person present is Satan," he said. After about an hour I closed my notebook and thanked him for the interview. Showing me to the door, he paused, as an afterthought, and asked if I'd like to meet a few of his friends. Of course, I said.

Stepping across the hall, he opened a door on a dimly lit room full of blaring rock music and entangled bodies. A gorgeous Filipina in a black Spandex mini-dress was dancing, rubbing herself rhythmically against her white-robed partner. Another man sat cross-legged on the floor, flashing a colored light at her legs. On sunken couches, a beautiful blond-maned Turk caressed an Egyptian woman for the benefit of a smiling male voyeur. At a bar in the corner, guests helped themselves to Johnnie Walker whiskey—$135 a bottle on the black market and its consumption punishable by flogging in the city square.

Swirling a glass of ice splashed with Scotch, the host seemed oblivious to the contradiction between what he'd just finished saying and what he was now showing me. After his second drink, he began to tell me about his failed marriage, to an American. "She insisted on riding around in my Rolls without covering her face. Of course, everyone stared at her," he said with distaste. After the divorce he had kept the children, as was his right in Saudi law. He had no plans to remarry. "I can have a woman any time," he said, nodding in the direction of the Filipina. "Last winter I paid a model to be with me for fifteen days in Switzerland."

I was baffled by this man's hypocrisy until I read Naguib Mahfouz's novel, *Palace Walk*, in which the main character is a man of strong faith who strictly sequesters his womenfolk, but each night goes out whoring with Cairo's famous singers. When a sheik chastises him for his fornication, he replies that "the professional women entertainers of today are the slave girls of yesterday, whose purchase and sale God made legal."

The Saudi clearly looked upon the women dancing in his disco room in a similar way. Most of them worked for Saudia, the national airline. It was one of the few jobs available for foreign women in Saudi Arabia, which generally didn't grant work visas to women other than housemaids. The airline needed foreigners since no Saudi women could be employed in a job that required unchaperoned travel and constant contact with men.

When I rose to leave, the Filipina asked if she could get a lift with my driver. She reached for her abaya—the Arabian version of the chador—and face veil. Aware of the men's eyes on her, she twitched the black silk slowly forward, letting it insinuate itself inch by inch over her cleavage and pour slowly down her thighs. Taking the piece of gauze that covers the face, she tossed her long tresses forward, leaning suggestively toward the men for a moment, then turning slightly to provide a view of her curvaceous rump. She flipped her head back, catching all her hair in the veil. It was a reverse strip tease. At the end of it she stood there, a black cone, the picture of Saudi female probity.

At first it surprised me that my hypocritical host would risk such a lifestyle in a country with such harsh laws against fornication. But eventually I realized that he was quite safe behind the high walls of his compound. In sexual offenses, executions and floggings usually take place only if the accused confesses. To get a conviction otherwise is almost impossible under Islamic rules of evidence, which demand that four male witnesses (or, since the testimony of a woman equals half a man's, two female and three male witnesses) testify to having seen penetration. Accusers without the right number of witnesses to back their testimony will be charged with slander and sentenced to eighty lashes.

But often, for women, none of these rules apply, because executions are carried out long before the accused ever gets near a court.

"My father died when I was nine years old," said Tamam Fahiliya, raking her nails through a wedge of curly, cropped hair. "Lucky for me. If he was here, maybe I would have been killed many years ago."

Tamam reached across the low coffee table in her apartment and stubbed out a cigarette. As she leaned forward, flesh rippled over the top of a low-cut bustier. Tamam lived alone, and lived dangerously, for a thirty-seven-year-old Palestinian Muslim woman. For three years she had had a lover: a handsome young Palestinian doctor who claimed to be a feminist.

"Of course, it was just talk. In the end he went back to his village and married his cousin. A man can always go back. But not me. No one would marry me now but a geriatric or a crazy man."

Tamam wasn't exaggerating to say her father might well have killed her if he had known of her affair. Every year about forty Palestinian women die at the hands of their fathers or brothers in so-called "honor killings" that wipe away the shame of a female relative's premarital or extramarital sex. Most of the killings happen in the poorer and more remote Palestinian villages. Often the women are burned, so that the death can be passed off as an accident. The killer usually becomes a local hero: a man who has done what was necessary to clear his family name. "Honor" killings are somewhat better docu-

mented among Palestinians than elsewhere because of the Israeli occupation: many, although not all, of the deaths come to the attention
of the Israeli military or civilian police.

Yet honor killings happen throughout the Islamic world. One of
the most notorious, the execution of the Saudi princess Mishaal bint
Fahd bin Mohamed in a Jeddah parking lot in 1977, was secretly
witnessed by a British expatriate. The airing of a film on the killing,
in a documentary titled *Death of a Princess*, created a diplomatic
incident that led to the expulsion of the British ambassador to Saudi
Arabia. In the United States, when PBS planned to air the film, a
major oil-company sponsor asked that it be canceled. Few of the facts
of the affair have ever been confirmed. The story told on British TV
held that Mishaal was a married woman who had run off with her
lover, Khalid Muhallal, the nephew of the man who is now Saudi
Arabia's information minister, and had spent a few nights with him
in a Jeddah hotel before trying to flee the country dressed as a man.
She was caught at the airport and handed over to her family.

But an American woman whose marriage into a prominent
Saudi family made her intimate with the people involved in the case
tells an even more extreme story. Mishaal, she says, was unmarried.
She was killed simply for flouting the family will and running away
from an arranged marriage in order to marry a man she loved. Her
grandfather, Prince Mohamed, the patriarch of Mishaal's branch of
the ruling family, ignored pleas for clemency even from his younger
brother, the king. Mishaal was shot; Khalid Muhallal was beheaded.
There was no announcement following the killings as there is with
executions that take place after due process of sharia law.

In either version of the story, under sharia rules of evidence
neither of the young people could possibly have been convicted. If the
documentary's account was correct, and Mishaal was a married
woman who committed adultery, the penalty would have been death,
but only if four witnesses had caught the pair in flagrante delicto at
the hotel. Circumstantial evidence, such as being together in the same
place overnight, would not have been sufficient. And as an unmarried
woman, Mishaal had not committed a capital offense under sharia
law.

It was unusual for an extrajudicial honor killing to be carried out by an upper-class family such as the al-Sauds. Generally, it is the women of poorer and less educated families who are most at risk.

Tamam's father had been uneducated and needy: he supported his seven children by working as a gardener. The family lived in the ancient city of Akko, in a crowded quarter close to the Crusader walls that run along the sea front. Because her family was among 156,000 Palestinians who stayed, and didn't flee, during the Arab-Israeli War in 1948, Tamam grew up an Arab with Israeli citizenship, speaking Hebrew as fluently as Arabic. She was the last of five daughters; her name, which translates as "enough," or "finished," was her parents' plea for an end to the long run of unwanted girls. Their prayer was answered, several years later, with the birth of two sons.

The brothers, too, could have been problems for Tamam. But because they were so much younger, and because she left home when they were still small boys, they never had a chance to feel proprietorial about their sister. "For most of us, our brothers are like big, barking dogs who feel that their whole purpose in life is to guard our bodies," she said. "It's a kind of oppression for them, too, that they have to go through their lives feeling this responsibility and worrying that at any moment we will snatch their honor away."

After she finished school, Tamam left home immediately to take a live-in job teaching disabled children. Later she trained as a nurse. By the time I met her in 1993 she had been living alone or with friends for more than ten years. She was the only Muslim woman I'd ever met in the Middle East who didn't live with either husband or family.

In June 1991, Tamam picked up the morning newspaper and read a short item about a murder in the village of Iksal, in the Galilee, not very far from where she'd grown up. The woman was nineteen years old, unmarried and seven months pregnant. Her incinerated body was found tied up in a burned-out car. The murderer was the girl's seventy-four-year-old father.

"I felt, 'This girl is me. She is any one of us. We are all fighting for our lives here.' "

For about six months before the murder, Tamam and a few of her friends had been meeting once a week, reading feminist books and discussing the problems of women in Arab and Muslim societies.

They had even come up with a name for their little group: Al Fanar—The Lighthouse. "We had big dreams about being a beacon for women in trouble. So I called my friends and said, 'If we don't do something about this case, what is the use of all our talking?'"

Tamam and her friends made placards which read: "Father, brother, support me, don't slaughter me." They called all the Arab women's groups they knew, asking for support. They didn't get much. None of the West Bank Palestinian newspapers would touch the subject, steering clear of any criticism of Arab society that could be used as propaganda by Israelis. West Bank women's groups argued that the time wasn't right, that the struggle for independence from Israeli rule had to come before questions of women's rights could be raised. The Israeli-Arab political parties also kept clear, not wanting to antagonize their constituents.

Tamam and her dozen friends put up the money to advertise the demonstration in two Arab-Israeli papers. Immediately her phone started ringing with harassment and threats. "The callers accused us of promoting promiscuity," Tamam said. One caller quoted the Koran's injunction that men are meant to be in charge of women, and accused her of heresy for challenging that notion. "They said if the demonstration went ahead we would all end up like the girl from Iksal."

Still, when about forty women gathered for the demonstration on a Monday afternoon in the main street of Nazareth, they found both supportive as well as hostile onlookers.

"Some yelled 'Whores' and other insults," said Tamam, "but several older women and even a few men joined us spontaneously." Encouraged by their success, the women began traveling to remote villages, distributing articles that argued not just against "honor" killings but also against forced marriages and the pernicious way gossip is used in small communities to control the behavior of women and girls. "We found it was best to go to the villages in the hours when the men were likely to be at work," says Tamam, "otherwise the husband would come to the door, take the flyer, look at it and tear it up before his wife even got a chance to see it."

In November another honor killing prompted a demonstration. This time the target was the Israeli police in the Israeli-Arab town of

Ramle. The police had picked up a sixteen-year-old Arab runaway they'd found driving around in a stolen car with a married man. The girl begged the police not to involve her parents. "She explained that they'd kill her, but the police took no notice," Tamam said. "They called the family and said, 'We've got your daughter here. She's very scared; you have to promise you won't hurt her.' Of course, the family said they wouldn't, so the police gave her back to them." Not long after, the girl was found murdered.

Al Fanar's activities began to attract the attention of the Israeli press. The women welcomed reporters, and then were dismayed by the articles that appeared. "We felt used for anti-Arab propaganda," Tamam says. "It was 'Look how the backward Arabs are killing their girls; look how the backward Muslims are attacking the women who fight it.' The reporters would come and see me and say, 'You're not like an Arab.' I'm sorry, I don't want Jewish people defining what an Arab is and telling me I'm different."

The attention from the Jewish press only heightened the fundamentalist backlash. "As well as calling us whores, now they began calling us traitors," says Tamam. Soon the women couldn't go to the villages without being abused or, worse, ignored. "Even the women began to see us as something so foreign to their community that nothing we said could possibly be of any relevance to them. We thought we knew our culture, but really we only knew our own small circle of friends. Now, if you go to an Arab village and ask the people what they think of Al Fanar, they'll laugh. We became a joke: the whores who thought they could change the way the world works."

The rejection led to arguments over tactics and approach within the group, and finally an acrimonious split. Two years after Al Fanar was founded, the group virtually ceased to function. "Society wasn't ready," says Tamam. "And we, also, weren't ready."

But at least they had tried. And at least the midwives of newly independent Eritrea are trying to undo the damage done to women through perversions of Islamic teaching. Many Muslims are content to claim that honor killings and clitoridectomy are not Islam; that they are customs that come from the national cultures and have nothing to do with the faith. With this assertion, many mainstream Muslims wash their hands of the twin brutalities that shape the lives of perhaps a quarter of the women of Islam.

It is understandable that progressive Muslims hate to see their faith associated with these practices. But what is less understandable is the way they turn their wrath on the commentators criticizing the practices, and not on the crimes themselves. An example is to be found in Rana Kabbani's book, *Letter to Christendom*, which she published as an answer to the attacks on Islam that followed Khomeini's fatwa against Salman Rushdie. Rana Kabbani was born in Damascus but grew up abroad and now lives in London. Her complaint is worth quoting at length: "I am always pained by Western misconceptions about the lives of Muslim women," she writes. "Western ignorance is often inseparable from a patronizing view that insists on seeing us as helpless victims, while hardly distinguishing between the very different cultures we come from. Recently, in London, I was visited by a novelist who had come to talk to me about a Muslim character she wanted to put into her next book. 'How can a feminist like you defend Islam,' she inquired, 'when it advocates female circumcision?' As chance would have it, that same day I read a piece by the historian Marina Warner in which she described Islam as a religion that practices clitoridectomy. Could these two writers not have taken the trouble to discover that this was an African practice which had nothing whatsoever to do with Islam?"

Could Rana Kabbani not have taken the trouble to reflect that one in five Muslim girls lives in a community where some form of clitoridectomy is sanctioned and religiously justified by local Islamic leaders? Or to note the chapters on "Women and Circumcision" appearing in many new editions of Islamic texts, especially in Egypt?

Until Islam's articulate spokeswomen such as Rana Kabbani target their misguided coreligionists with the fervor they expend on outside critics, the grave mistake of conflating Islam with clitoridectomy and honor killings will continue. And much more importantly, so will the practices themselves, at the cost of so many Muslim women's health and happiness.

Chapter 3

HERE COME THE BRIDES

"And of his signs another is,
that he hath created for you, out
of yourselves, wives, that ye may
cohabit with them; and hath
put love and compassion
between you."

THE KORAN
THE CHAPTER OF THE GREEKS

*R*ata-tata-tat-tat BOOM BOOM BOOM! Rata-tata-tat-tat BOOM BOOM BOOM!

I pulled another pillow over my head, but it was no good. Lifting a corner of the pile of bedclothes, I opened one eye and peered at the hotel's digital clock, winking greenly from the night table. It was 11:30 P.M. At least another hour, possibly two, before the noise would stop. I had to be up at 5 A.M. to catch a flight. But sleep was an impossible dream.

I got up and walked to the window. The street below was a traffic jam of wedding parties. I counted at least three bridal limousines stacked up in a holding pattern behind the one that had just pulled in to the hotel entrance. A bride had just emerged from a car and was making her slow procession up the hotel steps, surrounded by a squad of drummers. She was, by my insomniac count, the ninth bride of the night.

Rata-tata-tat-tat BOOM BOOM BOOM!

I was in Baghdad, visiting Iraq in what turned out to be the brief interregnum between Gulf War I (the foreign, subtitled version between Iraq and Iran) and Gulf War II (the American-made international blockbuster). In Iraq, any time bombs stopped falling a wedding boom began. Saddam Hussein had decreed that Iraqis should marry and breed to repair the demographic damage done at the battle front. To achieve his goal, he banned contraceptives and offered large cash incentives for weddings and births.

Since it didn't seem likely that I'd be sleeping any time soon, I decided to go down to the foyer and get a better look at the festivities. Unmuffled by sixteen floors and five pillows, the drums, cymbals and horns were deafening. Souha, the young woman at the center of it all, looked like an accident victim, stunned and trembling. Dressed as elaborately as a princess, she paraded amid the musicians toward a banqueting room set up with groaning trestles of food and a throne made of pink gladiolus. Elsewhere, perhaps earlier that night or perhaps some days ago, the groom and the bride's father had held hands under a piece of cloth provided by an Islamic clergyman. The father had said to the bridegroom: "I give to you my daughter, Souha, the adult virgin, in marriage according to the law of God and of his prophet." The bridegroom answered: "I take your daughter, Souha, in marriage, the adult virgin, according to the law of God and of his prophet." The father then asked, "Do you accept my daughter?", to which the bridegroom answered, "I have accepted her." The father said, "God bless you with her," and the bridegroom replied, "I hope in God she may prove a blessing." Then everyone in the room recited the brief and poetic first chapter of the Koran.

The marriage is legal once the groom and the bride's father sign the wedding contract, or *aqd*. Usually the contract's main purpose is to document how much the groom pays the bride on marriage, and how much more he will have to pay her if he later decides to divorce her. An Islamic aqd is akin to a Western prenuptial agreement—an unromantic, hardheaded document that faces the fact that marriages fail. A well-written aqd can counter some of the inequalities in Islamic family law, setting out a woman's right to work, to continue her education, and adding grounds for divorce to the very few allowed her under sharia law. Today, for example, many women add a clause known as the *esma*, giving her the right to a divorce if she asks for one. Others include a narrower stipulation, stating their right to divorce if the husband ever takes a second wife.

I stood on tiptoe and watched over the shoulders of the ululating women as the groom made his way to join the bride at the front of the room. The bride, Souha, smiled wanly as he raised her veil and kissed her on the forehead. This must have been a progressive family: at most Islamic weddings, even that modest little show of affection wouldn't have happened in public.

Across the hall, one of the earlier parties was already breaking up. Spilling out of the banqueting room, the guests clapped and ululated as the bride and groom disappeared into the elevator and headed for one of the hotel's luxury suites.

When done by the book, the Islamic wedding night tensions should be eased by tender rituals. When the bride is finally delivered by her family to her new husband, the groom is supposed to greet her by removing her shoes and washing her feet. It is an inspired way to vault the hurdle of a stranger's first touch. He is then supposed to pray and bless her, using the following words: "O Allah, bless me with her affection, love and her acceptance of me; and make me pleased with her, and bring us together in the best form of union and in absolute harmony; surely you like lawful things and dislike unlawful things." After the bride prays, the groom places his hand on her forehead and asks God that any child from their union be guarded from Satan.

It was hard to imagine this nervous, rumpled, exhausted-looking couple getting through all that. They were both under intense pressure. For the young man, the continuation of the marriage depended on his display of virility; if he failed to get an erection, his bride could repudiate him. The pressure on her was to prove her virginity. If she didn't bleed, she could be handed back in disgrace to a family that might become enraged enough to kill her. For generations, women had resorted to filling their vaginas with blood-soaked sponges or splinters of glass to compensate for lost hymens. Only peasants in remote villages still paraded the bride's stained garments for public inspection. But the issue of whether Souha was indeed "an adult virgin" still mattered, even in modern, urban families.

"Almost all of them check out with a stolen sheet in their bag, you know," said the hotel's lobby manager, leaning exhausted against a pillar. "Their older relatives still insist on seeing it." Almost a third of the hotel's rooms were booked by newlyweds. "There'll be a lot of you-know-what going on upstairs tonight," he grinned.

I wondered how it was going. Many of the couples were near strangers. Even in Baghdad, where men and women worked alongside one another, their personal lives remained highly segregated. During the war with Iran, when Iraqis were banned from foreign travel, I got used to being the only woman aboard flights in and out of the country. At the airport on my way home to Cairo, I would line up amid a planeful of Egyptian laborers for the Iraqis' intense security inspection. Once a young inspector had peered into my toiletries bag and pulled out a box of tampons. He prodded the contents, then called his supervisor. The two men emptied the box onto the counter and whispered together. Finally, holding one cellophane-wrapped tampon up to the light, the young inspector barked accusingly: "For what is this?" When I tried to tell him, he looked baffled, then horrified. Although he would have read in the Koran that menstruation is "an illness," I don't think anyone had ever explained to him the exact nature of a woman's monthly period.

Until this century, most Muslims married soon after puberty. Now, with the need for maturity in marriage widely recognized and the cost of weddings soaring, most young Muslims have to delay finding a spouse into their twenties and early thirties. Until she is married, a devout Muslim girl is expected to avoid even making eye contact with a strange boy. She will never so much as shake hands with a man, much less go out on a date or share a kiss.

In countries such as Egypt, where women had made their way into the work force, it was becoming more common for young people to meet prospective spouses before the family became involved. But in many countries marriages remain arrangements between strangers. In Saudi Arabia it wasn't until 1981 that a committee of Islamic scholars finally ruled that young women could meet their intended spouses, unveiled, before the wedding. "Any man forbidding his daughter or sister to meet her fiancé face to face will be judged as sinning," the committee found. But some Saudi women chose not to take advantage of even this small concession. Basilah al-Homoud, a thirty-eight-year-old school principal, had been twenty-one when her father told her that she had received a marriage proposal. "He said, 'Do you want to see him, do you want to sit with him?' I said, 'If you sit with him, it is enough for me.'" She glimpsed her husband, for the first time, from an upper window of her house as he arrived on the night of their wedding. "He was walking into the house with some of his relatives. My eyes went straight to him and I prayed that he was the one." She believed she had been right to trust her father. "Who wants my happiness as much as he does? Who knows me better? Done this way, my marriage is not two persons only. It involves my whole family, and my husband's whole family. And because the families are involved, I would think a thousand times before I say, 'Can I have a divorce?'"

But some young women weren't so confident. "Marriage for us is a complete risk," said Arezoo Moradian, an eighteen-year-old English-language student in Tehran. "A husband has so much power over you that you have to be mad to marry someone you don't know perfectly. But under the system we have here, it's impossible to get to know a boy perfectly. You can't go out with him, you can't spend time alone with him."

And once you marry him, his word is law, as the religious commentator in the *Saudi Gazette* pointed out to a correspondent in the January 9, 1993, edition of the newspaper. "In today's liberal world it is often assumed that the wife has absolute equal rights over her husband," wrote Name Withheld of Jeddah. "I think it would be good if you could explain the correct conduct of a wife."

Name Withheld was no doubt pleased with the explanation. "Leadership in the family is given to the husband," the commentator wrote. "For a wife to demand complete and full equality with her husband will result in having two masters in the family and this does not exist in Islam." Specifically, the commentator added, "To refuse to go with her husband when he calls her to bed is a grave mistake." Furthermore, "Leaving the house excessively is a bad habit for a woman. She should also not leave the house if her husband objects to her doing so."

If all this becomes too much, and she wishes to leave for good, obtaining a divorce can be fraught with difficulties for a woman.

Technically, Islam frowns on divorce. A hadith attributed to

Muhammad states that, of all lawful things, divorce is the most hated by God. The Koran gives an extensive and discouraging list of requirements to be fulfilled in ending a marriage, beginning with an instruction to bring arbitrators from the families of both bride and groom to attempt to patch up the rupture. In many countries Muslim authorities have expended much energy on debates over whether the arbitration is obligatory or merely recommended. "None came forward to ask why, if it is obligatory or recommended, whichever it may be, no practical steps are taken to comply with this clear commandment," wrote an exasperated Muslim scholar, Muhammad Rashid Rida, who, until his death in 1935, spearheaded an intellectual response to the encroachment of Western values in Muslim countries. Both he and the influential Iranian commentator on women's issues, Murtada Mutahhari, began a rereading of the Koran's pronouncements on divorce that, if followed through, could lead to the adoption of laws much more equitable toward women.

But, for now, both the Shiites and followers of all four major schools of Sunni thought have enshrined a mode of divorce that only the most convoluted and misogynistic reading of the Koran can support. That is *talaq*, or divorce by a husband pronouncing the words "I divorce you" three times. No grounds are required of him and the wife has no say. For her part, a Muslim woman has no natural right to divorce, and in some Islamic countries no legal way to secure one. The Hanbali school, followed by the Saudis, gives a woman almost no way out of an unhappy marriage without her husband's consent. Shiites and the Sunnis of the Hanafi school allow her to stipulate the right to divorce in her aqd, or marriage contract. Shiites, Hanafi and Maliki law all allow a woman's petition on the grounds of her husband's impotence, and Shiites and Malikis also allow petitions on the grounds of failure to provide support, incurable contagious disease or life-threatening abuse. Mental cruelty, nondisfiguring physical abuse or just plain unhappiness are rarely considered grounds on which a woman can seek divorce.

"I tell you, I hope I never fall in love," the young Iranian, Arezoo, said, impatiently pushing back the fetching black ringlets that kept escaping her magneh. "You know why? Because when girls fall in love here they lose their judgment. Yes, sure, they can put all kinds of conditions in the wedding contract, but who does it? It's always 'Ah, he loves me, he'll never hurt me.' I've watched them. Watched them walking with this stupid smile on their faces into the biggest risk you can take in this life.''

For some women, of course, the risk paid off. The happiest couple I knew also happened to be two of the most strictly observant Muslims I'd ever met. Khadija was a young Kuwaiti Shiite whose marriage had been arranged for her. She had consented to the match without meeting her fiancé, only stipulating that he should be someone who would agree to allow her to continue her studies. During the engagement the pair managed to meet, in secret, and found they liked each other enormously.

Khadija's husband was an importer who did most of his business with Iran. When he traveled to Tehran, he always took Khadija and the children along. Their idea of a fun night out was to go to one of Tehran's *husseinias*—Shiite study centers—to listen to a radical mullah lecturing on Islamic revolution. The two would, of course, sit separately—Khadija in her heavy black hijab always in the back with the other women, where their presence wouldn't distract the men.

Sometimes I would go looking for Khadija in her hotel room, only to find her husband there, minding the children, while she spent the day at lectures at one of the Islamic women's colleges. The hotel-room floor would always be completely covered in freshly laundered bedsheets, so that the toddlers, tumbling and playing on the floor, wouldn't pick up any germs from a carpet that might have been walked on by foreigners who didn't remove their shoes on entering a room.

When Khadija decided to do postgraduate work in London, her husband readily rearranged his business to accommodate her. The two of them never showed any physical affection in the presence of outsiders. But there was electricity in the looks they exchanged and warmth in the way they spoke to each other that made the intensity of their relationship quite obvious. When I asked Khadija why her marriage had worked out so well when so many other relationships looked empty, she smiled. "My husband is a good Muslim," she said. "He knows what the Koran actually says about relations between men and women, and that is what he lives by. It's as simple as that.''

Back in Egypt, my assistant, Sahar, had become engaged.

A few weeks after she began to wear hijab, she arrived for work bubbling with the news. She beamed as she showed me her fiancé's photograph. He was a newly qualified pediatrician and a second cousin. The picture showed a young face, grave and handsome, wearing the stubbly black beard of a devout Muslim.

Sahar had known him for years, seeing him often at family gatherings. But she hadn't considered him a likely suitor. At university he had been active in Islamic groups, risking prison for his opinions at a time when the government was keeping fundamentalists on a tight leash. "I always knew he would only marry a veiled girl," Sahar said. It was after he had seen her, veiled, at a family party, that he had told her parents he would like to propose.

Like many young Egyptian professionals, Sahar's fiancé hadn't found a well-paying post in Egypt. Instead, he had agreed to take a job in Saudi Arabia and would have to work there for several months before he could support a bride. Before her betrothal, Sahar's application to Harvard had been accepted; she could have used the delay to take the place in graduate school that she had been offered. Instead, she turned it down. It wouldn't be appropriate, she explained, for a devout Muslim woman to live alone in an American city. Her new plan was to look into Islamic studies at one of Saudi Arabia's segregated women's schools.

Before her fiancé left for Saudi Arabia, Sahar's family threw a lavish engagement party. Sahar sat on a flower-decked throne and received the gifts of jewelry from her husband-to-be that would become part of her dowry. "My aunt wanted me to take off hijab for the party," she said later. "She said, 'You want to look lovely for your engagement.'" Sahar stuck to her guns and sat on her throne with her hair wrapped away in a white satin scarf.

But it soon seemed Sahar's scarves wouldn't be enough to satisfy her betrothed. Within weeks of arriving in Saudi Arabia's austerely religious atmosphere, he was on the phone to Sahar, suggesting she lengthen her mid-calf dresses to floor length and put on socks to cover her sandaled toes. "I told him I'm not ready for that yet. I told him I want to go slowly, to be sure of what I'm doing," she said. "I've seen other women who go straight into gloves and face veils, and a few months later find they can't stand it. I don't want to put something on that I'm going to want to take off." As the months passed, I began to wonder whether her fiancé was drifting into a fundamentalism too narrow to admit Sahar's broad mind, no matter how correctly veiled.

Meanwhile, under her shapeless clothes, she started to gain weight. The elevator in our apartment building was so ancient it belonged in the Egyptian museum. It malfunctioned just about as often as it functioned. Sahar began to find the six flights of stairs an increasing trial. Sweating, she would sink into the chair by her desk and beg me to turn on the air conditioner, even on the mildest mornings. Because her coverings made her feel the heat, she no longer enjoyed walking with me when we'd go out reporting. She quickly became too out of shape to cover more than a block without gasping. She seemed to be growing old before my eyes.

Calls from Saudi Arabia invariably brought bad news. The medical center that had hired her fiancé had no patients. He would have to wait and see if business improved before he could set a wedding date. When it didn't, he began to search for a better job. But months had passed and he hadn't found one.

There were other disappointments. Once, a few months before she adopted hijab, Sahar had brought a videotape of her best friend's wedding to show me. It was a typical upper-crust Egyptian extravaganza, held at the Nile Hilton. Dancers pranced with candelabra on their heads, drummers and pipers provided the din. Everybody dressed to excess. Sahar told me she'd spent£60—a civil servant's monthly salary—getting her hair done. She watched the tape with her lips parted and eyes shining. Her expression reminded me of my five-year-old niece when I read her a fairy story. I couldn't believe that this serious, Harvard-bound woman admired this ostentatious display. But she did. "God willing, I'll have a wedding just like that," she said.

But it seemed that God, or at least her godly fiancé, had other ideas. Their wedding, he decided, would be small and austere. "I suppose he is right," Sahar said uncertainly. "At all those grand weddings, nobody ever says anything good about the bride or her family. If it isn't fancy enough, they criticize her stinginess. If it is very fancy, they criticize her for showing off." Her fiancé had even appropriated the task of buying the wedding dress. "The dresses are much finer in Saudi Arabia," Sahar said hopefully. That may have been so, but I couldn't help wondering what kind of gown a fundamentalist would choose for his bride.

None of my Egyptian friends seemed to have an easy time finding a mate. It became a race to see who would marry first: Sahar the fundamentalist, who had more or less arranged her own marriage, or my very unfundamentalist friend, who was having one arranged for her. She was named in Arabic for a beautiful flower, so I will call her Rose. She was unusual, even in the rarefied world of rich, Western-educated Cairenes. Like almost all unmarried Egyptians, she lived at home with her parents but, unlike almost all young women, she had a job that required her to travel abroad, alone.

On one of these trips she'd fallen in love with a Paris-based American and was, when I met her, in the midst of a passionate affair. He had offered to marry her, but she had refused. Although the Sunni branch of Islam allows men to marry other monotheists such as Christians or Jews, it doesn't offer the same liberty to women. Because Islam is passed through the paternal line, children of non-Muslim fathers are lost to the faith. Rose's lover came from a Christian fundamentalist family and argued that his conversion would kill his mother. For her part, Rose believed that marrying a Christian would cause a complete rupture with her family. "I would be living in sin," she explained. "And anyway, I want to marry a Muslim. I want my sons to be called Omar and Abdullah. I want to go to the sheik and have a wedding party with dancers and drums. I don't want to slink off to some French bureaucrat for a sly little civil ceremony."

The religious impasse finally ended the affair. As well as a broken heart, Rose had the gnawing anxiety of an Egyptian woman who was over thirty and edging toward irreversible spinsterhood. "I went to my father and said, 'All right. I give in. You've always wanted to arrange a marriage for me, so let's see what you can do. Bring 'em on.'"

Affluent, intelligent and beautiful, with the huge deerlike eyes extolled by Arabian poets, Rose had it all. Using their large network of extended family and business contacts, her parents soon compiled a long list of prospective suitors, and Rose worked her way through it as briskly as a pilot completing a preflight check. Her first meeting was with a young doctor, who came to her house with his father and sat down with Rose and most of her family for tea. "I asked him where he'd traveled and he said Alexandria and Ismailia. Alexandria and Ismailia! How can anyone get to the age of thirty-two and never have gone outside Egypt? His family's rich; he could have gone anywhere. I could never be happy with someone so unadventurous."

After that she vetoed meetings at home. "In the first five minutes I could tell it was pointless, but I was stuck there, being polite, wasting a whole afternoon." She insisted on meeting future prospects at their offices. "Usually they don't get past the first half hour," she reported after a few dismal encounters.

The wealthy young son of a merchant family survived his first interview and seemed promising. Rose even went on a three-week, closely chaperoned holiday to Los Angeles with the family. "I fell in love—with America," she reported on her return. But not with her suitor. "I had to want to do everything when he wanted," she said. "It was a disaster if I didn't like the film he was watching. And he didn't like the fact that I didn't drink. He said when he came home at the end of the day he'd like to share a beer. I said, 'I'll have a Coke and you have a beer; we'll still be sharing the moment.' He said, 'Yes, but we won't be sharing the beer.' It was too ridiculous."

At the Egyptian Foreign Ministry, one would-be spouse, a young diplomat, was preparing for his first posting abroad. "He would have been perfect," Rose sighed wistfully after her brief appointment. "He was witty, cosmopolitan. But he had dirty fingernails."

"Rose," I said, incredulous, "are you telling me you've ruled him out because he had dirty fingernails? For goodness' sake! You can always clean his fingernails." She raised her head and gazed at me sadly with her huge dark eyes. "Geraldine, you don't understand. You married for love. What's a dirty fingernail on someone you love? But if you are going to marry somebody you don't love, everything, *everything*, has to be perfect."

◆

I wondered if my Palestinian friend Rehab had expected perfection from her arranged marriage. If so, I could only guess at the depth of her disappointment.

Rehab lived on a hilltop west of Jerusalem, in an ancient stone village that seemed pinned to the earth by the spindly minaret of its mosque. To get there, it was necessary to drive past the cranes and bulldozers of half a dozen new Jewish settlements. The closest, a kibbutz, was just across the valley, its modern vegetable trellises lacing through the Arabs' ancient orchards like fingers locked in an arm wrestle.

Every time I arrived in the village I looked for Rehab and Mohamed. Rehab was a diminutive, feisty young women who worked as a hairdresser, going from house to house beautifying the village women for weddings and feast days. She kept track of every shred of women's news in town. Her husband Mohamed was an ebullient shopkeeper, strongly built, with muscular forearms, a tangle of thick dark curls and laughing brown eyes. He loved attempting jokes in his colorful, fractured English. I'd often been at their home, a couple of times with Tony along. We shared meals, played with their four-year-old daughter, admired the new coops they'd built for the "Palestine Liberation Chickens" that would free them from dependence on Israeli produce.

Tony and I loved hanging out with Palestinians. They were humorous, outspoken people who seemed to lack Egyptians' class consciousness and Gulf Arabs' reserve. What struck us most was the easy interaction of men and women. Women were in the demonstrations against Israeli occupation, in the hospitals treating the wounded, and at home, around the table, arguing politics with the foreigners as loudly as the men. Mohamed and Rehab's house always seemed full of friends of both sexes, and Tony and I were both equally welcomed.

One beautiful late summer day I arrived in the village alone, and met Mohamed at his shop in the tiny main street. He seemed distracted and upset. He had been impatient since my last visit, he said, because he wanted to ask me something important.

He needed a second wife. He couldn't mention his plans to anyone in the village because his neighbors, like most Palestinians these days, considered polygamy backward. Besides, if Rehab heard about his intention she'd go into a frenzy. Did I know any foreign woman who would secretly marry him? Could he get a visa to go abroad and find someone?

No, I said, stunned by his questions. I didn't know anyone, and visas were difficult to arrange without relatives abroad. Mohamed seemed angered by my answers. "You think I am a poor man? I am not!" he exclaimed, jumping up and dragging me by the arm behind the counter of his shop. Pulling down several boxes of goods, he reached back into the darkness and came out with his fists full of gold. I recognized the jewelry: gaudy bangles and necklaces made by the Indian goldsmiths of the Gulf States especially for bridal dowries. All of it was pure, solid, 22 or 24 carat, because that is what Arab buyers insist on. "I will give it all to her. It's just that I must have a son. My wife, after our daughter, they had to cut her up so she can't have another child. I am nothing in this village without a son." His voice cracked. "Please, you have to help me. Will you find someone for me?"

"May your womb shrivel up" is one of the worst Arabic curses it's possible to utter. Rehab had been cursed indeed. There was no way Mohamed could have raised the money to buy his secret stash of gold without scrimping on his family. I imagined the lies he'd told, as he denied her every little luxury. Four years of privation: the punishment for having only a daughter.

I remembered then that I'd never heard Rehab's kunya—her mother designation. Arab women don't take their husbands' names on marrying, but both men and women do take the name of their first-born sons. They are known to their friends ever afterward as "Umm Faris" or "Abu Aziz"—"Mother of Faris" or "Father of Aziz." Rehab, now infertile, would never have a kunya. Mohamed could get one if a new wife gave him a son.

It astonished me that Muslims, who put such store on emulation of their prophet, didn't wish to emulate him in something so fundamental as fathering daughters. Muhammad is thought to have had three or four sons, two or three by Khadija and one by an Egyptian concubine named Mary. None survived infancy. Instead, the prophet raised four daughters, one of whom, Fatima, he extolled as a perfect human being. "Fatima," he said, "is part of me. Whoever hurts her hurts me, and whoever hurts me has hurt God." Fatima was the only one of his children to outlive him.

The Koran, meanwhile, has a mixed message about female infants. It orders an end to female infanticide. One of its most beautiful and poetic chapters contains a poignant reference to the practice, then so widespread in Arabia: "When the sun shall be folded up; and when the stars shall fall; and when the mountains shall be made to pass away; and when the camels ten months gone with young shall be neglected; and when the seas shall boil; and when the souls shall be joined again to their bodies; and when the girl who hath been buried alive shall be asked for what crime she was put to death; and when the books shall be laid open; and when the heavens shall be removed; and when hell shall burn fiercely; and when paradise shall be brought near: every soul shall know what it hath wrought."

But elsewhere, in a discussion of the idol-worshipers in Mecca, the Koran mocks the Meccans' worship of three goddesses known as "the daughters of Allah." Why, it asks, would God have daughters, when even puny human males can have the more desirable sons?

As Mohamed thrust his fistfuls of gold under my nose, he seemed on the verge of tears. To calm him I muttered something about finding out about visas. His spirits lifted immediately. "Good," he said, smiling broadly. "Now I have something else to show you!"

He'd built a special hideaway at the top of the shop, from which he could spy on Israeli troop patrols. Grateful to get back to what I thought was the solid ground of reporting, I climbed the ladder to his secret nook and humored his insistence that I lie down on the thin mattress by the spyhole to examine the clear view of the street. When he lay down beside me to point out a Palestinian flag in the power lines, I jumped up immediately and climbed back down into the shop.

He had one more piece of news for my article, he said. The Israelis had imposed water restrictions, but the village had circumvented them by uncovering some ancient Roman-era cisterns on the village outskirts. He wanted to show them to me. We got into his rusty truck and rattled out of the village.

The cisterns were well hidden, at the base of a row of crumbling, abandoned olive terraces. As I scrambled down the rocky ground, Mohamed reached out to help me. His hand landed firmly on my buttock. It's a mistake, I thought. He didn't put it there on purpose. Without saying anything, I tried to prise his fingers loose. But he pushed my hand away, tightening his grip into a crude and unambiguous grope. Then, grabbing my arms, he pinned me in a sudden embrace that was more like a wrestler's hold. His bulk bearing down on me sent me stumbling against the wall of old stone. As he rubbed himself against me, I could barely breathe under his weight. I couldn't get my breath to scream, and there was nobody near this place to hear me. Wrenching one arm free, I started pummeling him, but he seemed oblivious. He reached for the edge of my shirt, trying to tug it up over my abdomen. His other hand pulled at the waistband of my trousers. "You should see what they did to my wife—here—right here, they cut her up—it is so ugly I can't look at it. I don't want to make love to such a body."

Suddenly, a rattle of stones made Mohamed look up. The vacant eyes of a sheep stared down at him. A flock was making its slow way across the upper terrace. Behind it, somewhere, would be a village child, shepherding. Mohamed would not want him to witness this. As his grip slackened I scrambled for my balance, leaping away up the stony hillside toward the road. I never saw him again.

I don't know if Mohamed ever found his second wife. But a few miles away, in a Palestinian refugee camp, I got to know a family in which the man had made a similar choice and brought a second wife into his first wife's home.

I met them first in the winter of 1987, just weeks after the Palestinian uprising had begun. I was driving through a hard, icy rain when a chunk of concrete slammed into the hood of my car and fanned in fragments against the windshield. The car fishtailed across the rain-slicked bitumen and twirled to a stop just inches from the wide trunk of an ancient cedar. In the rear-vision mirror I caught a flash of red. A group of youths, their faces wrapped in red-checked *kaffiyehs*, perched on the pile of rubble at the entrance to the camp.

I jumped from the car and ran toward them. Thinking I was an armed Israeli settler, they scattered like startled birds. "Please," I called in Arabic. "I don't have a gun. I'm a journalist and I'd like to talk to you."

One of the youths rematerialized atop the rubble heap. "Get out of here!" he cried in perfect English. "There are people in this camp who would kill you!"

I stood my ground and asked to interview him. "I'm too busy now," he said, eying the license plate of a passing truck to see if it was colored yellow, for Israeli, or blue for Palestinian. "And if I start on this subject I'll never stop." As a Fiat with yellow plates approached, he wound up like a pitcher and hurled his chunk of concrete at its windshield. It fell just short. "It hasn't been a good day for me," he said. "I've hardly damaged any cars."

The wail of an approaching army siren signaled that the day might be about to take a turn for the worse. Barking commands to his three accomplices, the boy turned and ran off into the camp, his kaffiyeh wound tightly around his face to prevent identification by camp informers. I turned and walked slowly down the camp's main street, hearing the commotion behind me as an Israeli jeep skidded to a stop and emptied its troops at the camp entrance. A few blocks farther, I glimpsed a flash of red in the window of a half-demolished building. It was the boy. His finger on his lips, he signaled to me to follow him.

Scrambling over rubble, we made our way through back alleys to a large metal door set in a concrete-block wall. The boy rapped gently on the metal and the door flew open. Two pairs of women's hands dragged him inside by his collar, quickly stripped his T-shirt and jacket and flung him a change of clothes. "In case anybody saw me," he explained. "This is Rahme, my mother," he said, introducing the smaller of the two women as she patted down his tousled hair. "And this," he said, turning to the other woman, "is Fatin, also my mother. Well, not my mother . . . excuse me, I don't know the

English word . . . but she is . . . married to my father after my mother."

"*Darra?*" I said. Co-wife. The Arabic word comes from the root "to harm."

"Yes," he said. "Co-wife."

At fifteen, the boy, Raed, was the oldest of fourteen children. Because Israeli authorities had closed the schools, all of them were at home on that wet day, crammed inside the four-room hovel. Cold seeped up through the bare concrete floors and rain dripped through the leaky roof. Most of the toddlers had runny noses. Over the next six years I visited the family often, sometimes spending the night on a thin mattress on the floor, wedged in with Rahme and Fatin and Raed's sisters. Raed and his brothers slept beside their father, Mahmoud, in another room.

Clearly, given the number of children in the house, the sleeping arrangements weren't always like that. Because it was impossible to have a private conversation in that crowded house, I couldn't raise such a sensitive subject with Rahme or Fatin. I asked a close woman friend from a similar background how people in such situations managed to have sex. What she described was depressing: "If there are three rooms, then the women take one, the boys one, and the husband and whichever wife he wants to have sex with will sleep in the third room," she said. "But in some homes in the camps there aren't three rooms, so the act is a quick, silent fumbling in a corner, hoping the children aren't awake. Of course, neither one of them would ever undress."

At first I visited the camp to write about the uprising. But soon I became more involved in the story of Rahme and Fatin. There is a poignant Berber folk song about the arrival of a second wife, and I thought of it every time I visited them:

The stranger has come; she has her place in the house.
Her tattoos are not like ours,
But she's young, she's beautiful, just what my husband wanted;
The nights aren't long enough for their play. . . .
Since she's come, the house is not the same,

As though the doorsills and the walls were sulking;
Perhaps I'm the only one who notices it,
Like a mule before his empty manger.
But I must accept my new lot,
For my husband is happy with his new wife.
Once I, too, was beautiful, but my time is past.

To an outsider, the relationship between Rahme and Fatin seemed to have little in common with that sad song. The two women seemed more like loving sisters than bitter rivals. If Fatin cooked, Rahme sewed. If Rahme made bread, Fatin kept an eye on the toddlers. When Raed finally got caught after throwing a Molotov cocktail at Israeli soldiers, it was Fatin, not his mother Rahme, who showed up in court to support him. And when Mahmoud, too, was taken to jail in a routine security sweep, the two women relied on each other to get through the long six months until his release. In all the time I spent in their house I never heard a cross word between them.

It was Raed who taught me to look deeper. Raed spent five years in jail for his part in the uprising. When he was released, in February 1993, the fiery fifteen-year-old who'd stoned my car had been replaced by a solemn twenty-year-old who celebrated his new freedom in long, long walks up and down the West Bank's stony hillsides. On one of these walks we stopped for a few minutes to chat with a woman he knew slightly. "Her life is complete misery," he said as we turned away. As we walked, he told me the story of the woman's unhappy marriage, her husband's eventual repudiation, and her return to her parents, her children, of course, left behind with their father. "It is my mother's story," Raed added unexpectedly, "except for the ending."

Rahme's story began in Jordan. In 1972, Raed's father's mother arrived there with her daughter, who had been promised in marriage to a relative in Amman. In Jordan, the mother spotted Rahme, a devout, rosy-cheeked young woman whose tiny stature made her look much younger than her seventeen years. She took the girl home to marry her fifteen-year-old son Mahmoud.

"What did he know at fifteen? Nothing," said Raed. "To him,

she was a good girl, a nice girl. But how could he love her? He didn't even know her."

Within a year, Raed was born. His brother Murad came a year and a half later, and two sisters in the three years after that. Rahme was still pregnant with her fourth child when she forced herself to face the fact that had the whole camp gossiping. Mahmoud had fallen for Fatin, a stunning eighteen-year-old who had recently moved in with relatives in the camp.

The two women couldn't have been more different. Where Rahme was shy and pious, Fatin was outspoken and political. Where Rahme was quiet and diffident, Fatin laughed and asserted herself. Fatin, tall and shining with confidence, seemed to eclipse the tiny Rahme. Finally, Mahmoud came home with the news that Rahme had dreaded. He had proposed to Fatin, and she had accepted him. Rahme, he said, could have a divorce.

Rahme knew that a divorce meant leaving the West Bank to return to her family in Jordan. In some ways, that would have been a relief. In six years the youth Mahmoud had grown into a fierce-tempered man who occasionally lashed out violently at both her and Raed, who even as a toddler was showing a streak of stubborn courage. To live with him as his only wife had been hard enough: she could barely imagine the greater humiliations and hardships that would come from being relegated to second place by a woman he really loved.

But when she looked up at Mahmoud and gave her answer, it wasn't what he expected to hear. "I don't want to divorce you," she said quietly. Under Islamic law, divorce meant leaving her children to be raised by Mahmoud and his new wife. "I want to keep my family," she said. "Will you allow me that?"

Mahmoud was bad-tempered and selfish, but he wasn't cruel enough to force Rahme to leave her children. If Rahme wished to stay, he said, he would continue to support her. But she would have to be content to be his wife in name only. Although the Koran declares that a man must treat all his wives equally, Mahmoud made it clear that it was Fatin, and Fatin alone, to whom he was sexually attracted. By choosing to stay, Rahme, at twenty-three, would be choosing a life of celibacy in a crowded hovel alongside a woman for whom her husband felt a passionate erotic attraction. Mahmoud made it clear that he would blame Rahme if the relationship between the two women was anything but placid and friendly.

Rahme choked back her tears and agreed to Mahmoud's conditions. A few weeks later she put on her best embroidered dress and danced to the drums at her husband's wedding.

When we returned to the house, I suddenly saw everything differently. Rahme was in the corner, performing her midday prayers, as Fatin laughed boisterously with Mahmoud. Fatin was pregnant with her eleventh child, and basking in Mahmoud's obvious pride in her condition.

Raed was less approving. Since his father's jobs on construction sites were irregular, Raed was working fourteen hours a day in a shoe factory to support the family. "It's stupid!" he fumed. "He can't support the babies he has, and he brings more and more."

Fatin had been nursing a newborn when I first met her in 1987. While I talked to Raed about the intifada, she'd sat in a corner of the room with the baby at her breast. She'd interrupted only once, when Raed's English stumbled over the word "peace." I'd asked him if the Palestinians in the camp were willing to accept peace with Israel. When he had trouble with the word, I tried the Arabic, *salaam*. "La salaam!" Fatin yelled suddenly. "No peace! The people of this camp want war!" Fatin, I reflected then, would be a formidable opponent if anyone crossed her.

Fatin's many pregnancies had stripped her of her girlish bloom. She showed me the gaps in her mouth from teeth that had fallen out during the latest one. Yet it seemed to be a price she was willing to pay to retain her husband's approval, and to underline her difference in status from Rahme.

"My mother is waiting only for us," Raed said. "As soon as my sisters are finished school and I can support them, she won't have to put up with this anymore."

I wondered, though, if the complex bonds in the family could be so easily broken. Raed himself said he didn't differentiate between his full siblings and his half brothers and sisters. He loved all of them, and felt responsible for protecting them from his erratic father. His feelings about Fatin also were complex. "I cannot say I hate this woman," he said. "I hate her only for being the cause of my mother's suffering, not for who she is herself."

In a rare private moment, when I tried to ask Rahme about her feelings, her rosy face broke into an enigmatic smile. She wrapped my hands in her two cracked and work-worn ones and whispered simply, "Insha'allah [As God wills it]." Then she went to wash and began her prayers, as the life of the household swirled unnoticed around her. In a few moments, following the prayer-time ritual, she knelt, touching her head to the floor.

Her religion, after all, was Islam—the Submission. It seemed to me that its rules had required her to submit to a lot.

Chapter 4

THE PROPHET'S WOMEN

"O wives of the prophet, ye are
not like any ordinary women."

THE KORAN
THE CHAPTER OF THE CLANS

*S*he was playing on her swing when her mother called
her. Noticing her dirty face, her mother took a little water and wiped
the grime away. The swing had left her breathless, so the two of them
paused for a few minutes at the door of the house until she recovered.

Inside, her father and his friends were waiting. Her mother
placed her in the lap of one of them, then everyone else rose and left
the room.

Aisha was nine years old, and that day, in her parents' house,
she consummated her marriage to the prophet Muhammad, who was
then over fifty. Ten years later, he died in her arms.

Today, if you ask Sunni Muslims about Aisha, they will tell you
she was the great love of Muhammad's later life, a formidable teacher
of Islam, a heroine in battle. But ask Shiites, and they will describe a
jealous schemer who destroyed the prophet's domestic peace, plotted
against his daughter Fatima, spied on the household and fomented a
tragic factional bloodletting that left the Muslim nation permanently
divided.

Aisha—Arabic for "life"—is one of the most popular girls'
names in the Sunni Muslim world. But among Shiites it is a term of

exasperation and abuse. When a Shiite girl misbehaves, her mother is likely to upbraid her with a shout of "You Aisha!"

Aisha went to live with Muhammad in the year 622 by the Christian calendar—the first year of Hegira by Muslim reckoning. Thirteen hundred and sixty-six years later, an interviewer for "Hello Good Morning" a live, national radio show in Iran, stopped a woman on a Tehran street and asked her who she thought was the best woman's role model. The woman answered Oshin, the heroine of a Japanese-made TV soap opera who had overcome all kinds of adversity by flouting Japan's staid traditions. The interviewer asked the woman why she hadn't named one of the prophet's wives or daughters as her role model. The woman replied that those women belonged to a far-off era that wasn't as relevant to her modern life. Ayatollah Khomeini, listening to the radio, was furious, and demanded that the show's producers be flogged. He relented when an investigation proved that the producers hadn't acted maliciously.

For once I found myself more or less agreeing with Khomeini. The lives of the prophet's wives and daughters were extremely relevant to modern Islamic women. Most of the Koran's revelations on women came to Muhammad directly following events in his own household. Like modern Muslim women, his wives had to cope with the jealousies of a polygamous household, the traumas of war, the hardships of poverty and the issues of seclusion and hijab.

To me, the hadith's intimate vignettes of life in the apartments around Muhammad's mosque were better than any modern soap opera. I couldn't get enough of these stories of intrigue, argument and romance. Aisha, undoubtedly, was the star, but the seven or eight wives in the supporting cast made for lively subplots.

When Muhammad's first wife Khadija died in 619, the forty-nine-year-old prophet was heartbroken. The Muslim community, especially the women who cooked and cared for him, believed a new wife might soothe his grief. A few months after Khadija's death, Muhammad's aunt, Khawla, suggested to her nephew that he marry again.

"Whom shall I marry, O Khawla?" asked Muhammad. "You women are best knowing in these matters."

Khawla answered that, if he wanted a virgin, he should take

Aisha, the beautiful child of his best friend, Abu Bakr. If he wanted a nonvirgin, there was the widow Sawda, a matronly older woman who had been an early convert to Islam and a devoted follower.

"Go," said Muhammad, "bespeak them both for me."

He married Sawda and Aisha in quick succession. But since Aisha was then only six, the marriage wasn't consummated, and she remained with her family. No one told the little girl of her change in status. But when her mother suddenly began restricting her play, Aisha later recalled, "It fell into my heart that I was married." By the time she went to live with Muhammad, the Muslims had fled persecution in Mecca and set up an exile community in the town of Medina. Muhammad lived in the mosque they constructed there—a humble structure of gray mudbricks roofed with the branches of date trees. Aisha and Sawda had a room each. When Aisha moved in, she brought her toys with her. Sometimes Muhammad would find her playing with them. "What are these?" he would ask. "Solomon's horses," or "My girl dolls," she would answer. If her child playmates ran away, intimidated, when he approached, he would gently call them back and sometimes join in their games.

Muhammad, according to many detailed physical descriptions, was a handsome man, of medium height with wavy black hair, a full beard, thick-lashed dark eyes and a radiant smile that revealed a gap between his front teeth. He was meticulous about his grooming, perfuming his beard and brushing his teeth at least five times a day. His only unattractive features were a tendency to bloodshot eyes and a protruding vein in his temple that is said to have become more pronounced when he became angry.

In the year or two after Aisha moved in, Muhammad married three more women, all war widows: Hafsah, the twenty-year-old daughter of his close friend Omar; an older woman, Zeinab, whose generosity had earned her the name "Mother of the Poor," and who died just eight months later; and Umm Salamah, a famous beauty whose arrival caused Aisha the first pangs of the jealousy that would blight the rest of her life. When Aisha learned about the marriage to Umm Salamah, "I was exceedingly sad," she said, "having heard much of her beauty." She called on the new wife and found her "twice as beautiful and graceful as she was reputed to be."

Muhammad tried to keep to the Koran's instruction that a man must treat all his wives equally. His practice was to see each of them, every afternoon, in a brief private meeting, but to have his dinner and spend the night with one at a time, in strict rotation. Aisha found the arrangement unsatisfying. "Tell me," she asked him one day, "if you were to come upon two camels, the one already pastured and the other not, which would you feed?" Muhammad answered that of course it would be the one not pastured. "I am not like the rest of your wives," Aisha replied. "Every one of them has been married before, except me."

Occasionally, if Muhammad wanted to spend time with a wife out of her turn, he would ask permission of the wife whose "day" it was. He soon learned better than to ask Aisha to give up her day. "For my part," she said, "I always refused him" and insisted on her scheduled visit. Sensitive to the young girl's needs and, perhaps, to the prophet's desires, the aging Sawda permanently relinquished her "day" to Aisha. But soon the arrival of several more wives spread the prophet's attentions even thinner.

Muslims argue that the many marriages of Muhammad's last ten years reflected the fast expansion of Islam, and his need to build alliances with diverse clans. At other times, they say, his choices reflected compassion for needy widows. Since women will always outnumber men in societies at war, they argue, surely it is better that women share a husband than have no man in their lives at all. Muhammad, they say, was setting an example by taking widows into his care.

Non-Muslims, particularly Islam's hostile critics, have taken a different view. Muhammad, they say, was a sensualist, whose increasing power and prestige gave him means to indulge his lusts after the death of the first wife who had been his patron.

These critics seem to overlook the austerity of the prophet's household. The mudbrick rooms of the mosque were hardly the quarters of a sensualist. Even as the Muslim community became rich on the spoils of military victories, Muhammad continued to live simply and to insist that his wives do the same. The poverty that he enforced in his own household became the source of much bickering between Muhammad and his wives.

Yet the devout view, of Muhammad as husband cum social worker for needy widows, isn't entirely convincing either. At least one hadith indicates that Muhammad knew polygamy was damaging for women. When his son-in-law Ali considered taking a second wife, the prophet expressed concern for the feelings of his daughter Fatima. "What harms her harms me," he told Ali, who abandoned the idea of a further marriage. (Shiites, who venerate Ali and Fatima, discount this hadith. They argue that Muhammad would never have criticized a practice that the Koran had declared lawful.)

Not all Muhammad's wives were pathetic cases or politically expedient matches. The beautiful Umm Salamah certainly wasn't needy. She had loved her first husband and, reluctant to remarry, had rejected a slew of eligible suitors when Muhammad began his dogged pursuit. She turned the prophet down at least three times. "I am a woman of an exceedingly jealous disposition, and you, O Messenger of God, acquire many women," she said, as one excuse for rejecting his suit. Muhammad replied: "I shall pray God to uproot jealousy from your heart."

Despite his attempts at fairness, the whole community seems to have become aware that Aisha was his favorite wife. Muslims who wanted to send him a gift of food began timing their presents for the days they knew he would be spending in Aisha's apartment. Since Muhammad lived so humbly, these gifts often provided his household's only luxuries. Umm Salamah, for one, bitterly resented the preference shown to Aisha. "I see that the rest of us are as nothing," she said when yet another basket of goodies arrived on Aisha's day. Enraged, she flounced off to complain to Fatima, Muhammad's daughter.

Muhammad's marriage to a child just a year or two younger than herself must have been difficult for Fatima in the wake of her mother's death. Her own marriage, to Muhammad's nephew Ali, was arranged soon after Aisha moved in. Whether it had its seeds in unrecorded childhood squabbles, or in the rivalry between Fatima's husband Ali and Aisha's father Abu Bakr for the role of Muhammad's chief lieutenant, a bitter enmity developed between Aisha and Fatima. Eventually it expressed itself in the Shiite-Sunni schism that was to sunder Islam. The temperaments of the two young women could hardly have been more different. Fatima was self-effacing and shy; Aisha was quick-witted and outspoken.

In any case, Umm Salamah knew where to look for an ally against Aisha. Fatima promised Umm Salamah to speak to her father about his favoritism. Muhammad's reply must have stung. "Dear little daughter, don't you love who I love?" he asked her. "Yes, surely," she replied. When she continued to put her case, Muhammad cut her off. "Aisha," he said, "is your father's best beloved." This brought Ali into the argument, chiding Muhammad for slighting his daughter by saying he loved Aisha best. The bitterness of the argument must have lingered, because soon afterward Muhammad ordered the door sealed between his wives' apartments and the apartment of Ali and Fatima. (Shiites deny this exchange ever took place: in their version, Muhammad extolled Fatima as "a human houri," or near-divine being.)

Aisha tried to undermine her complaining rivals with childish pranks. One day she noticed that Muhammad had lingered longer than usual on his evening visit with one of her rivals, enjoying a drink made with honey, his favorite delicacy. Aisha gathered some of the other wives together and concocted a practical joke. As he stopped by each woman's apartment, all of them pretended to be offended by his breath. Muhammad, fastidious about his person, was worried and confused. "All I ate was honey!" he exclaimed. The women muttered that the bees who made the honey must have fed on the nectar of a foul-smelling plant. Afterward, Muhammad refused honey when it was offered to him, until the more mature Sawda counseled Aisha that the joke had gone far enough, and that the poor prophet was depriving himself of one of his few pleasures.

Once Aisha and her coconspirators actually thwarted one of the prophet's attempts to add another wife to his growing harem. Aisha was distraught when Asma, the beautiful daughter of a prince, arrived with an elaborate escort for her marriage to Muhammad. Aisha and Hafsa, pretending to be helpful, volunteered to assist the young woman dress for her wedding. As they fussed around her, they shared "confidences" about the prophet's likes and dislikes. He would be inflamed with passion, they advised, if she pretended unwillingness. When it came time to consummate the marriage, they advised her to back away from the prophet's embrace and say, "I take refuge with Allah from thee."

The prophet, appalled at the thought of inflicting himself on an unwilling woman, immediately told Asma not to worry, that he would call for her escort and see her safely home. Asma went, devastated, and complaining bitterly that she had been the victim of deceit.

The multiple marriages fed such petty rivalries and added to the growing feud between Ali and Abu Bakr that was to threaten Islam's political future. They also began to shape the rules of the emerging faith. Muhammad's increasing number of divine revelations on women seemed more and more influenced by the need to achieve tranquillity in his own household. Aisha, for one, wasn't afraid to point out the coincidence. "It seems to me," she said tartly, "your Lord makes haste to satisfy your desires."

One such coincidence was the revelation that adopted children weren't to be considered as blood kin. This followed Muhammad's glimpse of the partially unclad Zeinab, wife of Zaid, the freed slave whom Muhammad had adopted and raised as a son. The community had been shocked by Zaid's divorce and Muhammad's intention to marry Zeinab, which flouted the ban on a father's marriage to the wife of a son. Muhammad was with Aisha when he had the revelation saying that it was a mistake by Muslims to consider adoption as creating the same ties as blood kin. From that point, the Koran says, Muslims were to proclaim the true parentage of any children they raised. God, the revelation disclosed, had arranged Muhammad's marriage with Zeinab to disclose to Muslims the error of their previous beliefs. When Zeinab moved into the mosque, she was able to taunt Aisha by claiming that her marriage to the prophet had been arranged by God.

The revelation on the seclusion of the prophet's wives came on Zeinab's wedding night. Sensitive to the ill feelings that the match had inspired, Muhammad had invited many guests to his wedding feast. Three of them lingered long after the meal, engrossed in conversation and seemingly oblivious to the prophet's impatience to be alone with his new bride. As Zeinab sat quietly in a corner, waiting for the guests to leave, Muhammad strode out of the room and wandered the mosque courtyard. He dropped in on Aisha, who politely inquired how he liked his new companion. Muhammad confided that he hadn't yet had a chance to enjoy her company, and wandered off to look in on each of his wives before returning to the room of the wedding feast. To his intense annoyance, the guests were still there. Irritable, he went back to Aisha's room and sat with her until finally someone came to tell him that the boorish guests had left.

Anas ibn Malik, a companion who had witnessed the whole scene, accompanied Muhammad back to the nuptial chamber. Muhammad had one foot in the room when he let fall a curtain between himself and Anas, and, as he did so, began reciting in the voice he used for revelations: "O ye who believe! Enter not the dwellings of the prophet for a meal without waiting for the proper time, unless permission be granted you. But if ye are invited, enter, and, when your meal is ended, then disperse. Linger not for conversation. Lo! that would cause annoyance to the Prophet, and he would be shy of asking you to go; but Allah is not shy of the truth. And when you ask his wives for anything, ask it of them from behind a curtain *(hijab)*. That is purer for your hearts and for their hearts."

These words now are inscribed in the Koran as the word of God. Obviously, such a verse is read very differently by a believing Muslim and a nonbelieving outsider. To a nonbeliever, it is hard to envision God troubling to micromanage matters of etiquette, like some kind of heavenly Miss Manners. To Muslims, though, there is nothing very extraordinary in God dealing with a situation that obviously left his prophet uncomfortable and unsure of how to act. In these latter years of Muhammad's life, with the community expanding rapidly, many new issues, large and small, had to be resolved. The Medina revelations are almost always far less poetic and more specific than the elegant reflections of the earlier verses revealed in Mecca. Often they came in direct response to new dilemmas facing the community.

What is so puzzling is why the revelation of seclusion, so clearly packaged here with instructions that apply only to the prophet, should ever have come to be seen as a rule that should apply to all Muslim women.

In Muhammad's lifetime the rule almost certainly was limited to his wives. It completely changed their lives. Muhammad had authorized Aisha, in his absence, to give religious advice, telling Muslims to "take half your religion from this woman." But after the revelation of seclusion, she no longer mingled freely with the visitors to the mosque. Some wives, like Sawda, famed for her fine leathercraft, had worked to contribute to the household's budget. The wives had even gone into battle alongside Muhammad, tucking up their robes and carrying water, or caring for the injured. Even Fatima had attended the battlefield, once cauterizing a bleeding head wound of her father's by applying ashes, a folk remedy that signified her skill as a nurse.

After the seclusion, Muhammad took one or two wives on campaign only as his sexual partners, drawing lots among them for the privilege. It was after one such battle that Aisha found herself facing the biggest trial of her married life.

As camp broke before dawn, Aisha walked off into the desert to urinate before the march. Returning to camp, she realized she'd dropped an agate necklace and retraced her steps looking for it. By the time she found it the men had led off the camel carrying her curtained litter, believing her to be already inside. She sat patiently on the sand, waiting for someone to miss her. A few hours later, a young soldier named Safwan found her waiting alone and carried her back to the city on his camel.

Her arrival with this young and handsome man created a scandal. Ali, Fatima's husband, took the opportunity to feed Muhammad's growing doubts of Aisha's virtue. As the scandal mounted, Aisha left her apartment at the mosque and returned in disgrace to her parents, who seemed just as ready to accuse her as everyone else. The gossip raged for over a month.

Finally Muhammad had a revelation clearing her name.

"Good tidings, O Aisha!" he cried out. "God most high has exonerated you."

"Rise and come to Muhammad," her parents urged.

"I shall neither come to him nor thank him," said the strong-minded young woman. "Nor will I thank both of you who listened to the slander and did not deny it. I shall rise to give thanks to God alone."

What became known as "the affair of the slander" made its way into the Koran. Why, God asks the believers, when they heard the allegations about Aisha, "did not the believing men and believing women form in their minds a good opinion and say, 'This is a lie manifest'? Why have they not brought four witnesses regarding it?" Since then, Islamic law has required four witnesses to sustain a charge of adultery: "The whore, and the whoremaster, shall ye scourge with an hundred stripes. . . . But as to those who accuse women of reputation of whoredom, and produce not four witnesses of the fact, scourge them with fourscore stripes, and receive not their testimony forever."

In the two years following his controversial marriage to Zeinab, Muhammad acquired five new women, including two Jews and a Coptic Christian. (There is a difference of opinion about whether he married all three of these women or simply kept one or two of them as concubines.) Mary, the Christian, became the focus of the harem's intense jealousy when she bore Muhammad a son. (The boy died in infancy.) Aisha, who hadn't been able to conceive, was particularly heartbroken. At one point she had complained to Muhammad about her lack of a kunya, or mother designation, since all the other widows had the kunyas of sons they'd borne to their previous husbands. Like the present-day Palestinian, Rehab, Aisha felt the lack of distinction keenly. Muhammad told her to call herself Umm Abdullah, after the son of her sister, to whom she was very close.

Aisha must have perceived Mary and her son as dangerous rivals for Muhammad's attention. Certainly an uproar followed the discovery of Muhammad having intercourse with Mary in Hafsa's room on Aisha's "day." The fallout from that upset, coupled with nagging from the women about the grinding poverty of their lives, caused Muhammad to withdraw from the harem and keep to himself for almost a month. The community worried that he might divorce all his wives, throwing into turmoil the alliances he'd so carefully crafted.

Finally he returned from his retreat and offered each of his wives a divinely inspired ultimatum: they could divorce him and have a rich settlement of worldly goods, or they could stay with him, on God's terms, which included never marrying again after his death. In return, they would be known forever as Mothers of the Believers, and reap a rich reward in heaven. All the women chose to stay.

It would be wrong to portray Muhammad's domestic life as

nothing but jealousy and scandal. The hadith also record moments of great tenderness in the little rooms around the mosque. One day, as Aisha and Muhammad sat together companionably, she at her spinning, he mending a sandal, Aisha suddenly became aware that he was gazing at her with a radiant expression on his face. Suddenly, he rose and kissed her on the forehead. "Oh, Aisha," he said, "may Allah reward you well. I am not the source of joy to you that you are to me."

Another hadith recounts an incident when several of Muhammad's wives were arguing with him over household finances. While the argument was in progress, Omar, Muhammad's stern lieutenant and the father of Hafsa, entered the room. The women, fearful of Omar's violent temper, immediately fell silent and hurried away. Omar yelled after the women that it was shameful that they should be more respectful of him than of the prophet of God. One replied, from a safe distance, that the prophet of God was known to be much gentler to women than his overbearing friend.

When Muhammad became ill and was dying, he at first kept to his habit of fairness among wives, moving his sickbed from one room to another depending on whose turn it was to have his company. But one day he began asking whose room he was to go to the next day, and the day after, and the day after that. The wives perceived that he was trying to calculate how long it would be until he was with his beloved Aisha. All decided to give up their turns to allow him to spend his last weeks with Aisha. He died in her arms and was buried in her room.

She was just nineteen years old. A lonely future stretched before her: childless, and banned from remarriage. All she had left was influence. Because she had spent so much time at Muhammad's side, she became a leading religious authority. Originally, 2,210 hadith were attributed to her: ninth-century scholars, dismissing the word of a mere woman, threw out all but 174.

On Muhammad's death, Aisha became a wealthy woman. She inherited nothing from Muhammad, who left all his own property to charity. But the community paid her for the use of part of her room —where she continued to live—as the prophet's tomb. The sum, 200,000 dirhams, was so vast that five camels were needed to transport it. The payment may have been extra generous because Muhammad's successor, or caliph, turned out to be Aisha's father, Abu Bakr.

Muhammad's death caused the boil-over of the long-simmering power struggle between Ali and Abu Bakr. Fatima, who had lived very quietly, raising four children, burst briefly into public life to fight for Ali's right to be caliph. By that time all her sisters had died childless, leaving her and her sons and daughters as Muhammad's only descendants. She argued powerfully that Ali had been Muhammad's choice. It was she who proclaimed that her father's command had been that the leadership of Islam should remain with his blood relatives. The Shiat Ali, or Partisans of Ali, rallied to support her. But she failed to convince the majority of the community. While Ali was prepared to mend the rift by accepting Abu Bakr's leadership, Fatima held out with the courageous stubbornness that continues to characterize modern Shiites. Convinced that her father's will had been flouted, she refused to offer allegiance to Abu Bakr. Perhaps as a result of the stress of that losing struggle, she fell ill and died just six months after her father.

Not everyone mourned the passing of Islam's prophet. In the southern Arabian region of Hadramaut, six women decorated their hands with henna, as if for a wedding, and took to the streets beating tambourines in joyful celebration of Muhammad's death. Soon, about twenty others joined the merry gathering. When word of the celebration reached Abu Bakr, he sent out the cavalry to deal with "the whores of Hadramaut." When his warriors arrived, the men of the settlement came to their women's defense but were defeated. As punishment, the women had their henna-painted, tambourine-playing hands severed at the wrists.

Who knows what motivated the women to make their rousing and reckless celebration? To them, at least, it must have seemed that Muhammad's new religion had made their lives more burdensome, less free. And much worse was coming. Repression of women was about to be legislated into the religion on a large scale by Abu Bakr's successor as caliph, the violent misogynist Omar.

That Aisha supported Omar's bid for leadership shows the depth of her loathing for Fatima's husband, Ali. Her opinion of Omar was not high. Knowing his cruelty to the women of his household, she had cleverly helped foil a match between him and her sister.

Omar cracked down on women in ways that he must have known flouted Muhammad's traditions. He made stoning the official punishment for adultery and pressed to extend the seclusion of women beyond the prophet's wives. He tried to prevent women from praying in the mosque, and when that failed, he ordered separate prayer leaders for men and women. He also prevented women from making the Hajj, a ban that was lifted only in the last year of his life.

On Omar's death, Aisha supported Othman as his successor. When Othman was murdered by members of a rebellious faction, Ali, who had had to wait twenty-four long years since Muhammad's death, finally got his chance to lead. When he became the Muslims' fourth caliph, Aisha's well-known enmity soon made her a lightning rod for dissidents. She spoke out stridently against Ali's failure to punish Othman's killers.

As opposition to Ali's rule mounted, Aisha made a brave and reckless move that might have changed forever the balance of power between Muslim men and women.

She led the dissidents into battle against Ali in a red pavilion set atop a camel. Riding ahead of her troops, she loudly exhorted them to fight bravely. Ali, realizing the effect this was having on his men's morale, ordered her camel cut down under her. He then routed her forces. Hundreds of her partisans were killed, including her dearest friends and relatives.

The defeat proved disastrous for Muslim women. Her opponents were able to argue that the first battle of Muslim against Muslim would never have happened if Aisha had kept out of public life as God had commanded. After the battle, one of Muhammad's freed slaves reported a hadith that has been particularly damaging to Muslim women. The man said he had been saved from joining Aisha's army by recalling Muhammad's remark on the news that the Persians had appointed a princess as ruler: "No people who place a woman over their affairs will prosper." Whether or not the former slave's convenient recollection was genuine, that hadith has been used against every Muslim woman who has achieved political influence. In Pakistan it was frequently cited by opponents of Benazir Bhutto.

After the rout, Aisha finally made her peace with Ali. She retreated from politics but remained an eminent religious authority. Most accounts describe her in later life as a sad and self-effacing woman whose one wish was to be forgotten by history.

It is said that she wept whenever she recited the Koranic verses: "O wives of the prophet . . . remain in your houses."

Chapter 5

CONVERTS

> "Marry not women who are idolaters, until they believe: verily a maid-servant who believeth is better than an idolatress, although she please you more."
>
> THE KORAN
> THE CHAPTER OF THE COW

At sunrise, before the heat slams down and the air becomes heavy with diesel fumes, Tehran smells of fresh-baked bread. At neighborhood bakeries women wait in line with their flowery household chadors draped casually around their waists. Their faces seem less lined than they will look later, as they struggle through the crowded city burdened with parcels and children and the countless worries of women in poor countries. During this pause they have the brief luxury of watching someone else's labor.

Sometimes, when I tired of the stares and questions I got as the lone woman registered at the Laleh Hotel, I would head for the northern suburbs to stay with a family who had become good friends. They lived on a winding road of mosques, shops and every kind of housing from villas to hovels. In the mornings I would find my way to the local bakery by following my nose. The air carried both the sweetness of seared crusts and the tang of woodsmoke from ovens sunk into the bakery floor. Inside, a four-man assembly line blurred in a heat shimmer of deft hands and flying dough. The bakers made *lavosh*—thin, flat sheets of bread soft as tissue. They worked like jugglers: one boy weighing dough, another rolling it flat, a third flinging it from stick to stick to stretch it thin, a fourth slapping the wafer against the oven wall. Watching the other women, I learned to reach for the hot bread with my hands wrapped in a fold of chador. I would carry it home that way to the Mamoudzadehs' breakfast table.

Like houses everywhere in the Islamic world, the Mamoudzadehs' gave nothing away from the street. Its huge iron gate shut out the world completely, securing the family's privacy within. The gate opened to a courtyard with flower gardens, children's bikes and a shady mulberry tree from which Janet Mamoudzadeh made the jam that spread deliciously over the steaming lavosh. I kicked off my shoes into the pile by the front door and stepped onto the softness of handmade rugs and kilims. Just inside, I flicked my chador onto a rack that contained two or three of the coats and scarves that Janet wore for ordinary use; the more concealing, nunlike magneh she wore to her job as an English teacher at her daughter's grade school, and the chador she kept for religious occasions.

Janet's husband Mohamed was a trader at the Bazaar-e-Bazorg —the Grand Bazaar—dealing in Persian carpets and foreign currencies. She had met him at college in Pittsburg, Kansas, where he was studying engineering and she was taking computer science. She fell in love, converted to Islam, and traveled home with him to Iran.

Janet married Mohamed before the revolution, when it was possible for non-Muslims to live in Iran with their Muslim spouses. These days, conversion is obligatory, in line with the Shiite view that permanent marriage (as opposed to sigheh) can take place only between Muslims. The prophet's sunnah on this matter doesn't really help to clarify the Koranic verses.

The prophet had relationships with at least two Jewish women and one Christian, but Islamic sources differ as to whether the women converted or, if they kept their own faith, whether they became full-fledged wives. Safiyah, the wife of the leader of the Jews of Khaiber who died in battle with the Muslims, converted to Islam and is mentioned in all the sources as a full-fledged wife of the prophet. The status of the other two women isn't so clear. Some sources say that the other Jew, Raihanah, decided to remain as a slave/concubine in the harem, so that she could keep her faith and remain free of the restrictions of seclusion. Mary, the Coptic Christian, who never changed her religion, is described as a concubine in all but Egyptian sources.

Janet converted to Islam because her husband wanted his children raised as Muslims and she believed that having the same religion would make her household more harmonious. She looked upon her conversion in a matter-of-fact way. "Allah, God—it's the same guy, isn't it? And if you read the Koran, Mary is in there, and Jesus—it's just that they're called Maryam and Isa."

Janet's conversion had been a simple matter. In her family's living room in Kansas, in front of two witnesses, she had simply proclaimed the *shehada,* the Muslim profession of faith: "There is no God but God and Muhammad is the Messenger of God." Because her husband is Shiite, she also added the additional, optional sentence: "Ali is the friend of God." Once she said the simple formula, she was a Muslim. To be a *good* Muslim, she also had to live by the other four of the faith's Five Pillars: praying five times a day; fasting in Ramadan; giving alms to the poor—usually set at 2.5% of a person's net worth, not mere income—per year; and making the pilgrimage to Mecca at least once in her life, if she could afford it.

I was intrigued by Janet's decision. Early one morning in the winter of 1984, I had made a similar choice. I'd gone to a dank room in a Cleveland suburb, submerged my body in a tiled pool of rainwater, and come up pronouncing the words: "Hear, O Israel: the Lord Our God, the Lord Is One." Later, I celebrated with my rabbi and my fiancé over matzo-ball soup and potato latkes at a nearby Jewish deli.

My conversion had more to do with history than faith. If I were going to marry a Jew, it seemed important to throw in my lot with his often threatened people. I didn't know then that I would spend the best part of the next decade in the Middle East, where being on my husband's side made me an automatic enemy to many of those we lived among.

Janet, too, wanted to be on her husband's side. But in Iran in the late 1970s, her nationality was an obstacle that her new faith couldn't entirely overcome. "It wasn't a great time for a bride from Kansas City to be setting up house in Tehran," she recalled with a wry grin. Within a couple of months of her arrival the city was paralyzed by demonstrations, fires, gun battles. When Khomeini returned from exile in 1979, Mohamed was exultant. Like many young, well-educated Iranians, he despised the corruption of the old order and admired the way Khomeini thumbed his nose at the great powers who had vied with each other to exploit the wealth of his homeland.

Janet had to sit through family gatherings listening to Mohamed's relatives pillory her country. As her Farsi improved, she began to challenge them. "They would say, 'Oh, Janet, you know we like American people, it's just the government we hate.' I would say, 'Yeah? Well, in my country, buddy, the government *is* the people.' "

When Iranian students occupied the U. S. Embassy in Tehran in 1979, the State Department told all United States citizens to leave. Janet watched as an exodus emptied the city of the thousands of American expatriates who had once made fortunes there. Soon only a handful of Americans remained, most of them wives of Iranians too financially or ideologically committed to their country to leave. "The State Department said we'd be on our own if we stayed here. And we have been. But if you love your husband, you stay."

Janet also gradually found herself coming to love many aspects of her life in Iran. She found that Iranians lavished affection on the few Americans who stayed. Some Iranians had warm memories of American teachers or technicians who had helped the country, while even those who saw Americans only as rapacious exploiters felt that Janet, by staying, had aligned herself with Iran. Instead of being greeted with hostility, she found herself welcomed everywhere—pushed to the front of food lines, given the best meat, and helped in every possible way. "They treat me like a queen here," she said.

But convincing her parents back in Kansas City took some doing, especially after Betty Mahmoody published her memoir, *Not Without My Daughter*. The book is a nightmare tale of an American wife who agrees to visit her husband's family in Tehran only to find herself trapped there by Iranian laws that forbid women to leave the country without their husbands' permission. It gives an unremittingly bleak picture of life in Iran, describing wife beatings, filthy houses and vermin-infested food.

"My father would get on the phone and say, 'I know Mohamed is beating you,' and I'd say, 'Dad, he'd no more beat me than you would.' I even took pictures of my freezer to show how much food we have.'' She tried to describe the split-level luxuries of her spacious villa, the leisure provided by her regular cleaner and her easy access to good child care for her three children. It was a life that many Americans would have found enviable. But her parents weren't reassured. So she agreed to see me in the hope that her parents might believe a report by an outsider. She invited a friend, a Californian also married to an Iranian, to meet me as well.

Janet gaped as she opened the door to her friend. It was the week of Khomeini's funeral, and the whole of Tehran was shrouded in black. Black crepe decked public buildings, men wore black shirts, women packed away their colorful scarves for the forty days of official mourning and donned their black chadors. Amid all this gloom, Janet's friend stood out like a clown in a convent. Six feet tall and seven months pregnant, she wore a huge cotton caftan splashed with pink and red roses, and a pink silk scarf that barely covered her sun-bleached hair.

"Good grief, I hope Hajji Yousefi didn't see you!'' gasped Janet, referring to her next-door neighbor, a member of the local Komiteh responsible for enforcing Islamic discipline. The woman, whom I will call Margaret, just shrugged and flopped into an armchair. "Who cares?'' she said. "I got abuse on the way over here, with some old bag in a chador coming up to me and saying, 'How can you dress like that? Don't you know the imam is dead?' I said, 'What's it to me? I'm an American.' I told her I knew better than she did what the Koran says women should wear, and it doesn't say anywhere that it has to be a big old black rag.''

Margaret knew what the Koran said because she spent every morning sitting cross-legged on the floor beside her mother-in-law, studying the holy book line by line. Margaret had wed a scion of the Islamic Republic's aristocracy: the son of a long line of eminent ayatollahs. The family tolerated a lot from their son's odd choice of bride because she had done two things to earn their approval: converted to Islam and quickly become pregnant. Her mother-in-law fervently believed that winning a convert was a passport to paradise and, as none of her children had yet given her a grandson, she had high hopes for Margaret's pregnancy.

Margaret also spoke frankly about the sexual power she believed she wielded over her husband. Growing up in California's hedonistic beach culture, she had acquired a sexual repertoire undreamed of by an Iranian boy closeted among clerics. "He runs after me like a puppy," she giggled. All this, she believed, protected her from conforming to the iron disciplines of Iranian society that Janet barely questioned. In Tehran, all government buildings have female guards who strictly enforce Islamic dress codes, and Margaret had recently been turned back at the door of a post office for wearing lipstick. "I asked for a Kleenex, and she said, 'Here's your Kleenex,' and slapped me across the face." Margaret complained to her family and they had the guard sacked.

A few days after our meeting at Janet's house, I invited both women to join me for lunch in town. Margaret chose her favorite place, a once grand French restaurant with linen tablecloths and red banquettes. The restaurant waiters greeted her like a long-lost sister. Complimenting her on her colorful dress, one of them asked why her two friends were wearing such dowdy black hijab. Margaret replied with a quick Farsi crack. The waiter looked startled, then laughed. "I told him you were ass kissers," she grinned.

But even Margaret had learned that there were limits. Once, her irreverence had almost gone too far. She had been annoyed for days by some anti-American graffiti scrawled on a wall at the end of her street. One night she'd taken a can of paint and altered the lettering to turn the insult back against the Iranian government. At daybreak the new message caused a furor and a witch hunt. Margaret, delighted by the frenzy she'd created, confided to her husband, thinking he'd enjoy the joke. "I never knew he could be so angry," she said. Furious, he screamed at her, calling her a madwoman: "Do you want to be killed? There are some things even I can't save you from." In the end, no one managed to identify her as the culprit.

For me, Janet's friendship offered a window into women's lives in Iran. Mohamed's huge extended family included the poor and the affluent, the religiously convinced and the skeptical. Whenever I was in town it became understood that I was included in all family events. For me, being Jewish had remained an abstraction: something that had defined the kind of wedding I'd had, and afterward meant a once-a-year family feast at Passover, a fast at Yom Kippur, a certain awkwardness at Christmastime and a label, often an inconvenient one, that I had to write on visa forms when I visited Middle Eastern countries. But, for Janet, religion shaped every day's routine.

No one in the Mamoudzadeh family lived a secular life. Mohamed's mother rose every morning before dawn to ready herself for the first of the five prayers she would offer each day. Mohamed and Janet were less meticulous, but even Janet said she enjoyed the moments when she joined her mother-in-law at prayer. "It's just such a peaceful few minutes in your day," she said. "If the kids call for you, or someone comes to the door, you just raise your voice and intone 'Allah' to signal that you're praying, and no one can interrupt you."

To prepare for prayers, Janet and her mother-in-law would wash carefully, scrubbing the face, feet and hands, rinsing the mouth, and rubbing damp hands over the hair. Women can't wear nail polish in Iran because of the law that hands have to be clean for prayer, and a coating of polish is considered polluting. At the airport, even foreign women are handed petrol-soaked rags to wipe varnished nails. But perfume is encouraged at prayer time, so Janet and her mother-in-law would sprinkle themselves with scent, enfold themselves in their prettiest floral chadors, roll out a special prayer rug, and begin the series of bows, kneeling and prostration that accompany the Muslims' melodious poem of devotion: "Praise be to God, lord of the creation, the compassionate, the merciful, king of the last judgment . . . You alone we worship, and to you alone we pray for help. . . . Guide us to the straight path, the path of those whom you have favored, not of those who have incurred your wrath. . . ." Men must recite the prayers audibly enough for someone nearby to distinguish the words. Women, whose voices are considered sexually arousing, are supposed to whisper.

Every year Mohamed put his name down for the lottery which selected the pilgrims who would make the annual Hajj. The month of Hajj follows immediately after the purifying month of Ramadan. These days, about two million Muslims from all over the world descend on Mecca annually, ritually dressed in simple white garments.

NINE PARTS OF DESIRE

Because the Iranians' politicized view of religion doesn't sit well with the Saudis, Saudi Arabia imposes a tight quota on the number of Iranian pilgrims it admits each year. Finally, in 1993, Mohamed's name was drawn. He planned to take his mother and Janet on the month-long journey. But Janet, after studying the obligations of the pilgrimage, decided not to go. "There is so much more to it than circling the Kaaba and praying for forgiveness on the Plain of Arafat," she said. Pilgrims not only had to refrain from having sex, she learned. "Even thinking about sex can destroy the value of your Hajj." As well, there could be no irritable words or malicious thoughts. "I don't think I'm spiritual enough to do it properly." Instead, she offered her place to Mohamed's sister, who delightedly embarked on a special Hajj course of study to prepare herself.

Almost every week of the Mamoudzadehs' life contained some religious observance bound up in the rituals surrounding births, betrothals, marriages and funerals. During one week-long visit to the family, I learned a lot about Iranian life from two very different deaths.

Mohamed had lost a great-aunt—a ninety-year-old matriarch. Together, we set off for her Shabba Haft—Seventh Night—an evening of ritual grieving that takes place one week after a death. The woman's children, grandchildren and great-grandchildren were so numerous that the gathering spilled from her own large house into a neighbor's. Both homes were decked with black crepe, their courtyards filled with carpets and cushions and strung with fluorescent lights. Mohamed parked the car and we split up, he heading with the other men to the neighbor's house—neighbors generally lend their homes for the men's gathering, since women often come encumbered with toddlers who might make a mess. Janet and I joined the women and children crowding into the reception room of the dead woman's home.

Next door, among the men, a mullah read from the Koran, his voice piped through to the women's gathering via loudspeakers. Mullahs who do such readings are chosen for their fine voices, and after the Koran chant he began to sing a low, mournful song extolling the virtues of mothers. Around the crowded room, women sobbed gently. Then, with the end of his song, the mood changed abruptly. Servants spread huge sheets of plastic over the carpets and laid out mountainous trays of lamb, chicken, rice and vegetables.

Such gatherings bring families together, but this Shabba Haft also revealed how ten years of war and revolution had torn this Iranian family apart. A picture of the dead woman's grandson, a "martyr" in the war with Iraq, hung in the center of the living-room wall. Underneath the portrait sat the young man's sister, who had recently been released from prison after serving a seven-year sentence for shouting "Death to Khomeini." Her brother, the martyr, had denounced her to the Revolutionary Guards.

"You will find something like this in almost every middle-class Iranian family, if you can get them to talk about it," Janet said. "The revolution really divided people here—passionate believers and passionate disbelievers all under the same roof." We were sitting next to the young woman's aunt. The aunt had lost all three of her own children—two fighting for the regime, the third struggling against it. A daughter died in training for the volunteer women's militia. At her first practice on the rifle range, she was so startled by the burst of automatic weapons fire that she stood up in her trench and was shot in the head. One son went to the Iran-Iraq front and was listed missing in action. I didn't tell his mother that I had been to the battle lines where her son had fought. I'd gone from the Iraqi side, since Iran didn't take women reporters to the front. I arrived the afternoon of a major Iraqi victory, and the Iranian dead lay sprawled and flyblown in their trenches like ragged sacks of rotting meat. The Iraqis had already set to work reinforcing the few meters of desert they'd captured. Giant earth-moving equipment rumbled right over the corpses, leaving the sand smeared with a paste of mashed flesh. There would be no identification for such bodies. Hundreds, maybe thousands of young men will always be "missing" in those sands.

The hardest death had been her second son's. He had been executed by the Islamic Republic for membership in a militant opposition group named the People's Mujahedin. He was, she said, a confused young man who had been preyed on by a well-organized group that lived off Iraqi handouts and brainwashed its recruits. I wanted to ask her if she blamed the Iranian government for not showing her son some mercy, but Janet, who was translating, shook her head slightly and didn't put the question. Instead, I asked gently if she felt that all her sacrifices had been worth it. She nodded without hesitation. "Our village was the first to tear down the Shah's statue," she said, "and we haven't wavered from that path, no matter what you Westerners think." We talked about her work as a teacher in the village school. After all her losses, she said, she tried now to think of her pupils as her children.

A few days earlier, Janet and Mohamed had attended another Shabba Haft. Unlike the death of the ninety-year-old matriarch, who had gone to her God gently and in good time, this other death had been sudden and shocking.

Annahita was just thirteen years old. In the weeks before her death she had come under enormous pressure from a teacher who was vice-principal of her school. First the teacher had chided her over the way she wore her magneh, telling her the cowl-like hood was pushed too far back, letting her hair spill out provocatively. Another day the teacher took exception to her shoes, saying they were too fashionable for a modest schoolgirl. Then the teacher found a group of girls looking out a particular schoolroom window that had views of an area frequented by young men. Annahita later told her parents that she was sitting nearby, innocently doing her knitting, when the irate teacher pounced on the pupils and marched them all off for a reprimand, then singled her out to stand, humiliated, outside the classroom. It was Ramadan, and Annahita had been fasting, without even a sip of water, since dawn. She stood there, in the hot sun, for the rest of the long schoolday. That evening she confided her misery to an older brother, a medical student. "Every day they harass me. If it's going to be like this every day I don't want to go on." Her brother had no idea how deeply she meant what she said.

At school the next day the vice-principal excoriated Annahita's mother over her daughter's behavior. Annahita, the vice-principal said, was well on the way to expulsion. She would, in all probability, grow up to be a whore. Her mother bitterly refuted the teacher's claims, saying that Annahita hadn't yet realized there was such a thing as the opposite sex: "She's still a little girl," she told the teacher. "I have to hold her on my lap like a baby and force her to have her hair brushed, she's so uninterested in how she looks." The argument was still going on when Annahita, distraught, left the school, walked home, climbed to the roof of her house and threw herself off.

A few days later another young girl, also complaining about pressures over hijab and sexuality, killed herself the same way. In her pocket was a picture of Annahita torn from a newspaper account of the earlier suicide. The two cases prompted weeks of soul searching in the Iranian media. "We are sending our kids to school with thousands of hopes for their future," read the headline on an article about the suicides in a magazine named *Today's Woman*. Where, asked the article, are we going so wrong? Like most articles on the subject, this one laid the blame on an overly disciplinarian teacher, calling for more teacher training in child psychology. No one questioned whether the Islamic burden was being laid too soon, and too heavily, on the frail shoulders of little girls.

When I met Janet's daughter Leila, she had just turned nine, the age when girls assume all the responsibilities of their religion. In Iran, a nine-year-old girl is required to wear full hijab, to rise for dawn prayers and to fast during the daylight hours of Ramadan. Boys, considered less mature, aren't required to fast or pray until they turn fifteen. On his return to Iran, Khomeini threw out the Shah's 1975 Family Protection Law, which had banned child brides and polygamy. Now, in Iran, a nine-year-old girl is legally old enough to marry.

Leila had grown up in Iran but vacationed every other summer with her grandparents in Missouri. In Kansas City she enjoyed the freewheeling games of her American pals. But back home the walls of the courtyard closed in on her. When a car-repair shop opened across the street, she had to put away her bike. "There are always young men there, talking about their cars," Janet explained. "If she rides around in the street with her brothers, she'll be stared at."

The conversion of a house to a mechanic's shop hadn't pleased Janet, but she felt powerless to fight it. For one thing, the young proprietor had been a prisoner of war in Iraq and had opened his business on the proceeds of a government grant to help veterans. "And anyway," Janet sighed, "the local authorities wouldn't have any sympathy for me saying I wanted my daughter to be free to play outside. In their eyes, she belongs inside, whether there's an auto shop across the street or not.''

Leila already had her first chador, cut down to size and lace-embroidered on the hem. She loved to wear it. "It makes her feel grown up, I guess," Janet said. "I suppose I'm lucky that she isn't rebellious against it." Janet worried about how her own decision to embrace Islam would ultimately affect her daughter and watched anxiously for signs of a rebellion that would make Leila's life difficult outside the home.

But, as Leila grew from cute kid to lovely young teenager, religion became one of her favorite school subjects. At prayer time she enjoyed needling her fourteen-year-old brother, who hadn't yet begun to do his daily prayers.

"Moma, why isn't Yusef praying?" she would call, loud enough for her brother to hear over the TV show that was engrossing him. "He's not fifteen, he doesn't have to," Janet would sigh wearily. "But, Moma, our teacher says if he knows the prayers and understands them, then he should pray, no matter how old he is, and you know Yusef knows the prayers."

Janet stopped worrying about rebellion and began to dread the onset of a narrow fanaticism that would raise tensions within the family. Janet had one American friend whose daughter had become so intensely devout that she refused to accompany her mother on visits to the "spiritually polluted" United States.

Leila's schoolday started with prayers followed by a ritual chant: "*Marg bar Amrika* [Death to America]!" Her school, the Martyr of Knowledge, was a reasonably progressive institution within the Iranian spectrum and didn't require its pupils to wear chadors. Chador-wearing for schoolgirls had become controversial following several serious car accidents when drivers at dusk hadn't seen the black-veiled little figures trying to cross busy streets. Instead, Leila's school uniform was a dove-gray tunic worn over pants and topped with a magneh. The girls kept their hoods on as they ran and laughed in the playground, even though the school was off limits to all men—even the pupils' fathers. Pupils passed into the high-walled compound through a curtained entrance zealously guarded by an elderly security man.

Inside, the usual grade school decorations of cut-out animals and nature collections shared space with banners declaring "Death to America." But the school's official anti-American fervor was belied by the scramble to get into Janet's English class. Teaching English fell from favor in government schools during the first decade of the revolution, but after Khomeini's death it began to creep slowly back. Leila's school had two English teachers, but it was Janet's class that was constantly oversubscribed by parents pressing for their children to learn the language with a Midwestern accent.

"This is a pen! This is a desk! I am a girl!" Twenty-three bright little six-year-old faces, framed in their gray magnehs, chanted in unison. One by one, Janet called on the girls to recite the ABC, or to write the unfamiliar Latin alphabet on a board usually covered with the curvaceous script of Farsi. For those who knew their work, the reward was a candy and a round of applause.

Every time I saw Janet she seemed more settled in her community and contented in her private life. So far, Leila has managed to be religiously devoted without drifting into dogmatism. In Iran's family-centered world, Janet and Mohamed saw more of each other and divided their parenting more equally than most Western couples. The Friday weekend for them was always a family day, spent taking the children to the nearby mountains, to a kebab joint, visiting relatives, or just hanging out at home with the latest videos.

"At first, when my husband brought me here, I hated it," said one of Janet's American buddies, stopping in one afternoon for tea. "I just hated every step I took." The woman had left her husband and gone back to the States. "Back there, I couldn't believe the rat race. My job demanded every ounce of energy I had. I kept longing for the slow pace of life here, where the home and the family come first, and the job just gets done somehow in between. Then I got cancer, and I felt so alone there. I had relatives, of course, but they couldn't just drop everything for me. I kept thinking, if I were in Iran the family *would* drop everything. As soon as I was cured, I came back here, and it really is a good life."

But tales of domestic contentment didn't tell the whole story, any more than Betty Mahmoody's domestic nightmare had. I had lost touch with Janet's friend Margaret. Two years had slipped by since our first meeting. But one day we made contact again, and she invited me to one of her mother-in-law's *rosees*. For devout women, these gatherings—a cross between an afternoon tea party and a religious-studies class—are the major means of socializing.

When I arrived at the house I barely recognized the black-chadored figure who opened the door. Margaret had scrubbed her pale face of makeup and bound her blond hair out of sight. Even her dramatic height seemed shrunken by a weary stoop. As we walked together through her mother-in-law's courtyard, I admired its center-piece, a pretty blue-tiled fountain. "My mother-in-law washes there for prayers. It's my job to scrub it, tile by tile, to make sure it's *puk*—religiously clean. I also have to sweep every rug, every day, with that," she said, pointing to a short-handled bundle of straws. "I've got a vacuum cleaner, but I'm not allowed to use it because my mother-in-law isn't sure it gets the rugs puk. Because I'm a convert, I have to do everything better than a born Muslim just to convince them I'm not still a dirty infidel." She sounded tired and bitter. All the feisty insolence seemed to have been scrubbed and beaten away with the specks of mold on the blue tiles and the motes of dust in the rugs.

She ushered me into a salon stripped of furniture except for one empty, ornate carved chair, shrouded in black. The other guests—some dozen women—sat on large cushions lining the walls. As the mullah arrived, they pulled the edges of their chadors down over their faces. Without even a greeting, the mullah took his place in the chair and began intoning in a sad, hypnotic voice. Within minutes, most of the women were sobbing. Margaret's mother-in-law began to keen violently, her shoulders heaving underneath her black chador. From under their veils, women groped blindly for the boxes of Kleenex set out on the floor between them.

The mullah was telling the story of Hussein, the prophet Muhammad's grandson, leading his army to defeat by treachery on the plains of Karbala, thirteen centuries ago. It is a story every Shiite knows by heart. I was surprised that its retelling could unleash so much emotion. "They are not just weeping for Hussein," whispered Margaret, sitting on the floor alongside me. "They are weeping for all the terrible things in their own lives—the babies they've miscarried, the children who've died of disease, the brother killed in the war, the husband who divorced them. In a third-world country like this, women have plenty to cry about."

The mullah's singsong voice built to a crescendo, then suddenly ceased. As abruptly as he'd entered, he rose and left the room. The second he was out the door, the women threw off their chadors. They were dazzlingly dressed in silk suits decked with ropes of pearls and gold. A dozen conversations started up all at once. Margaret immediately jumped up and went to the kitchen, returning again and again with platters of fruit, tiny crisp cucumbers, sweet cakes and tea. The guests primped their elaborate coiffures and wielded tissues on each other's blurred mascara, then piled the sugar into their tiny tea glasses.

After a while I rose to telephone for a taxi. A few minutes later, when the phone rang, Margaret nudged me and nodded in the direction of her sister-in-law, who was picking up the receiver carefully wrapped in a fold of her chador. "It's the 'dirty infidel' business I was telling you about," Margaret whispered. "Because you're not Muslim, she can't stand to touch something you've touched until she's had a chance to scrub it—or have me scrub it." In that case, I thought, it was lucky that Margaret's sister-in-law didn't know I was Jewish, or she might have felt obliged to throw the phone away altogether. Fear of pollution from Jews is so strong among some Iranians that once, long before the Islamic revolution, the government passed a law requiring Jews to stay indoors during rain or snow showers, lest water that had touched their bodies flow into streams that Muslims might use to wash before prayers.

After Margaret had finished serving everyone, taking directions from the wizened mother-in-law propped up on pillows in the corner, she signaled me to come for a quick private chat in her room.

The "room" turned out to be a narrow alcove, divided from the main salon by a flimsy curtain. She shared the alcove with her son, now almost two. There was no space and little privacy. Her husband had gone on a long business trip to America and, instead of taking her for a visit to her parents, had chosen to leave her behind to do the chores for his mother and sister. "My mom's not too pleased," she said. "She calls up and says, 'You waiting on his relatives again?' She knows they're working me to death. She wants me to come home."

Margaret walked with me into the lane behind the house as I waited for my taxi. The neighbor's kitchens all backed onto the laneway, and the air was rich with the spicy scents of Persian cooking. As my cab made its slow way toward us, I asked why she didn't take her mother's advice and go home for a while. She straightened her hunched shoulders and kneaded the small of her back with a clenched fist. "I can't," she said. "My husband doesn't want me to." It was up to him to sign the papers that would allow her to leave the country. As she waved goodbye, I saw her sister-in-law appear at the door. Margaret's hands flew to her head, yanking her scarf back over a few stray wisps of blond hair.

Chapter 6

JIHAD IS FOR WOMEN, TOO

"O true believers, if ye assist
God, by fighting for his religion,
he will assist you against your
enemies; and will set your
feet fast."

THE KORAN
THE CHAPTER OF WAR

At first Hadra Dawish had trouble with the prone position on the rifle range. "I was always wondering, 'Does my uniform cover me enough? Is there a man walking around behind me?'"

But five months later, when she graduated top of her class at the United Arab Emirates military academy, Hadra Dawish had learned to empty her mind of everything but the target. She had mastered the M-16 assault rifle, Russian rocket-propelled grenades, multipurpose machine guns, hand grenades and 9mm pistols. She knew how to rappel from a hovering helicopter and conduct a night reconnaissance patrol through desert terrain. In 1992 she became the first woman from an Arabian Gulf country to enroll for officer training at the British military academy, Sandhurst.

No one seemed more surprised by any of this than Hadra herself. She had been born in 1967 into one of the most conservative Muslim societies. In those days most women of the Emirates lived in strict seclusion. Outside the family they wore the long black abaya and a cloth veil over their faces. Even at home, many women wore the *burka*—a black and gold canvas or leather mask that conceals everything but the eyes. Sending a daughter to an all-girls school was considered a risky step: less than a decade ago, conservative families wouldn't allow their sons to marry any girl who had been seen by anyone, man or woman, outside the family circle.

Hadra's family had been progressive enough to send her to school and allow her to work as a therapist with handicapped children —a job that didn't involve any contact with men. She went to and from her job wearing a cloaklike abaya and *niqab*, or face veil. "I never questioned it," she said. "The truth is, I still prefer to dress this way when I can. It's just that it isn't possible for a soldier." Now she wears desert-camouflage fatigues with a jacket cut long and loose to hide the curves of her body. Under her soldier's cap, a tightly wrapped scarf covers her hair.

Hadra became a soldier for the same reason most people do: "I love my country," she says. "I don't want to see it destroyed." In 1990, Hadra watched in horror as Iraq invaded neighboring Kuwait. Kuwait's flimsy forces, mostly staffed by foreign recruits, quickly collapsed. Kuwaiti refugees fled to the Emirates with tales of rape and destruction.

The United Arab Emirates is a mirror image of Kuwait: rich, tiny, and tempting to tyrants. In the palace of the Emirates' president, Sheik Zayed, strategists racked their brains to figure a way to boost their own small army of 50,000 men. The Emirates, after all, had less than half a million citizens to draw on. It was Zayed's wife, Sheika Fatima, who argued that the tiny state could no longer afford to waste half its population. Her radical solution: recruit women.

Sheika Fatima wasn't Zayed's first wife, or his only one. The sheik, a tribal leader in the days before the Emirates united to form a modern state, had married often, like the prophet, to cement treaties and further political alliances. Usually the wives would stay with him for a few years before being divorced and sent back to their families with honor and a sizable fortune. But Fatima had won his heart, and also his respect, and became the official first lady of the Emirates. She had married the sheik as a child bride with little education beyond basic study of the Koran. She had used the resources of the palace to pursue her education, studying English and classical Arabic. In 1973 she started the Abu Dhabi Society for the Awakening of Women, aiming to eradicate illiteracy and train women in trades.

Still, by the 1990s, Emirates women were only gingerly arriving in the work force. Just a handful had started taking jobs that put them in contact with men. One of them was a friend of the sheika's, a trailblazer named Hessa al-Khaledi, the Emirates' first woman civil engineer. With Zayed's approval, the sheika delegated Hessa to solve the problems of recruiting the Emirates' first women soldiers and reconciling the religious establishment to their existence.

Hessa took a year's leave from her job at the Public Works Department and went straight to her Islamic history books. At issue was the matter of *jihad*, or holy struggle to spread the faith and defend the Muslim community. Jihad is obligatory on all Muslims but can take many forms. In the Western mind, jihad has become synonymous with acts of terrorism carried out by extremist Islamic groups. But teaching the faith, or spreading the word through an exemplary life, are also forms of jihad.

Women's role in jihad was an issue even at the time of the prophet. In the first years of the faith, when the Muslim community had to fight to establish itself in the face of hostility from existing religious groups, some women clamored to contribute. Victorious soldiers were blessed by God and enriched with a share of the spoils of the defeated enemy. A hadith records this exchange between the prophet and one of his followers: "I am the delegate of women to you. This jihad was made obligatory on men. If they win, they are given worldly rewards, and if they are killed they are alive with their Lord, well provided for. But we Muslim women, we serve them; what do we get for that?"

Muhammad replied: "Convey to the women you meet that obedience to their husband, and the acknowledgment of their favors, is equivalent to that jihad."

The Emirates' Muslim authorities quoted that hadith in their arguments against recruiting women soldiers. But Hessa al-Khaledi countered with historical evidence showing that women *did* fight alongside Muhammad, and were honored for it.

Nusaybah bint Kaab is perhaps the most celebrated of the many women warriors, since she helped save Muhammad's life in the battle of Uhud. When the Muslim army was dispersed in an enemy charge, she was among the ten fighters who managed to hold their ground, shielding the prophet's body with their own. She received thirteen wounds during her valiant stand; one, a near-fatal sword cut to the side of her neck, took more than a year to heal. Lying close to death the day after the battle, she heard Muhammad calling for volunteers to pursue the enemy and tried to rise to answer the call, but fainted from loss of blood. In a later battle she lost a hand. Muhammad clearly honored Nusaybah's contribution. He often visited her house and took dinner there.

Some of the Muslims' most formidable opponents also were women. The notorious Hind bint Utbah, wife of the leader of Mecca, was a fearsome presence at the battle of Uhud, screaming warlike poetry to exhort her side's fighters and humiliate the enemy. One of her anti-Muhammad chants has survived, in rough translation, as:

> We reject the reprobate!
> His God we repudiate!
> His religion we loathe and hate!

Omar, Muhammad's misogynist lieutenant, came back with this crude, and revealing, response:

> May God curse Hind
> Distinguished among Hinds,
> She with the large clitoris,
> And may he curse her husband with her!

Hind was unintimidated. When the Meccans defeated the Muslims, inflicting heavy losses, Hind searched among the Muslim dead for the man who had killed her father in an earlier battle. When she found the corpse, she cut out the man's liver, sliced off his nose and ears and strung them into bracelets which she wore, as she stood on a rock yelling verses of victory while Muhammad's wives and the other Muslim women scrambled to retrieve the bodies from the field before more could be desecrated.

Stories of Muslim women's battlefield courage abound. Muhammad's aunt, Safiyah, was the first Muslim woman to kill an enemy in battle; Asma bint Yazid killed nine men of the opposing forces at the battle of Yarmouk. Khawla bint al-Azwar rode to battle with her mantle pulled close around her face. As she charged the enemy, observers asked each other if they knew the name of the brave man riding beside the prophet.

After Muhammad's death, women continued to take part in campaigns. When the Muslims attacked a Persian seaport, a band of women, led by Azdah bint al-Harith, turned their mantles into banners and, marching in phalanx toward the enemy, were mistaken for fresh reinforcements.

Armed with these examples, Hessa gradually wore down opposition to the new women's military academy. "I would ask them, if it wasn't forbidden then, why forbid it now?" Even the conservatives couldn't argue against the example of the prophet. But one question kept coming up: Who would train the women? The Emirates' only qualified instructors were men, and that was unthinkable. A male officer couldn't supervise unveiled women's physical fitness training, or barge into a women's barracks to enforce discipline; he couldn't touch a woman to adjust her stance with a rifle.

The answer was obvious to anyone who had watched the U.S. military descend on nearby Saudi Arabia. There, U. S. Army women were flying troop transports, maintaining missile batteries, trucking munitions to the front lines. The Emirates asked the U. S. Army if it could spare a few of its senior women to run a basic training course. Fort Bragg chose ten specialists whose average length of service was fourteen years. Their commander, Major Janis Karpinski, was already serving in Saudi Arabia.

Before they began work, Hessa arranged for each of the U.S. soldiers to spend two days living with an Emirates family so they would at least glimpse the cultural background from which the recruits were coming. As she arrived at the huge house of an Emirates army officer, Tracy Borum, a military police captain from Nashville, Tennessee, felt nervous. "I worried they'd see me as a Western woman invading their home and challenging their ways," she said. Instead, she found herself an honored guest. She feasted on camel meat ("sweet and sort of greasy"), tried on a burka ("a weird feeling —like I was trying to hide from somebody") and watched the women perfume themselves by placing burning incense braziers under their long robes ("I was sure they'd set themselves on fire").

Meanwhile, Hessa was screening applications from over 1,200 women who had answered advertisements seeking volunteers. She chose 74 women, ranging in age from seventeen to thirty-one, and in education from completion of sixth grade to achievement college degrees. "At first I tried to screen out women with small children," she said, "but that was impossible." In the Emirates, women still marry quite young and start their families as soon as they can, so almost all the women in the right age group had young children. But because most of them lived in extended families there were plenty of mothers and aunts in most households willing to provide child care. Hessa found that many of the applicants came from families with a brother or father already in the military. The chosen group included about seven sets of sisters. At first, as the United States trainers divided the recruits into three platoons, they considered splitting the sisters, but decided against it when they saw that the women seemed to work better with a sister's support. None of the women had been physically active; most had never spent a night away from home. Tracy Borum remembers their extreme shyness. Raised from childhood with the Koranic injunction to "lower their gaze and be modest," the women now found themselves hollered at to square their shoulders and stare their officers in the eye. "At first I had to go around lifting their chins to get them to look at me," Tracy recalls.

The Americans had to adjust some aspects of their training. "The drill sergeants, yelling at them to get in formation or get in the barracks, were just about scaring these poor women to death," recalls Janis Karpinski. "American recruits expect that—they've seen all the movies." The drill sergeants learned that lavishly praising recruits who got it right worked better than abusing those who got it wrong. The women had been raised to please, Tracy Borum discovered, "so we tried to become the people they wanted to please." Other modifications included arranging the drill schedule to include prayer times and rescheduling heavy physical training for nighttime during the month of Ramadan, after the women had broken their day-long fast. Janis Karpinski and a few of the instructors fasted all day along with their troops. "I wanted to show solidarity with them, but I also wanted to know exactly what their physical condition was. If one of them said she couldn't make it through a four-mile run, I'd say, 'You can, because we can, and we were fasting too.' "

Except for Ramadan, the day started with the prayer call at about five-thirty each morning. After prayers, recruits in black sweatsuits lined up for physical training. "We do the PT before any of the male administrators show up," said Tracy. That way, the recruits could work out with their hair uncovered, although they usually kept their scarves tied around their waists, just in case.

Only fifteen women dropped out of the course. Some couldn't cope with the presence of a few male administrators in the military school. Others missed their families, or their maids. Those who stayed thrived. At first the American trainers had revised their fitness targets downward, to accommodate women who'd never had to walk to the grocery store, much less complete a forced march. But within weeks the targets had been raised again, as the women easily mastered a hundred push-ups a day. One recruit shed forty-four pounds during the five-month training.

As the course wound toward its end in May 1991, "we saw this metamorphosis take place," says Janis Karpinski. "In the last thirty days, I never saw these women but their shoulders were squared, their heads tall." When Hadra Dawish took leave to visit her family, they were shocked at the changes in her. "They told me I'd changed too many things, from the way I walk to the way I act with them," she said. "Some they liked. Some, no." Hadra found her women friends hardest to convince. Sitting in their gilded salons, with foreign maids passing trays of sweet pastries, they shuddered at Hadra's tales of digging foxholes and standing guard all night in desert camps. "They kept saying to me, 'You have to come out, you've made a terrible choice.' But I knew I'd made the right decision."

Meanwhile, some senior officers in the Emirates' army found it hard to credit the fine results the women recruits were achieving. Lieutenant Colonel Mohamed Nasser, the commander of the academy, had admitted from the beginning that he felt lukewarm about the whole idea of women warriors. "If we had a bigger population, I'd rather see women stay at home," he said. But slowly he had to revise his view of their capabilities. At first he refused to believe the women's shooting scores. "When I see results of thirty-eight out of forty, I have to be surprised," he said. The women, after all, had grown up in an atmosphere in which girls never even played at aiming a toy gun. The lieutenant colonel wondered if the high scores reflected a defect in the newly built shooting range at the women's academy. To find out, he commandeered the men's academy shooting range and ordered the women to redo the test. There he watched in growing astonishment as bullet after bullet slammed home, right smack in the center of the target.

Before I went to the Middle East, I'd always found myself on the dovish side of every argument. Despite glaring evidence to the contrary (Golda Meir, Margaret Thatcher) I believed that a world with more women in positions of power would be a more peaceful place. So it seemed odd, and a little sad, that of all the rights a woman might aspire to, the one that Hadra and her friends had won was the right to kill and be killed. And yet it was impossible not to celebrate the strength the Emirates women had discovered in themselves, the skills they'd mastered and the confidence that seemed to shine from every face I encountered on the base.

I had grappled with this paradox once before, in Eritrea, huddling in a trench burrowed out of an African mountaintop. A few meters away, Ethiopian soldiers stared through binoculars, waiting for someone on our side to make a move. Of the hundred or so soldiers on the Eritrean side of that front line, about fifteen were women, including the commanding officer.

Those Eritrean women guerrillas had witnessed the worst that war could offer. One had seen a friend take a Kalashnikov round full in the face, blasting away half her jaw. Another held the hand of a comrade as her mine-shattered leg was amputated without anesthetic. The women talked of these things with a sad pragmatism. Most had been born since the fighting with Ethiopia started in 1962 and had known nothing but a country at war.

As in the Emirates, Eritrean women had joined the guerrillas because they felt they had to; there simply weren't enough men to challenge the might of black Africa's biggest army. If anything, their society had been even more resistant to the notion of women warriors than that of the Emirates. In the 1960s in Eritrean villages, women's position was so lowly that a wife presumed to speak to her husband only if it was absolutely necessary. From the Koran's pronouncement that menstruation is "an illness," during which women must refrain from sex and prayer, Eritrean villagers had developed a tradition of forcing menstruating women to leave their homes for a week each month and seclude themselves, day and night, in a pit reserved for the "unclean."

When war broke out with Ethiopia, a few women insisted on fighting. "At the beginning, they were needed, so there wasn't the luxury of refusing them," said Chuchu Tesfamariam, who became a fighter herself at the age of seventeen. The valor of the fighters won new respect for women in general and broke down many taboos. The Eritreans, desperately poor, had few factories. But, as a gesture to the comfort of the women fighters, they had invested some of their scarce resources in a plant to produce sanitary napkins.

Living conditions at the front line were desperately harsh. The troops, slight and undernourished from years of drought-reduced rations, lived on a porridge of lentils scooped up in spongy bread. Their World War I-style trench system burrowed for miles across high mountain ridges. Supplies had to be hauled by hand up the near-vertical rock face, work that the women shared equally with the men. Everyone slept on the ground.

The guerrillas came from a wide range of backgrounds. Some, like the university-educated idealists who returned from exile to enlist, found it natural that women and men should fight together. Others, simple villagers, had difficulty adjusting to the idea.

Ismail Idriss, a twenty-three-year-old goatherd and a devout Muslim, had never spoken to a woman from outside his family when he suddenly found himself taking orders from one. "Women fighters I knew about from the beginning; even when I was wandering with my goats I'd seen them," Ismail explained, sunning himself on a rocky ledge during a rare break in the fighting. "But I never believed a woman could give orders to a man." Ismail's company commander was a stocky, taciturn woman of his own age named Hewit Moges, a thirteen-year veteran of front-line fighting who came from a Christian background. "Now I have seen it in practice I have had to start to accept it," he said, in a voice that still sounded hesitant about the idea. "When it's a hard climb she runs up the mountain, when it's a battle she's in front of the troops, and when someone is wounded she's the one who carries him from the field." He spread his palms and raised his shoulders in a wide shrug. "What can I say against it when I have seen such things?"

A few nights later the war took a rare break for a wedding. Fighters always married in large groups; a single couple couldn't afford the traditional feast of goat meat. A young dancer dressed in a costume made of grain sacks marked "Gift of the Federal Republic of Germany" leaped and twirled across the sand, followed by 120 brides and grooms, all clad alike in the same shabby khakis they'd worn into battle shortly before. The couples paired up and held hands, waiting for their division commander to read out their names and declare them husband and wife. Each couple received a wedding certificate, produced in the fighters' underground printshop, carrying a quote from the 1977 Marriage Law stating that the union was "the free will of the two partners based on love."

I sat on the sand listening to the long list of names. Nura Husseini was marrying Haile Gabremichael. Abdullah Doud was wedding Ababa Mariam. Muslims and Christians were marrying each other by the dozen. "It's possible that these people come from parents who were taught that you starve before you share food from the plate of someone of a different faith," said Chuchu, sitting on sand beside me. But in the trenches of this long war these young men and women had shared much more: fear, and victories, and belief in a cause. In the dark I could just make out Chuchu's profile. A sad half smile played across her face. "Not everything that comes from war is bad," she whispered.

And unfortunately, not everything that comes with peace is good. In 1994 I returned to Eritrea, which by then had been an independent country for almost a year. The capital, Asmara, had fallen to the guerrillas without a struggle. Unscathed by the fighting that had reduced so much of the country to rubble, its Italianate buildings glowed in a gentle wintry light, their terra-cotta walls splashed with sudden tumbles of scarlet bougainvillea. The streets were clean and safe to walk, even late at night. During the war, even schoolteachers had carried AK-47s. Now, no one was armed, even at the airport or entrances to government buildings. One of the world's most militarized populations had put away its guns.

For once, a guerrilla movement had come to power and not been instantly corrupted by it. The movement's leaders still wore the cheap plastic sandals they'd fought in, and none of them, including the president, drew a salary. Like the other fighters, they donated their labor to the rebuilding effort.

But, for the women fighters, peace had brought some unexpected disappointments. The new government offered women political participation and new legal rights, such as the right to own and inherit land. It also banned genital mutilation in hospitals, and sponsored a radio series in which both the Muslim mufti and the Christian bishop stated clearly that such practices weren't religious obligations.

Still, the traditions of the wider society outweighed the culture that had developed at the front. Suddenly, fighters had come back home to families who had spent the war under occupation by Ethiopian forces. Often, the guerrillas' progressive mores were at odds with the deeply conservative values of their parents. "Most of them respect us—they understand we lived a different way," said Rosa Kiflemariam, a thirty-three-year-old who spent eight years at the front. "But others say to us, 'That was then—this is now, and now you have to live our way.' "

In 1989, Rosa had married a fellow guerrilla in one of the front-line wedding ceremonies. The couple, serving at different fronts, had spent only one month together before peace came. Now she and her husband were trying to get to know each other in the midst of enormous family pressure. Rosa's mother-in-law didn't approve of her son's wife going out to work and wanted her to give up her job as a financial officer in the Eritrean Women's Union. "Every time she sees me she starts saying, 'Why don't you have children? Why don't you stay at home?' "

In the villages, particularly, families found it difficult to accept the tough young women who were used to absolute equality, or even positions of command in military units. In those cases, families urged divorce, offering their sons young, tractable village girls as alternative wives prepared to wait on them hand and foot. Such tensions were exacerbated if the husband and wife were from different religious backgrounds.

For a young, unmarried woman fighter, the future was problematic. On the one hand, she was a heroine, but that didn't necessarily make her marriageable in villages that still valued modesty and certain virginity.

To Rosa and many other women, a new struggle had just begun. "We have to fight now to make them understand that everyone has the right to live freely. It's another war, I think."

Chapter 7

A Queen

"I found a woman to reign over them,
who is provided with everything
requisite for a prince, and hath
a magnificent throne."

THE KORAN
THE CHAPTER OF THE ANT

*T*he ancient trade routes of Arabia are potholed highways now. The groaning strings of camels that Muhammad led for Khadija from coastal port to inland fortress are gone as well. Instead, trucks thud and grind from Aqaba to Mecca through a miasma of diesel and dust. What passes for an oasis these days is a gray concrete truck stop, innocent of a palm tree or even a blade of grass.

In the spring of 1989, I went to cover a riot in one of these places —a dismal shanty town named Maan in the middle of the Jordanian desert. The Jordanian prime minister had raised the price of gas, and Maan's truck drivers had poured into the streets to protest. The riots spread from there all over the country, troubling the stability of King Hussein, the Middle East's longest-reigning monarch. It was a story I'd written a half dozen times: a poor country needs aid, the International Monetary Fund comes in and demands economic reform, its terms are too tough, the people revolt.

But this time, as I perched on what was left of a chair in the burned-out ruins of a Maan bank, the story took a sudden lurch away from what I expected to hear. Sitting opposite me on the upturned drawer of a filing cabinet, an edgy Bedouin in a grimy robe played with the fringes of his kaffiyeh. He had been with the mob as it rampaged through the town a week earlier. "The demonstrators want lower prices, yes. They are poor already, and the increase will take the food from their children's mouths. But that wasn't all they were shouting for." He looked around, to make sure no one was listening. "They were shouting for the king to divorce the queen."

Like most Middle East correspondents, I knew vaguely that King Hussein had married an American, but I'd thought of her as photogenic fodder for the social pages, not as someone likely to emerge as a slogan in a price riot.

"People here have many questions about the queen," the Bedouin said, letting go of his kaffiyeh and reaching into the pockets of his robe for worry beads. As the beads traveled through his grease-stained fingers he listed the questions one by one: "Was she a virgin when she married the king? Is she really Muslim? If so, why doesn't she cover her hair? Is it true she supports Christian causes? Her family is from Halab [the Arabic name for the town of Aleppo, in Syria, where her grandfather was born before moving to Lebanon]. Halab has many Jews. How do we know she doesn't have Jewish blood? We have heard that she is from the CIA, sent to poison the king."

The Bedouin was troubled by a familiar bundle of Middle Eastern bogeys: America in general and the CIA in particular; Jews, or if not Jews, then Christians; women's sexuality—both the fear of a "past" and the dread of present emancipation signaled by the absence of a veil.

It was hard to take his ranting seriously. Yet, in Iran and Egypt, rulers' wives had served as lightning rods for dissent, or at least criticism of them had been a barometer of troubles to come. The shah's empress Farah and Sadat's wife Jehan both had been aggressively modern, high-profile women who had fought for reform. What was Queen Noor doing to earn so much opprobrium?

At fifty-four, her husband, King Hussein, was the Middle East's great survivor. At thirteen, he'd narrowly missed being killed in the hail of assassin's bullets that murdered his grandfather. In 1951, at fifteen years old, he'd inherited a wobbly throne, survived the loss of the West Bank—half his kingdom—to Israel in 1967, put down an armed insurrection by Palestinian refugees in 1970 and, by 1989, had ruled for thirty-eight years. "He's been to the funerals of all of those who said he wouldn't last a week," said Dan Shifton, an Israeli analyst of Jordanian affairs. Within days of the riots, the survivor in the king did what was necessary: he sacked the prime minister, Zaid Rifai, and promised his restless subjects their first general election in twenty-two years. I wondered if his marriage to Noor, his fourth and longest, would also have to be jettisoned in the interests of his survival.

When riots broke out, the king and queen were in Washington, dining at the White House. Pictures of Noor, resplendent in a navy-blue chiffon gown, and word that her sister had attended the dinner on the arm of the film producer George Lucas, only fed the angry talk about her American values and extravagance.

I had a standing request at the palace for an interview with the king. Not really expecting a reply, I fired off a new telex asking to see the queen as well, to talk about the way she'd become a target of the rioters. To my surprise, I got an answer back almost immediately: both Their Majesties had agreed to see me, and a car from the palace would collect me from my hotel.

Along with my chador, I always traveled with what I called my "king suit"—one decent Italian outfit in pin-striped silk that wadded up into a corner of a carry-on bag and emerged respectable after a quick press in a hotel laundry. I put the suit on, along with a pair of high heels that I hadn't worn since my wedding, and went down to meet a pistol-packing soldier at the wheel of a silver-gray Mercedes.

The royal palace sits on a hilltop near the center of old Amman, the town whose Roman name was Philadelphia—the city of brotherly love. The royal court does its business behind tall iron gates designed to protect those inside against brotherly hate. I had been inside the palace compound before, but only as far as the king's offices, the Diwan, where Circassian soldiers in high fur hats stand guard and obsequious courtiers wait for the royal summons. I expected that our meeting would take place in the king's book-lined office. But the car swished past the grand stairway of the Diwan and deposited me under the thudding rotors of a Black Hawk helicopter. The king was already in the pilot's seat. "Hop aboard," he cried, beckoning me into the seat behind him.

The king pushed the control stick forward and we heaved off the ground, hovering low over the palace and Amman's dense honeycomb of flat-roofed houses. Within seconds, the city was gone. We skimmed groves of ancient olive trees and ribs of bleached white stone. In Amman, fast-food joints named New York New York Pizza and giant supermarkets with bagels in the deep freeze gave Jordan a familiar, Western facade. But the modern layer was thin as a crust of sand. Beneath was an ancient, biblical landscape peopled by tribesmen who lived by their goats, their olives and their blood alliances just as they always had.

Winston Churchill used to boast that he'd created Jordan on a Sunday afternoon with the stroke of a pen. At a meeting in Cairo in 1921, Churchill and T. E. Lawrence (Lawrence of Arabia) doodled the amoeba-shaped state of Transjordan onto the map of the Arabian Peninsula to provide a throne for their ally, Abdullah, who had helped Lawrence fight the Turks in World War I. Abdullah's father, Sherif Hussein, the thirty-fifth-generation direct descendant of the prophet Muhammad, had ruled Mecca and the Hijaz region until the al-Sauds swept down from the Nejd desert in the North and pushed him aside.

A Palestinian assassinated Abdullah in 1951. His son, Talal, was mentally ill and abdicated two years later. The teenaged Hussein inherited the throne of a state in which the desert Arabians like himself were quickly becoming outnumbered by Palestinian refugees, pouring across the border after each war with Israel. Jordan, alone among Arab states, gave citizenship to the Palestinian refugees from the West Bank. But in the "Black September" of 1970, Hussein felt the Palestinians were trying to take control of his kingdom. He crushed them, with many casualties.

I stared at the king's crash helmet, which had "Hussein I" stenciled on the back. In the West, it was easy enough to see the king simply as a smooth-talking, Harrow- and Sandhurst-educated diplomat. But out here he was something much more potent: the avatar of his ancestor the prophet Muhammad, prayer leader, warlord and father of the tribes. Such a leader has to be seen by his people—and not just on TV, talking the dry argot of diplomacy with foreigners. Hussein, busy with foreign policy, had lost touch with his people. He was on his way to mend the rift.

The United States never seemed to lose its ability to be amazed when one of its foreign-leader buddies was overthrown. Partly, I thought, it was because we only saw these men as they appeared in their dealings with the West. We had no sense of them as they seemed to their own people: that giant constituency to which even the greatest despots are eventually accountable.

As Hussein landed the helicopter on the outskirts of a desert town, the chant of the waiting crowd defeated even the thump of the rotors. *"Bil rub, bil damm . . .* [With our soul and with our blood . . . we sacrifice for you, O Hussein!]" Through the swirling dust, the faces straining toward the king were twisted, almost pained. Bodies surged forward, held back by cordons of soldiers who cracked skulls and thumped shoulders as though they were dealing with the nation's mortal enemies. The king, usually a grave, gray figure, beamed as he tossed off his crash helmet and threw a red and white kaffiyeh atop his balding head. He plunged into the crowd.

I climbed out of the helicopter in his wake and was instantly swept away from him and his tight capsule of bodyguards. The crowd, moving like a single, demented entity, had closed ranks behind the king and carried him forward. I felt myself being dragged in the other direction. I heard the bat squeak of ripping silk as the jacket of my king-suit caught on the hilt of a Bedouin's dagger. Tottering on the unfamiliar high heels, I tried to keep upright. One of the burly soldiers of the king's bodyguard spotted me. Cursing and swatting a path through the press of bodies, he grabbed me in one hand and, continuing to rain blows on everyone around us with the other, propelled me back toward the relatively calm eye of the storm that his colleagues were maintaining around the king.

The surge was carrying us toward an array of tents. As we approached, a gurgling moan rose above the chants. Just in front of the king, a camel stumbled to its knees and then, like an inflatable toy losing its air, slowly collapsed forward, thudding with a tiny splash into a glossy pool of its own blood. Across the curve of the animal's long neck the butcher's ritual dagger had inscribed a parody of a smile. As tradition demanded, the king strode through the welcoming sacrificial blood and the bodyguards propelled me after him. Days later, when I unpacked my shoes, I imagined I could still see the rusty tidemark, halfway up the heel.

As we reached the shade of a black goat-hair tent, a white-robed tribesman with shaky hands poured coffee from a long-spouted pot into a tiny handleless cup. Trembling violently, he raised the cup to his mouth and downed the contents, to prove it wasn't poisoned. Then, still shaking, he poured a second cup for his king.

That whole long, scorching day passed in a blur of tableaux from *The Arabian Nights:* a barefoot poet, chanting his verses in praise of the king; an old Bedouin woman swathed in black veils and marked on the face with blue tattoos, pressing a petition into the king's palm; the king at lunch, plunging a hand into a platter of steaming lambs' heads set atop piles of rice; tribesmen, old enough to be his father, kissing him reverently upon shoulders and nose, but addressing him, in their egalitarian desert way, by his *kunya* Abu Abdullah.

I lost count of how many settlements we visited, flitting between them by helicopter, the king's grave countenance losing more of its grayness as the day wore on. By late afternoon I was almost surprised to find the helicopter easing down once more in Amman, and the king's soft voice asking me to join him at al-Nadwa, his pink stone palace. "Noor is waiting for us," he said.

Inside the grand doorway he discreetly pointed me toward a bathroom, then bounded away, over the Persian carpets, past the display cases of antique guns and swords, up the grand staircase, taking the steps two at a time like a boy.

I splashed my face with the hot water that gushed from gold faucets and attacked my wind-knotted, dust-crusted hair with a gold-backed brush set out on the gleaming marble bureau. When I emerged, the queen was drifting down the stairs in a long, Palestinian-style dress with panels of silk in plum and dull gold. Her hair, a brighter gold, fell in loose tresses down her back. She was a striking woman, slender and very tall—at least five inches taller than her husband. In official portraits she was always posed to look shorter than he. I wondered whether he perched on a box or she stood in a hole.

She smiled and held out her hand for a firm, American-style

shake. "I asked His Majesty how you were, and he said, 'Well, she's a bit dusty,' " she said. "But you don't look dusty to me. Let's talk in the garden. It's the best room in the house. In 1970 they had to put bulletproof glass in all the upstairs windows. I think it makes the inside claustrophobic."

She swished through french doors onto a terrace giving way to lawns and flower beds. The afternoon light fell in solid golden shafts. We wandered over to a group of chairs near a tangle of fragrant jasmine. I perched my notebook on my knee. "You need a table," she said. Spying a piece of cast-iron garden furniture across the lawn, she strode over and hefted it herself, waving away the dismayed-looking servant who rushed to help her. She had always been athletic: cheerleader and a member of the hockey team in the first coed class at Princeton in 1969 and an avid skier during a semester spent waitressing at Aspen. Now, she rode, played tennis and did aerobics two or three times a week.

A waiter brought me fresh orange juice in a gold-rimmed glass. The queen took a sip of an astringent-smelling herbal tea, trained her green eyes straight on me and, simply and frankly, unfolded her thoughts on the riots, their meaning and their aftermath. "We flew straight home from Washington when it happened," she said. "And, as soon as I got home, one of my friends sat me down and told me what had been going on—the absolute *rubbish* in the air about me." The friend was Leila Sharaf, Jordan's only woman senator and one of the queen's confidantes. "Some of it was so preposterous that you have to meet it with a sense of humor, otherwise it crushes you. I mean, someone in my position will always be talked about, whatever I do."

It was no secret that wealthy Amman wished the king had married one of its own daughters instead of an outsider. His first wife had been Dina Abdul Hamid, a university-educated intellectual with Egyptian roots, seven years his senior. After eighteen months and the birth of a daughter, there had been a sudden divorce. Dina, holidaying in Egypt when she received news of the split, later said that she had been allowed to see her daughter only once during the next six years. The king's next choice was Toni Gardiner, nineteen years old and the daughter of a British military officer. The king met her at a dance and ignored all warnings about the possible pitfalls of the match. He renamed her Muna al-Hussein—Arabic for "Hussein's wish." They had two sons and twin daughters, but when his wishes changed, in 1972, he divorced her to marry a Jordanian of Palestinian roots named Alia Toucan.

Alia was the first of his wives on whom he bestowed the title queen. She was the perfect choice to heal the scars of Black September and unite the kingdom in the time-honored tribal way. Her son, Prince Ali, born in 1975, vaulted over Hussein's older sons by Princess Muna to take second place in the succession after Hussein's brother, the crown prince Hassan. Alia also had a daughter and fostered a baby whose mother was killed in an airline crash. Alia suffered her share of malicious gossip while she lived, but her sudden death in a helicopter crash in February 1977 made her certain to be remembered as the king's great love and the country's perfect queen.

So twenty-six-year-old Lisa Halaby had a hard act to follow when the king married her just sixteen months later. There was little in her background to prepare her. She had grown up in a wealthy and influential Washington family. Her mother, the daughter of an immigrant from Sweden, married and later divorced Najeeb Halaby, the son of a Syrian immigrant. Najeeb was a success story of the American melting pot who grew up speaking only English and rose to the top in both business and government service. He became chief executive of Pan Am and directed the Federal Aviation Authority under Presidents Kennedy and Johnson. His interest was domestic politics, not foreign policy, and his daughter could barely remember a discussion of Middle East issues at home. Still, she claimed a stubborn attachment to her Arabic heritage. "The fifties were all about conformity, and I suppose I rebelled against that," she said. "When everybody wanted to be the same, I clung to the things that made me different." For a while she even tried to persuade her bemused fellow pupils at the Washington's Cathedral School to call her Lisa Man-of-Halab, since that was the literal translation of her Arabic surname.

At Princeton she completed a BA in architecture and urban planning and, in the four years following her graduation, worked her way around the world as a draftswoman on town planning schemes in

Tehran and architectural projects in Sydney. In Jordan, she'd taken a job as a designer with the national airline. It was at a reception celebrating the delivery of the Jordanian airline's first jumbo jet that Najeeb Halaby introduced his daughter to King Hussein. The king invited her to lunch at the palace and entertained her for five hours, showing her the palace and introducing her to his children. For the next six weeks they ate dinner together almost every night. Afterward, they'd roar around the hills of Amman on the king's motorbike, with bodyguards trailing at a discreet distance.

Lisa, working at the airline and living at the Intercontinental Hotel, kept the romance secret. Rebecca Salti, an American married to a Jordanian, had come to know her quite well. She remembers running into her outside the hotel that summer. "It was very hot, and the two of us just sat down on the pavement there and chatted about this and that. Looking back on it, I guess she seemed a little distracted." Later that day the royal palace officially announced the engagement of King Hussein to the woman who from then on would be known as Noor al-Hussein, the Light of Hussein. The official announcement stated that Noor had adopted the Islamic religion.

"When he proposed, I thought long and hard about accepting," said Noor. "Not because I was unsure of my feelings for him. My feelings were so strong for him that I was thinking of him, perhaps, more than myself. I was well aware that I wasn't a typical, traditional wife. I didn't want to be a source of controversy for him."

And now she was. It wasn't difficult to pinpoint what had gone wrong. At first the people of Jordan had been warm. "I hadn't expected the outpouring of affection," she said, thinking back to the early days of her marriage. Others in Jordan remembered it too. "She tried to give a speech in Arabic, and halfway through she got a bit flustered and looked as though she was about to cry," recalled Metri Twall, a young Amman businessman. "The whole audience was behind her. People were calling out, 'Don't worry, we love you, you're doing great.'" The births of four children in six years also had pleased a population obsessed with family.

Those were the oil-boom years, when bright Jordanians could make a fortune working in the Gulf. Coming home, they built bougainvillea-splashed villas where thick-pile carpets muffled the foot-falls of Filipino servants and the only sound was the tinkling of decorative fountains.

In that era of conspicuous consumption, Noor at first stood out as being rather less ostentatious than the elite among her new subjects. Her wedding, in June 1978, was low-key by royal standards, held in the gardens of the king's mother's palace. Engagement and wedding photos show an unregal-looking bride, with a scrubbed face and lank hair. But that unstudied coed style soon vanished. With the media's need for a new Grace Kelly, international photographers such as Norman Parkinson made their way to Jordan, trailing famous makeup artists. Anthony Clavet, who specialized in creating distinctive "looks" for celebrities such as David Bowie and Sophia Loren, gave Noor a look of sleek, queenly glamor, accented by fine jewelry and French couturier clothes. The king and his beautiful wife became fixtures on the royalty and head-of-state circuit. It was possible to find them at their London address, opposite Kensington Palace, or in their hilltop retreat near Vienna as well.

But times had become harder in Jordan since then. The oil boom busted, and the bright young Jordanians who formerly would have been able to make their fortunes in the Gulf were staying at home, underemployed. Hardship bred frustration, and frustration fundamentalism. America's support for Israel, even during the violence of the intifada, had inflamed ever present anti-American sentiments.

In Amman, after the riots, everyone seemed ready to attack the queen as an extravagant clothes horse. "She has become our Imelda Marcos," sneered a young businessman. Even government officials joined in. "People remember the young girl who came here wearing blue jeans. They expect someone down to earth, not dripping with jewelry and jetting off to Europe," said one prominent politician.

The city, he said, was abuzz with the latest outrage. While the king had been in Kuwait seeking aid to patch up Jordan's ravaged economy, the queen had gone shopping. "She bought a piece of jewelry that cost three quarters of a million dollars," he said. "A Kuwaiti newspaper got ahold of the check and printed it under a headline, 'While the king begs, the queen spends.' " I asked him if I could borrow his copy of the article. "Well," he said, "I didn't actually see it myself. My friend saw it." For the next few days I chased this article across Amman. The friend would refer me to a neighbor who'd refer me to a shopkeeper who'd swear his son would be able to show me a copy. But he couldn't. I tried combing every Arabic information service and checking with press attachés at foreign embassies. Nothing. Finally I got out the Kuwaiti telephone directory and called each of the emirate's newspapers, one by one. At every paper the answer was the same: no such article had ever run. But in the minds of Jordanians it was as real as if they'd held the dog-eared clipping in their hands.

The king had joined us in the garden. Now, he interjected gently, in his soft, deep voice. "It's natural that someone close to me should become a target." The ancient bonds between the Bedouins and their leader, especially a leader descended from the prophet, created strong taboos against direct criticism. Women, on the other hand, were easy targets. Any time things started to go wrong in the Middle East, women suffered for it first. A fundamentalist revolution couldn't instantly fix a national economy, but it could order women into the veil. If Jordanians were unhappy, they couldn't punish their king. But they could make his wife's life a misery.

King Hussein had always been an accessible ruler who understood the Western press and rarely shied away from the chance to put his point of view on Middle Eastern affairs. But in the late 1980s things started to change. By the time I became Middle East correspondent in 1987, he had become harder to reach, walled off by an impenetrable defensive line of palace advisers. They were all men, all middle-aged, all of a type: intelligent and elitist, yet deferential to the point of groveling before the king. The fired prime minister, Zaid Rifai, had been a brave diplomat, astute at analyzing the shifting moods of Jordan's dangerous neighbors—Syria, Iraq, Israel and Saudi Arabia. But his domestic politics were a disaster. His authoritarian streak led him to distrust the ordinary people of Jordan and disregard popular opinion. Under his direction, control of the press and TV was total, and a whisper of dissent, especially from citizens of Palestinian background, often led to a jail cell. It was ironic to me that in 1987 and 1988, when Israel was engaged in a virtual civil war with its Palestinians, I could go to a refugee camp anywhere on the West Bank or Gaza and talk to whomever I wanted. But across the river in Jordan a trip to a Palestinian camp required a permit and an intimidating escort of secret police whose presence stifled any possibility of a frank discussion. The riots had been a reaction to Rifai's repression, and the king had already eased the rules on free speech.

Hussein looked at his wife as if apologizing for what she had borne on his behalf. "It's sad and difficult for Noor, who has done so much here and in the outside world for Jordan."

Noor acknowledged that some of the criticism had to be addressed, and was trying to distinguish between behavior that she was prepared to change and behavior she wouldn't sacrifice. She had more or less decided that her style would change, but not her substance. After the riots she switched to clothes that were almost all Jordanian-made, from ballgowns to blue jeans. The big jewels vanished into a vault somewhere, to be replaced by down-homey pieces such as a charm bracelet decked with ornaments chosen by her children. Just after our first meeting she invited me to go with her to Jerash to inspect the preparations for that year's arts festival. She wore a mid-calf khaki skirt; mine came just to my knees. In the newspaper the next day I was amused to find myself in a picture standing just behind the queen. The photograph had been retouched to give me a modest pair of trousers. Sensitivities were obviously so great that even someone in the queen's entourage had to be covered.

But the queen was not going to submit to demands that she wear Islamic headscarves. "I don't play to one group or another, and I don't plan to start now," she said. "I think it's possible to—and I think I do —balance a respect for what's traditional in this society with what's practical for the role I have to play."

That role—her projects—would all continue, although, she said wistfully, "some of them will take years to be understood." When she married the king, she had asked him what she should do. "He said, 'Whatever you decide I'm sure will be right,' " she recalled. At the time she had been buoyed by his confidence in her. But her first visits to government officials were less encouraging. One minister strongly advised her to confine her public role to cutting an occasional ceremonial ribbon.

"Everyone would have understood that," said Ranya Khadri, a

Jordanian law graduate. "If you just sit home and have kids, that's fine with everyone. The minute you try to do something different as a woman in this society, you open yourself up to gossip and criticism."

But Noor couldn't imagine a life without something resembling a job. "I'd always worked," she said. At first she involved herself with projects linked to her former career: urban planning, building codes and environmental issues. As her children were born, she became increasingly involved with issues of mother and child health and education, then women's training and employment, then sports and culture. By 1985 she was heading a large foundation from an office in a refurbished palace that had belonged to King Abdullah. Her projects tended to focus on women, especially the women of isolated rural areas. Many Bedouin tribes had stopped wandering with the seasons and settled down year round in makeshift settlements that lacked transport, clean water, health care. Lisa Halaby, the town planner, looked at these places and imagined them differently. Noor, the queen of Jordan, goaded the politicians to make them so. The men who ran Jordan weren't used to taking orders from a young woman.

And the men whose wives she was helping didn't always like the effect of her help. A rug-weaving project on a wind-swept hilltop named Jebel Bani Hamida had been a roaring success because the women could do the work at home on simple, traditional looms made of sticks and stones. The queen had helped with design and organization, then bought the rugs as gifts for Jordan's official visitors. She also visited the women, squatting beside them in the dust and listening to their problems. The money for the rugs went straight to the women, giving them a measure of independence for the first time in their lives. One of them used the money from her first rug to pay for bus fare to the city to file for a divorce.

Noor had other interests that didn't sit well with religious extremists. There had been threats to disrupt the arts festival at Jerash, of which she was the principal patron. The festival had been growing every year, drawing traditional artists such as Arabian poets but also increasingly attracting European performers, such as foreign ballet companies, whose acts the fundamentalists considered lewd. They also opposed the creation of a scholarship boarding school, which the queen had sponsored. The school was to be coeducational—anathema to Islamic hard-liners. The "Christian causes" that had so worried the Bedouin in Maan entailed working with denominations such as Mennonites, Anglicans and Roman Catholics who had refugee-relief programs running in Jordan.

Whenever Noor spoke about becoming a Muslim, she always stressed Islam's compatibility with the values of the Judeo-Christian tradition in which she'd been raised, and of the need to "promote an accurate image" of Islam's humanism and universal character. She criticized "extremists" for conveying what she said was a distorted picture of the faith.

Her sudden return from Washington in the midst of the riots had left her staring at a diary of empty, unscheduled days. She had to decide how to fill them: to hide from the criticism or to go out and face it. She went out. "It might be easier to retire slightly or retract slightly," she said, gazing at a fading beam of sunlight falling gently on a bed of soft pink roses. "I'd have more time with the children"— her own were then aged nine, eight, six and three. "I could exercise more or even read a book. But I feel I have a responsibility to those young people who believe in the same ideals as me but don't have the power to carry them out. If I pull back, I'm letting them down— especially the women." Her first public appearances had gone well. "I was so relieved to find that the rubbish in the atmosphere hadn't had any impact, thank God. I'd worried whether the rumors could affect the way people related to me. It was a mood that came, and seemed to pass . . . although you never let go of the knowledge that people could feel that way."

Later, when I got to know her better, she confided that she'd considered an alternate answer to her critics: having another baby. "I thought, 'That's something I can do that would please everyone.' " But in the end she decided against it. "I'd love to have another baby, but I also want to be a good family-planning model," she said. I laughed and said that the king's eleven children rather militated against that. She pointed out that fertility rates—Jordan has one of the highest in the world—are calculated on offspring per woman, not man. "By Jordanian standards, four children is still considered a large small family. If I had five, it'd be a small large family."

That evening in the garden she hinted that the riots had not been quite the calamity for her that I had assumed. I had asked the king whether he felt the riots were a one-time explosion of emotion, or whether unrest could occur again. "I think it was a one-off," he said. The queen shook her head. "I don't think you can assume that, Sidi," she said. Sidi, meaning leader, was what the king's closest deputies called him. I wondered if she was the only one of them brave enough to contradict him. She went on to say that much would depend on whether people believed the promised changes to be genuine. She spoke warmly of the king's decision to call elections and the freeing of comment in the local press. A few days earlier an outspoken Palestinian journalist who had had her passport confiscated and her career ended by Zaid Rifai's government had been invited to the palace for a meeting of reconciliation. "I was so glad," said Noor. "These are things that I have been pushing for and that His Majesty has always wanted for Jordan. But some of the people around him have tried very hard to prevent them from happening."

Between the lines, what had happened was clear. The queen's Western values had been at war with Zaid Rifai's authoritarianism. The riots had proved the queen right and Rifai wrong. Rifai was gone; the queen wasn't going anywhere.

Later that year the king's democratic initiative bore fruit in an election that left Islamic hard-liners dominating the Parliament. Just before the election, a delegation of liberal-minded Jordanians had come to the palace to brief him on the persecution of Toujan Faisal, a candidate whose campaign for greater women's rights had made her a target of extremist threats and harassment. The night before the vote, Hussein went on television and warned against religious extremism. The division of his country along religious lines, he warned, would never be tolerated while he lived. The extremists seemed to get the message and stopped short of violence against Toujan or her supporters.

Until August 1990, Jordan ticked along, the fundamentalist parliamentarians making a proposal, such as the banning of male hairdressers for women, and the rest of the community panning the idea and carrying on much as it always had. Free speech was exposing the fundamentalists' agenda to a healthy airing, and most people, it seemed, weren't buying it. One initiative that cost the Islamic bloc credibility, even with very religious Jordanians, was a proposal to ban fathers attending their daughters' school sports days. "Are they saying I'm so dirty-minded that I can't even be trusted to watch my daughter play basketball?" fumed one intensely religious father who had previously been in sympathy with the Islamic bloc.

Then Saddam Hussein invaded Kuwait, the United States sent troops to Saudi Arabia, and Jordan erupted in an outpouring of support for Iraq. I went to a sermon at one of Amman's largest mosques and heard the preacher whip the overflow crowd into an anti-American frenzy, warning the U. S. Government that "your pigs will only come back to you in coffins, God willing."

It was the queen's moment. Suddenly, she could serve her adopted country in a way that no Arab-born consort could have. When Washington snubbed the king, sending Secretary of State James Baker and other officials to every other country in the region but Jordan, she got on a plane and went to her old hometown, lobbying senators and congressmen, asking them to understand the king's quest for a negotiated settlement. It was interesting to compare the press coverage she gleaned on these trips with the articles that had appeared on her first visit to Washington after her marriage. "I'd Be Delighted to Have His Child" cooed the headline on a 1978 *People* magazine article, full of her thoughts on sport and shopping. This time she spoke at the Brookings Institution and appeared on "Nightline," no longer asked about hairstyles and child rearing, but required to field hard questions about Jordan's foreign policy. She did it well, with poise and clarity.

Back home in Amman, she encouraged the king to brief reporters hurrying to and from Baghdad through Jordan, the only gateway to Iraq that U.N. sanctions had left open. She arranged small dinners in a salon at her office for ten or twelve reporters at a time to meet the king and hear his version of events.

I saw a lot of her as I passed back and forth between Saudi Arabia and Baghdad. Sometimes she invited me to the palace for supper. It was damage control, done with the lightest touch. And it worked. It was impossible to sit with the two of them for hours on end and not emerge with a better understanding of the king's delicate balancing act between Iraq and the hard place of American disapproval.

There was a guilty pleasure in these visits. My hotel room in Jordan was littered with packs of dried food, jerry cans for petrol and a pallet of bottled water: the gear I needed for trips to the front in Saudi Arabia or to the ruins of Iraq. Hanging in the closet were my khaki pants, marbled with baked-bean stains from my last stint with the United States marines, when we'd crouched on the sand, eating our slops from makeshift plates of torn-up cardboard.

Nadwa palace was the non sequitur in my wartime travels. When Noor excused herself to "see about dinner," what usually followed was a battery of servants carrying in a choice of two soups, three middle courses and four main dishes—always including the light, healthy things she liked, such as seaweed soup, grilled fish or spiced lentils with yogurt. The king rarely ate any of what he jokingly disparaged as Noor's health food. Every evening he picked at the same meal: a skewer of grilled lamb on a bed of rice. As soon as etiquette allowed, he pushed his plate away and lit a cigarette. Noor, anxious for his health, would furrow her brow if he lit more than one. "When people say, 'Do you mind if I smoke?' I always say, 'I mind for you,' " she said. "I hate to think of people doing that to their bodies." Her oldest son, ten-year-old Hamzah, was an ally, berating his father in *sotto voce* Arabic.

The dinners, even the least formal ones around the circular cane table in the family room, were always lit with little candles in glass bowls edged with feathery greenery. The conversation was both a journalist's dream and worst nightmare. For once, here was a source who actually knew what was going on and was prepared to talk about it. On the other hand, most of what was said was off the record. Listening to talk like that is dangerous when it induces a sense of having the truth, when all one might actually have is self-serving spin.

Still, the king had known every United States president since Truman and been friends with most of them. He could be witty, and sometimes scathing, about Arab leaders. But he didn't dominate the conversation. Unlike many husbands, he seemed genuinely interested in what Noor had to say. Even Hamzah wasn't excluded. Although the boy's command of English was perfect, he preferred to speak Arabic, and would force his father to act as translator.

One day I flew with the queen to the border camps, where a flood of Egyptians, Sri Lankans, Sudanese and Bangladeshis were pouring out of Iraq, leaving behind their jobs and the fruits of years of hard work. It was a pathetic scene: rows and rows of tents packed with despairing people. Noor would wander through the hospital tent, talking to anyone who spoke Arabic or English, pulling a tissue from her pocket to comfort a crying Sri Lankan woman, feeling the forehead of a child to check for fever. With the camp administrators, she would pore over the plans for the tent camps, figuring better layouts for services such as water and food distribution points. Back in her office in the palace grounds, she would work the phones, calling Richard Branson, the head of Virgin airlines, to ask for extra planes to ferry the people home; asking other wealthy connections to help pay for a mountain of blankets. Suddenly, her star-studded Rolodex was a national asset.

She would arrive home late and collapse, rumpled and exhausted, into the cotton-covered cane sofas of the palace's upstairs family rooms. Across Jordan, a dozen years of her work was unraveling. Jordan had made a good living as the transit point for trade with Iraq, but the U.N. boycott had left ports idle and drivers unemployed. "We're seeing a rise in the school dropout rate for girls because their families' incomes are falling and girls' schooling is the first place they economize," she sighed. The first signs of malnutrition were showing up at child health centers. "People are cutting down on the protein in their diet and it's starting to affect the children's development." Often the palace phone rang as aid workers, her friends, called her at home to ask for her help to cut through red tape.

Sometimes we would watch the war news on CNN, sipping our seaweed soup from mugs. If Hamzah was still up, he sat by us on the couch, hunched over his Gameboy, fighting imaginary enemies as CNN showed footage of the preparations for a real war just across the border. Sometimes the king would borrow the Gameboy, to ease his nerves. There were stacks of videos piled up by the TV—Clint East-wood Westerns for the king; romantic dramas for the queen. And there were videos they'd taped themselves during the crisis, including a Ross Perot appearance with Larry King, in which Perot, then a little-known Texan businessman, eviscerated Bush's Gulf policy.

Hussein played the Perot tape for me and laughed out loud at the Texan's account of the mysterious workings of Arab diplomacy. Much of what Perot was saying wasn't very flattering. In his folksy drawl, Perot was telling Larry King that the Arabs, left alone, would go inside some tent, rearrange the sand and come out with some deal Americans would never understand. It was an odd scene: the king, a master diplomat facing the negotiating challenge of his career, laugh-ing his head off as Perot boiled down his life-and-death dilemmas to a series of quips.

A few days later Hussein received word of the first bombing of Baghdad in a predawn phone call. Noor, lying in bed beside him, felt his body go rigid as he held the receiver and listened to the bad news. He got up, put on his fatigues and went to visit his troops.

Since that morning the king had visibly relaxed. It was as if he'd tried everything to avert the war, done his best, and now was willing to leave it to fate. I visited the palace two nights after he'd gone on Jordan TV and made a speech that had enraged the Bush White House. Hussein had accused the United States and its allies of trying "to destroy Iraq," and had praised the bravery of the Iraqi people in the face of the onslaught. That night at the palace the king, watching CNN, learned that the United States was considering cutting Jordan's $50 million aid package. He shrugged and flipped off the remote con-trol. "The noose is tightening," he said. "But I'm not prepared to subject every word I say to censorship or criticism from any source." In fact, he knew he didn't have to: the Americans needed the king to keep Jordan stable, and despite hard words on Capitol Hill, they kept up a clandestine flow of assistance.

Downstairs, in the formal sitting room, I'd been keeping my eye on a side table full of silver-framed pictures of world leaders. Since the start of the Gulf crisis, the pictures had been in constant motion. Saddam Hussein had slipped from the front row after his invasion of

Kuwait. Egypt's President Hosni Mubarak had disappeared altogether, while George Bush had been pushed behind a lamp. That night George Bush had reemerged, positioned cheek by jowl with Saddam, as if to send the message that Jordan was, after all, a neutral party in the conflict. In front was a picture I'd never seen before: Pope John Paul II, who had just called for an immediate end to the war.

Upstairs, Noor, wearing blue jeans, was on the phone to friends in the States, offering to fax them copies of the king's speech, so that they could read his remarks in context. On the street in Jordan, her efforts were winning praise in the salons and the mosques. Even the fundamentalists thought she was doing a good job of putting Jordan's case to a hostile outside world. It was the first time I'd heard the mosque crowd praise any woman for taking an active role.

Without the Gulf crisis, it was impossible to know whether she would have been able to live down gossip and criticism. But the war had won her a measure of popularity unimaginable a year earlier. One young taxi driver I rode with had a picture of her tucked into his sun visor. She was wearing military fatigues, as if she were about to literally do battle with America. Did he know, I asked him, that she was American? "She is Arab," he replied fiercely. "She is one of us."

But just a year after the war the rumor mills were grinding again with whispers of divorce. This time most Jordanians were hoping it wasn't true. The king, the rumors claimed, had fallen in love with a twenty-five-year-old Palestinian-Jordanian journalist and had promised to marry her. The young woman had worked for CNN during the war and had recently been tapped as the king's press secretary as part of an effort to get some younger staffers into the royal court. "If you put young people in the palace, and some of them are women, and one of them is beautiful, then you are bound to get these kinds of rumors," said one Amman journalist.

A cynical Arab businessman had a different view. "All the king's marriages have been state marriages," he said. "When he needed to be close to Nasser, he married an Egyptian. When he needed England, he married an English rose. When he needed to mend fences with the Palestinians, he chose a woman from a West Bank family. The 1980s were the American decade, so the marriage for the eighties was with an American." In the 1990s, the business-man said, the king might sense the need for a different alliance.

But most Jordanians seemed to discount the story. They rea-soned that, even if Hussein were infatuated with a younger woman, a divorce at his age would seem frivolous. What's accepted, even ex-pected, for a man in his twenties is unseemly for a man of fifty-seven, even if he is a king. Some put the talk of divorce down to professional rivalry from men who had had their eyes on the press secretary's job. A scandal had traditionally been an easy way to dispose of an incon-venient woman.

Noor was now forty-one years old, had been married to the king for fifteen years, and was much better understood and respected in Jordan because of her role during the war. Her sons had been seen on TV on religious holidays, reading the Koran in flawless classical Arabic. Some Jordanians had even started to murmur about the suc-cession, saying that if the king lived long enough to raise these boys to adulthood there was no reason why one of them shouldn't be considered for the crown. Fifteen years living alongside the Middle East's great survivor had taught Noor a thing or two about securing her own position.

Still, the rumors proved unusually durable, and when press re-ports of an impending divorce made the papers in the United States and Britain, the Jordanian embassies took the unprecedented step of issuing denials. In Washington a friend who saw Noor at a small reception in her honor found her nervous and brittle, her usual com-posure and charm completely deserting her.

A few weeks later another explanation for her nerves emerged. The king had been rushed into hospital in the States to be operated on for cancer. The disease had attacked his urinary tract, and while the surgery was said to be successful, his condition would require regular monitoring.

In Jordan the mood was somber and uncertain. When the king arrived back after his surgery, the crowd that thronged the road to the palace was the biggest in the country's history. Their cries of *"Aish*

Hussein [Long Live Hussein]'' had a desperate intensity. It was hard to imagine another country in the Middle East where the outpouring of support for a leader would be as spontaneous or as sincere.

There would be no more gossip. No one now, not even the extremists, would risk a whisper of criticism of the king, even indirectly through attacks on the queen. For however long her husband had left to live, Queen Noor seemed certain to be secure on her throne.

If there had been a marital rift, it wasn't obvious when the couple came to the United States in 1994. After a checkup at the Mayo clinic at which the king got a clean bill of health, the couple were spotted in Washington, shopping for Harley-Davidson and BMW motorbikes. Together, they picked out three new bikes to be shipped back to Jordan, and took away about $2,000 in matching motorcycle clothes. The spending spree would help them reprise their courtship bike rides around the hills of Amman.

The king's recovery from life-threatening illness also seemed to reinforce the risk-taker in him. Perhaps he sensed that time was short. In 1993, just after Israel and the Palestine Liberation Organization signed their sudden and controversial peace accords in Washington, Hussein allowed Jordan's scheduled elections to go ahead as planned. Foreign diplomats and most of his own government ministers had warned against it, fearing that a political campaign would become a front for agitation by Islamic extremists and hard-line Palestinians who didn't want peace with Israel. Jordan, they said, would be destabilized.

Instead, the elections went off without a hitch. Behind the king's resolve, I was sure I saw the queen's quiet influence at work, and his world view gradually becoming identical with hers. Not long after the elections, in the winter of 1994, a satirical revue lampooning the pomposity of Arab leaders opened in Amman. Some of Jordan's neighbors were not amused, and tried to have the revue shut down. The king stood up to the pressure and said the show must go on, including the skit that skewered his own sometimes ponderous rhetorical style.

Jordan was one of the first countries I'd visited when I moved to the Middle East in 1987. In six years I saw it transform itself from a tense police state to the most promising cradle of political freedom in the region. The fundamentalists were still there, but so were the feminists. No group's rights had been trampled for the sake of another's. The struggle went on, but it went on in the open. And the weapons were words, not bombs or gunshots or mass arrests.

To me, it was clear that much of the credit for that transformation belonged to a woman.

Chapter 8

THE GETTING OF WISDOM

"Read, in the name of thy Lord,
who hath created all things; who
hath created man of congealed
blood. Read, by thy most beneficent
Lord; who taught use of the pen;
who teaches man that which he
knoweth not."

THE KORAN
THE CHAPTER OF CONGEALED BLOOD

*I*n Saudi Arabia the road north from Riyadh is a flawless strip of six-lane bitumen slicing through wind-sculpted sand dunes. Every few miles, through the shimmering heat haze, it is possible to glimpse the ruins of yellow mud lookout towers cut with rifle slits. They are eroding, like children's sand castles.

My Saudi friend took a hand off the steering wheel, reached into the refrigerated glove compartment of his luxury four-wheel drive and tossed me a frosty can of soda. Then he threw one to the American in the back seat, a colleague he had enlisted for the day to play the role of my husband.

My Saudi friend, an urbane, Western-educated professional, wanted me to meet his uncle, an old man who lived out among the sand dunes near the hometown of Mohamed Abdul Wahhab, the preacher who had taught a form of Islam so severe it banned even whistling. The uncle was a true Wahhabi, strict and austere. It wasn't certain he'd agree to speak to me—"he's never spoken to a woman outside his family before," my friend said, but he thought it would be worth a try so that I could understand the forces stacked against change for women in Saudi Arabia. The "husband" in the back seat was essential. "My family is used to a lot of strange things from me, but showing up alone in my car with a foreign woman would be pushing their understanding a bit too far."

The uncle, Mohamed al-Ghazi, lived in a flat-roofed house beside a grove of date palms. High orange sand dunes cradled his fragile little farm. When I opened the door of the air-conditioned jeep, a blast of hot air hit me like a gust from a crematorium. My eyeballs felt desiccated, like dried peas. T. E. Lawrence described the heat of these Arabian sands: "The sun came up like a drawn sword and struck us speechless." And he wasn't wearing a black abaya and opaque stockings at the time. I squinted enviously at my friend and his uncle embracing each other in their cool white robes and sandals. An irreverent thought occurred to me: if God really liked women, He would have revealed the Koran to an Inuit fur trader rather than an Arabian camel-caravan manager.

Calling to his wife, Mohamed al-Ghazi signaled me to follow her to the women's quarters. My friend placed a hand on his uncle's arm and explained that he wanted me to sit with them, in the men's reception room, to talk about local history. I stood a small distance away, my abaya billowing in the hot wind, as a rapid-fire dialogue in Arabic ensued. Finally the uncle shrugged glumly and, without looking at me, beckoned me inside.

The men's *majlis*, or reception room, stretched the length of the house. Mohamed al-Ghazi was an important man in his tiny village. Five times a day he led the prayers at the local mosque. As prayer leader, or imam, he was the villagers' spiritual guide, and for performing that service he received a stipend from the government. Before oil wealth had allowed the government to afford such handouts, Mohamed had eked out a living from his dates, rising before dawn each morning to hand-water trees so few and precious that he had given each of them a name. He had been fifteen years old before he even had time to learn to read the Koran, so demanding was the toil required to wrest a subsistence living from the desert. Now, oil had brought electricity to power a water pump, and enough income to employ a foreign laborer. Every Friday, after community prayers, the imam slaughtered sheep and covered the floor of his majlis with platters of lamb and rice. The men of the village joined him for lunch and a discussion of the issues of the day.

I asked how, if he never had spoken before to women outside his family, he was able to serve as spiritual counselor to the village women. My friend looked at me strangely. "They put their problems to him through their husbands, of course," he said.

"But what if their husband is their problem?"

That possibility hadn't crossed either man's mind.

The Friday before our visit, Mohamed's majlis had been abuzz with rumors about the women who, demonstrating for the right to drive, had dismissed their chauffeurs and taken to the wheels of their cars in downtown Riyadh. The old man was appalled by the prospect of women driving. He clapped a bony hand to his heart and gazed heavenward: "I hope I never see it in my lifetime," he said.

But once, many years earlier, he had become a radical in his small rural community. He had petitioned the government to open a boys' school in the village. Some of his neighbors were scandalized by the idea of secular education. Imams in neighboring towns sermonized against education, substituting the word filth, or *mingissa*, for the word for school, *madrassa*. To them, the only subject worthy of study was the Koran, and their boys were already learning that at the local mosques. Of what use were history, geography and foreign languages, they argued, when such studies brought knowledge of ungodly lands and peoples?

But Mohamed al-Ghazi knew that the prophet's lieutenants had spoken foreign languages, and that they had used that knowledge to spread Islam. And what was the danger, he argued, in teaching the geography and history of Islamic lands? In the cities, the *ulema*, or religious regulators, had already fought these battles, making sure that the curriculum banned subjects such as music, which is considered too sensuous by Wahhabis, and art, which could lead to the creation of graven images. Mohamed al-Ghazi's campaign eventually won the village its school. Two of the imam's sons who studied there had gone on to university; the third had joined the military.

His daughters were another matter. To the gnarled old imam, sending his daughters out of the home—to walk in the streets, even if veiled, to sit among strangers, even if all girls—was wicked. His daughters learned what he felt they needed to know, which was to recite the Koran, in the seclusion of the women's quarters of their house.

Today in Saudi Arabia, fathers like Mohamed al-Ghazi can still make such a choice for their daughters. Schooling for girls, although now widespread, has never been compulsory if their fathers disapprove. Many men believe in the saying that educating women is like allowing the nose of the camel into the tent: eventually the beast will edge in and take up all the room inside.

Saudi Arabia didn't get its first girls' school until 1956. Its opening was contrived by Iffat, the wife of King Faisal, and the only Saudi ruler's wife ever referred to as queen. Iffat, who had been raised in Turkey, wanted to broaden education to include more science and more Western subjects, but she had to proceed cautiously even in opening such a school for her own sons. The girls' school was an infinitely more delicate matter. When Dar al Hanan, the House of Affection, opened in Jeddah in 1956, it did so in the guise of an orphanage. Since the Koran repeatedly orders Muslims to care for orphan girls, such an institution was beyond reproach. It had been running a year before Iffat felt able to risk explaining the institution's real intention.

In an article in a local paper titled ''The Mother Can Be a School in Herself If You Prepare Her Well,'' the objectives of Dar al Hanan were described as producing better mothers and homemakers through Islamically guided instruction.

Iffat, through Faisal, based her case for women's education on a famous set of verses in the Koran that have become known as Umm Salamah's verses. Umm Salamah, the beautiful widow whose marriage to the prophet had so upset Aisha, is said to have asked Muhammad one day why it was that, when God sent his revelations, the language in them was always addressed to men.

According to a hadith, Umm Salamah was in her room by the mosque, combing her hair, when she heard the prophet's voice from the *minbar*, or pulpit. ''I hastily did up my hair and ran to one of the apartments from where I could hear better. I pressed my ear to the wall, and here is what the prophet said:

" 'Lo! Men who surrender unto God, and women who surrender, and men who believe and women who believe, and men who obey and women who obey, and men who speak the truth and women who speak the truth, and men who persevere, and women who persevere, and men who are humble and women who are humble, and men who give alms and women who give alms, and men who fast and women who fast, and men who guard their modesty and women who guard their modesty, and men who remember God much and women who remember—God has prepared for them forgiveness and a vast reward.' "

What the verses made clear was that the obligations of the faith fell without differentiation on men and women. To carry out those obligations, Iffat argued, women had to be educated and informed. By 1960 the ulema had been brought to grudging acceptance of this principle, and cautiously agreed to the spread of girls' schools throughout the country. The provisos were that the schools would remain under the control of the ulema and that no father who objected would be obliged to send his daughters to them.

But for some Saudis that wasn't enough. In the town of Burayda, not far from Minsaf, men rioted in protest at the opening of the first girls' school in 1963. At around the same time as the United States was calling out its National Guard to enforce racial desegregation of schools in the American South, King Faisal had to call out the National Guard to keep the Burayda school open by force. For a year, the only pupil in the school was the headmistress's daughter.

Many fathers continued to exercise their option of keeping daughters ignorant. By 1980, only 55% of Saudi girls were attending primary school, and only 23% were enrolled in secondary education. Only 38% of women were literate, compared with 62% of men.

Still, some girls managed to get the best education that money could buy. At Dar al Fikr, a private school for girls in Jeddah, the German-built campus is about as magnificent a school building as it's possible to imagine. Inside the privacy of a towering white wall, glass doors swish open into a crisply air-conditioned foyer of polished stone. The layout is star-shaped, with classrooms radiating from large indoor recreation areas. High ceilings and huge panes of glass give an open, airy feeling to art studios, a gymnasium, science labs and a

computer center humming with Commodore and Macintosh desk-
tops.

No class has more than twenty pupils. There is a day-care center, being used when I visited by the teachers' infants, but available to
the students in a country where early marriage and pregnancy are
accepted and encouraged. In addition to an academic curriculum that
stressed languages, girls could choose courses in cookery or dressmak-
ing, karate or ballet, desktop publishing or motor mechanics. The
motor mechanics course puzzled me, since Saudi women weren't allowed to drive. "If her driver says there's something the matter with
the car, I want her to know if he's telling the truth," explained the
headmistress, Basilah al-Homoud.

The pupils had the well-tended look of the very rich. They were
tall, with lustrous hair swept back in thick braids. The headmistress, a
svelte, silk-clad thirty-eight-year-old, had the unlined skin of a teenager and the taut body of an aerobics addict. "The gym is the most
important room in my house," she said. Twenty years earlier, her
older sister had wanted to study dentistry, impossible then for women
in Saudi Arabia. Basilah's father had moved the whole family to Syria
so her sister could study at Damascus University. She came home as
the first Saudi dentist and opened a clinic to treat both men and
women. But she soon found that some Saudi men used to strict segregation couldn't cope with having a strange woman touch them, even
with a dentist's drill. Tired of propositions and misunderstandings,
she separated her clinic into men's and women's sections and hired
male dentists to treat the men.

Basilah, too, preferred professional segregation. Dar al Fikr had a
neighboring school for boys and a male board of directors. When
Basilah had to have a meeting with the board, or with her boys'
school counterpart, she used closed-circuit TV. "I might need a colleague's support, but I don't need to be sitting in a room with him,"
she said. "If the men could come in here and be with us, they would
end up dominating and telling us how to run things. I prefer to run
my own show."

Basilah also used closed-circuit TV at the university, where she
was studying for her MBA. Women were first admitted to university
in Saudi Arabia in 1962, and all women's colleges remain strictly

segregated. Lecture rooms come equipped with closed-circuit TVs and telephones, so women students can listen to a male professor and question him by phone, without having to contaminate themselves by being seen by him. When the first dozen women graduated from university in 1973, they were devastated to find that their names hadn't been printed on the commencement program. The old tradition, that it dishonors women to mention them, was depriving them of recognition they believed they'd earned. The women and their families protested, so a separate program was printed and a segregated graduation ceremony was held for the students' female relatives. Two thousand women attended. Their celebratory ululations raised the roof.

But while the opening of women's universities widened access to higher learning for women, it also made the educational experience much shallower. Before 1962, many progressive Saudi families had sent their daughters abroad for education. They had returned to the kingdom not only with a degree but with experience of the outside world, whether in the West or in more progressive Arab countries such as Egypt, Lebanon or Syria, where they'd breathed the air of desegregation and even caught a breath of secular culture. Now a whole generation of Saudi women have completed their education entirely within the country. While thousands of Saudi men benefit from higher education abroad at government expense, women haven't been granted such scholarships since 1980. The government's position is that women's educational opportunities have improved within the kingdom to the point where a woman's needs can all be met within its borders. The definition of her educational needs, as set out in a Ministry of Higher Education policy paper, are "to bring her up in a sound Islamic way so that she can fulfill her role in life as a successful housewife, ideal wife and good mother, and to prepare her for other activities that suit her nature such as teaching, nursing and medicine."

The result is a cadre of older Saudi women professors who are vastly more liberal than the younger women students they now are teaching. When some of these women professors took part in the driving demonstration, it was their women students who turned on them first. One student barged into one professor's office and started pulling at the professor's hair and abusing her for demonstrating. Young women objecting to the drivers led an angry protest from the campus mosque. Among the calls of the zealots following the demonstration was for the women's university to be permanently closed.

Lack of opportunity for education abroad means that Saudi women are trapped in the confines of an education system that still lags men's. Subjects such as geology and petroleum engineering—tickets to influential jobs in Saudi Arabia's oil economy—remain closed to women. Three of Saudi Arabia's seven universities—Imam Mohamed bin Saud Islamic University in Riyadh, the University of Petroleum and Minerals and the Islamic University in Medina—don't accept women. Few women's colleges have their own libraries, and libraries shared with men's schools are either entirely off limits to women or open to them only one day per week. Most of the time women can't browse for books but have to specify the titles they want and have them brought out to them.

But women and men sit the same degree examinations. Professors quietly acknowledge the women's scores routinely outstrip the men's. "It's no surprise," said one woman professor. "Look at their lives. The boys have their cars, they can spend the evenings cruising the streets with their friends, sitting in cafés, buying black-market alcohol and drinking all night. What do the girls have? Four walls and their books. For them, education is everything."

When Saudi women did go abroad to be educated in the 1950s and 1960s, one of the places they often selected was the American University of Beirut. In 1866 a Vermont missionary named Daniel Bliss laid the foundation stone for the men's college that was to become AUB, declaring that the school was for "all conditions and classes of men without regard to color, nationality, race or religion. A man white, black, or yellow, Christian, Jew, Mohammedan or heathen, may enter and enjoy all the advantages of this institution . . . and go out believing in one God, in many gods, or in no God."

The AUB opened a Women's School of Nursing at the university as early as 1905 and accepted its first woman student to the general campus in 1921. She arrived fully veiled and accompanied by her husband. By the mid-sixties, the last all-male bastion, engineering, had fallen to coeducation.

For a while, the transplant of American liberalism seemed to work. Leila Sharaf, a Lebanese Druse, witnessed the birth of dozens of political and philosophical movements on the campus in the 1950s, and fostered the rise of Arab nationalism. "There were so many clubs," she says. "The Arab Cultural Club, the Loss of Palestine Club, the Baathists." Women sat with men in the coffee shops fringing the campus, arguing passionately into the night. Leila Sharaf met her future husband, a Jordanian Muslim, at one of the clubs and returned with him to Jordan, where she eventually became minister of information in the Jordanian government and a close adviser to Queen Noor.

But by the middle of the 1960s the return to Islamic fundamentalism began to emerge as an ideology in competition with Arab nationalism. The university's liberalism, and its American name, began to make it a target of extremists.

The heart of the liberal program at AUB has always been a cultural studies course that takes students from the Epic of Gilgamesh through Homer and Virgil to Locke, Descartes and Hobbes. In 1966 the imams of some Beirut mosques got hold of a required text from the course that quoted the medieval Christian theologian, Thomas Aquinas, saying that the Islamic faith's swift expansion didn't indicate the religion's inherent truth. Police burst onto the campus to arrest the heretical author. "I told them Mr. Aquinas wasn't available at the moment," recalls Tarif Khalidi, a medieval historian who helped develop the cultural studies program. He found himself hauled off to be interrogated instead. It was one of his students, Hanan Ashrawi, who raised the alarm and brought the president of the university and the Lebanese interior minister to have him set free.

By the 1980s the attacks were no laughing matter. One day in 1984 a crowd of Hezbollah activists poured into the campus and planted a green Islamic flag atop one of the buildings. Sheik Fadlallah, the spiritual leader of Hezbollah, gave a speech about the prophet's daughter Fatima and her importance as a role model for Muslim women. "It wasn't that he said anything particularly controversial, but you can speak about the weather, and everyone knows what is meant," says Wolfgang Köhler, a German scholar who happened to be on campus that day. To him, the message was that Hezbollah's power extended even within the gates of the most important American institution in Lebanon.

That message was conveyed brutally in January 1984, when the university president, Malcolm Kerr, was murdered near his office by gunmen with silenced pistols. AUB faculty and staff also became kidnap victims. In 1985, in the wake of the Kerr murder, the cultural studies program came under fire again. This time the issue was the teaching of sacred texts—one of the gospels, an epistle of St. Paul, parts of the Koran—that was led by a Christian member of the faculty. "With the growth in the number of fundies in the arts faculty, more and more students found it objectionable to be taught the Koran by a Christian," Tarif Khalidi recalls. "So we decided to throw out the sacred texts, much to my regret. How can you understand, say, St. Augustine, if you haven't read any Old and New Testament?"

Mostly, the university resisted sectarian pressures. Men and women continued to mix freely on the tree-shaded, seaside campus, and more women still wear blue jeans than veils. And that is a thorn in the side of extremists. In 1991 a powerful bomb tore the heart out of the campus, leaving a pile of rubble beneath the gate inscribed with the university's motto: "That they may have life and have it more abundantly."

Tarif Khalidi has no doubts about where he and his colleagues stand with fundamentalists, both Christian and Muslim. "I have reason to believe they hate our guts. I know myself I set out consciously to sow doubt in their minds." One area in which he likes to sow doubt is the role of women. His mother was one of the first Arab women to appear in public without the veil. "She was always reading the Koran and shaking her head," he recalls. "The line about 'men are in charge of women' used to make her really angry."

To go from the liberal, tolerant campus of the AUB to the gates of the Islamic University of Gaza feels like traveling backward in time. In fact, it is the Gaza campus that offers the more accurate vision of the future as Islamic groups gain increasing influence.

The campus of the Gaza university is split down the middle, with one section for men and one for women. When I visited the women's campus in the spring term of 1993, I wore a scarf and a loose-fitting, long-sleeved ankle-length dress, since I knew the institution strictly enforced hijab. But my arrival at the women's gate caused a flurry anyway. "We have to find you a *jalabiya*," explained Asya Abdul Hadi, a recent graduate, pointing to her own neck-to-toe button-through coat. "Even on the women's campus, we have men professors."

Eventually, someone found a baggy blue serge garment that belonged to a student at least five inches taller than I. Grabbing a fistful of fabric so I could walk, I tottered after Asya into the high-walled campus and past a jumble of low, asbestos-roofed huts.

What Berkeley was to the antiwar movement of the sixties, the Islamic University of Gaza is to the holy-war crowd of the nineties. Most of the campus supports Hamas, the Islamic group that calls for a war to the death against Israel. The university's militance was so menacing to the Israelis that the army declared the campus a closed military zone from 1987 to 1991 and hauled most of the faculty and a large swatch of the student body to prison.

We wandered to the students' common room, where a few women sat sipping Cokes and chatting. All of them wore jalabiyas in dull shades of brown, olive or navy. Asya introduced me to some of her friends who worked in the university administration. I asked if I could meet some of the women professors as well. "We don't actually have many women professors," said Majida Anan, a thirty-year-old administrator. "The priority here is for men to teach, because the man is the one who needs a career. The woman will be married and her husband will take care of her. And besides, if the university hires a woman, she can only teach here, on the women's campus, whereas a man can teach both here and across the street with the men. When we achieve our Islamic state there won't be any mixing at all."

Khomeini's daughter Zahra taught philosophy to mixed classes at Tehran University. I asked Majida her opinion of that. "There are no opinions in Islam,'' she responded brusquely. "Islam says that men and women can mix if it is absolutely necessary. If there is no necessity, then they mustn't do it."

I'd hoped to find something different at Gaza University—perhaps the emergence of an Islamic feminism. Palestinians had always been among the most progressive on women's issues, and I thought the fusion of that spirit with militant Islam might produce something interesting.

But in Gaza the militants had latched onto a brand of Islamic radicalism that threatened to do worse than set the clock back for Palestinian women. What Majida was proposing had never been part of Palestinian culture. Instead, her ideas were imports: they had "Made in Saudi Arabia" stamped all over them.

Hamas devotes two articles of its thirty-six-article charter to the role of Muslim women. Women, it says, "manufacture men and play a great role in guiding and educating the [new] generation. The enemies have understood that role, and therefore they realize if they can guide and educate [the women] in a way that would distance them from Islam, they would have won that war. Therefore you can see them making consistent efforts by way of publicity and movies, curriculi [sic] of education and culture, using as their intermediaries their craftsmen who are part of the various Zionist Organizations which take on all sorts of names and shapes such as: the Free Masons, Rotary Clubs, gangs of spies and the like. . . . Therefore, we must pay attention to the schools and curriculi upon which Muslim girls are educated, so as to make them righteous mothers, who are conscious of their duties in the war of liberation. They must be fully capable of being aware and of grasping the ways to manage their households. Economy and avoiding waste in household expenditures are prerequisites to our ability to pursue our cause. . . ."

When I'd first visited Gaza in 1987, girls, unveiled and wearing blue jeans, had been in the streets alongside the youths, throwing stones at Israeli soldiers. Mothers had been right behind them, ready with wet cloths or cut onions to counter the effects of tear gas. Women had gained stature from their role in such protests. Now, thanks to Hamas, women had been sent back home, to manufacture male babies and avoid waste in household expenditures.

"The struggle has changed," said Asya, a tall, intense woman with large dark eyes and heavy brows. "Throwing stones, it's for kids now. The activists who have real weapons don't stay in their homes; they are always moving from place to place, sleeping here and there. A woman cannot do that."

The struggle had changed, and so had Gaza. Driving from the huge military roadblock that divides the Gaza Strip from Israel, I hadn't seen a single unveiled woman. "There is no coercion," said Majida. I gazed down at my dowdy serge sack. "Of course, we can impose it here, inside the university. But outside we don't impose it. The relationship is with God and each woman can decide for herself."

I sipped my Coke and said nothing. I had been in the emergency room of a Gaza hospital when a young Palestinian nurse came in, shaking, her uniform covered in wet, brown stains. "It was the boys in the market," she said. "They told me to cover my head. I told them I was Christian, but they said it didn't matter. They said, 'The Virgin Mary covered her head, so why not you?' They threw rotten fruit at me and told me next time it would be acid."

Most of the classes were finished for the day. If I wanted to sit in on a women's religion class, Asya told me, I'd have to come back in the morning. "Why don't you stay with me tonight?" she said.

I hesitated. "It's too much trouble for you to put me up," I said.

"What's the matter?" she laughed. "Are you afraid to stay in the camps? We are hospitable people here."

I *was* a bit nervous. That week, an Israeli lawyer working on development projects in Gaza had been hacked to death with an ax as he met with his Palestinian clients. My journalist colleagues in Jerusalem had warned against even staying in a Gaza hotel. "Word gets around that you're there—anything more than one night is definitely unsafe," one journalist said.

I told Asya that I'd be delighted to stay with her.

She walked ahead of me to the gatehouse, where I would have to hand back my long robe. "By the way," she said over her shoulder, "what is your religion?"

"I'm Jewish."

Asya spun around. Her mouth narrowed to a thin line. Her eyes darted across my face, then drifted off to scan the horizon. I tried to read her expression. Angry? Offended? I couldn't tell.

I'd only lied about my religion once, just after I'd arrived in the Middle East. It left me feeling so ashamed and cowardly that I resolved never to do it again. Since then my policy had been to tell anyone who asked. Usually the people I told were intrigued rather than hostile. An interrogation usually followed: What did I think about Zionism? Did anyone in my family give money to Israel? But Asya said nothing.

I put a hand on her arm. "If you'd rather I stay at the hotel, I'll understand," I said.

"No," she said, snapping out of her trance. "You must sleep at my home." Striding ahead of me, she hailed a cab, and we bumped over the potholes toward the refugee camp of Dier el Balah. As the taxi sped out of Gaza City and through orange groves fragrant with spring blossoms, Asya changed the subject from religion to books. Her degree was in English literature. She talked of the novels she had liked best in her studies: Thomas Hardy's *Tess of the D'Urbervilles* and Jane Austen's *Pride and Prejudice*. I smiled. It was hard to think of two Western books more in tune with an Islamic world view than Hardy's tale of a woman ruined by sexual dishonor or the Bennet sisters and their parlor-based quests for suitable spouses.

Asya's home wasn't anything like the cramped hovels of the camps. It stood right at the edge of Dier el Balah, where the claustrophobic, ill-drained alleys opened to farmland and the sweet scent of the sea beyond. The house was solid, generously built, and walled off from the street with a high, graffiti-covered brick fence. Asya lived with her widowed mother, a stooped, potato-shaped, uneducated woman who seemed more than a generation removed from her tall, intellectual daughter. Two younger sisters, a brother and his wife also shared the house. Asya's younger brother was in prison, accused of being an activist of Hamas. The others were scattered across the map of the Palestinian diaspora. One was a Palestine Liberation Organization fighter in Iraq, one a teacher in Saudi Arabia, one a worker in Greece. Diaspora remittances had built the house.

The brother she lived with usually worked as a laborer in Israel, but for several weeks, because of a series of murders by Palestinians,

Israel had barred Palestinians from Gaza and the West Bank from going to their Israeli jobs. That left Asya, who worked as an assistant to a Palestinian journalist, as the family's main breadwinner. When she walked in the door, her mother and little sisters hovered around her, bringing tea, a change of clothes, a hairbrush, bustling to serve her with a respectful attentiveness I'd usually seen lavished only on men.

Asya threw off her hijab, pulled on leggings and fluffed out her shoulder-length hair. When her sister brought her a knitted jersey, she pushed it away, asking in Arabic for a prettier one. The sister returned with a black polished-cotton smock with maroon flowers hand-painted around the hem. "You see," she said, "I look a lot different now." She did, of course. She had high cheekbones that were lost behind the scarf, and a lithe, athletic figure. I realized I'd disappointed her. She'd expected a compliment along the lines of the old black and white movies where the secretary lets out her hair and takes off her glasses: "Why, Miss Asya, you're lovely!" But I had become too used to these kinds of transformations to be surprised by them anymore.

When her sister-in-law brought supper, it was a collection of Egyptian staples: *foul, tamiyya* and *molokiyya*—mashed beans, fried chickpeas and an okralike green. Egypt had ruled Gaza between 1949 and 1967, and the Egyptian influence remained strong. Squatting on cushions, we scooped up the various vegetables on flat bread that Asya had baked before leaving for work that morning.

Asya usually slept in the women's reception room, which she shared with her younger sisters, but tonight she decided we would have a room to ourselves. She dragged two thin mattresses into a large salon, empty but for a closet against one wall. My instinct would have been to spread the mattresses out, to give us each a measure of privacy and personal space. But Asya placed both mats in one corner, side by side, almost touching.

Asya reached for her radio and twirled the dial. I smiled as I recognized my own habit of reaching for the radio last thing at night and first thing in the morning, to catch the news. Through the static, she found, in turn, the BBC's Arabic service, Cairo's Voice of the Arabs, Radio Monte Carlo. She frowned intently as she recognized a voice she knew: the spokesman for the Hamas activists deported to Lebanon by the Israelis. In heated tones, he was denouncing the resumption of peace talks between Israel and the Palestinians. A peace agreement, he said, would open the *bab al fitna*, the door to civil war. Asya nodded. "He's right. Hamas will never accept such an agreement." But when Arafat *did* sign a peace agreement that fall, no civil war broke out between Hamas and the PLO. While opposing the pact, Hamas vowed it wouldn't shed Palestinian blood. Instead, the Islamists stepped up their attacks on Israelis, and waited for the deal to founder.

As the news ended, Asya rose and turned out the overhead light. She left a small night light glowing in the corner. In the semidark, we chatted in whispers, like teenagers at a pajama party.

Asya had become religious because of the example of her younger brother—the jailed Hamas activist. She had begun to wear hijab ten years earlier, at the age of nineteen. "Everyone was so surprised," she said. "It was, 'Why is Asya wearing that?' You see, this was a long time before the Islamic movements became very strong here, as they are now. Before I put on hijab, I used to be afraid of everything; afraid of ghosts, afraid of being alone in a room. When I put it on, the fears vanished. Now I know that this life is just a game, a house for testing people. Once you submit to that, there is nothing in this life that can frighten you."

Asya had just won a British Council scholarship to study journalism in London. "Do you know any journalists who wear hijab?" she asked. I said I couldn't think of any in the mainstream media, except in Iran, where there were women TV crews, sports reporters, photojournalists.

"Perhaps I will be the first one in London," she said.

Being twenty-nine and unmarried made Asya unusual in Gaza. She had already been through the initial stages of a number of proposals. "First, his mother and sister come to visit, to get a look at me out of hijab. If they admire me, they say they'd like to bring their son to meet me. But I say, 'Not so fast.' First, I must know, is he religious? What is his work? If he prays and he has a good job, I send somebody to ask his neighbors about him; friends bring me detailed reports. In most cases that's enough: I say to his mother, 'Don't bother to bring him, I'm not interested.' "

Because she worked, she also had the opportunity to meet men by herself, unfiltered by the rigmarole of matchmaking. But she ruled out anything like a Western-style romance. "The first time a man says to me that he likes me, that will also be the last time," she said. "I will tell him, 'Don't say these words to me. Here is the name of my brother. Go and see him with what you have to say.' " After Asya had interviewed for her job with the Palestinian journalist, her brothers conducted their own interview of her prospective employer to make sure that he and his office were suitable for their sister. They were. Her boss, himself a devout Muslim, worked out of his home with his wife and kids underfoot at all times, acting as chaperons.

Asya lay on her back with her hands linked behind her head, continuing her monologue. "Actually, I'm not very interested in men. Only to have babies."

Was this, then, the logical end to the ideals of segregation? A profound rejection of the opposite sex? As I lay there, listening to Asya, I thought of all the smart young Islamic women I knew: Hamideh, my translator in Iran; Nahid, the former medical student and one of the four or five most beautiful women I'd ever met; Hadra, the soldier in the Emirates; a Kuwaiti political activist, a Jordanian journalist, a Kurdish teacher—all of them were single, long after the normal marriage age for women in their societies. And all of them, now that I thought about it, had talked about the problems of meeting men that they could talk to, who understood them, that they could trust.

"Yes, yes," Asya was saying, as if she had followed my thoughts. "It would be very nice to have a good relationship with a man that you marry, but that's not so easy with Eastern men." It wasn't, she stressed, the Islamic part of their heritage that made them difficult. "I would like to marry an Islamic preacher—a *Western* Islamic preacher."

"Good luck," I said, and we both giggled.

Asya turned on her side to face the wall. I thought she was ready to sleep. I rolled over myself and was almost dozing when she spoke

again, her face still turned away from me. "Every time, when someone comes here to research about Islam, it turns out they're Jewish.
Why do you think that is?"

"I don't know," I said. I really didn't. My interest in Islam had
everything to do with being a woman and zero to do with being a Jew.
But I knew what she meant. Many of the Western reporters in the
Middle East were Jews. "Perhaps it's because Jews grow up more
interested in Middle Eastern issues," I said. "Or maybe it's because
Jews and Muslims are fighting each other here, and Jews think understanding Islam might help find ways to solve the conflict?" Asya was
silent. "Perhaps," I mused, "some of them are convinced that Islam
is dangerous, and they come here to find evidence to support that
view."

"That's what I thought," she said. "Good night."

At the university the next morning, we made our way to a class
in the religion faculty, where women students were due to hear a
lecture on Islamic regimes. "You'll find it very lively," Asya said.
"Lots of questions and argument."

But when we arrived, the lecture room was deserted. A veiled
student told Asya that the women had decided to protest the previous
day's announcement of a resumption in peace talks with Israel, and
had gone to a sit-in outside the home of Dr. Haider Abdul Shafi, the
head of the Palestinian peace negotiators. The only class under way
was a math tutorial.

Asya and I braved the men's campus in search of the university
spokesman. The corridors were full of bearded students, all conscien-
tiously averting their eyes as we swished past them in our jalabiyas.
Ahmad Saati, the spokesman, was a short, fleshy man who, like most
of the faculty, had done his time in an Israeli prison, suspected of
being an activist for Hamas. He apologized for not offering a hand-
shake. "We have a saying: 'It's better to stab yourself in the hand
than to touch a woman's hand.' "

"But doesn't intention matter?" asked Asya. "I thought it was
all right to shake hands if you have a good intention." Ahmad, himself a graduate of the Islam Institute of Higher Studies in Egypt,

corrected her politely. "*Your* intention might be okay. But what about mine? How can you know the other person's intention?"

When I asked about coeducation, Ahmad almost exploded with excitement. "Coeducation is prevented in Islam! We know the disastrous results of coeducation. We have names, we have numbers." *Zina,* or out-of-wedlock sex, had taken place at Birzeit, a coed Palestinian university on the West Bank, he said. "This is disastrous, especially for young girls."

It could be disastrous, I agreed, since fathers and brothers still killed their teenaged girls if they suspected them of having sex. "We are not for these extrajudicial killings," he said. "Islam is not for them. Islam demands proof. Not just a witness: four witnesses. Not just a confession: a credible confession."

Then why didn't learned Islamic scholars, such as the university faculty, speak out more vehemently against these killings, instead of turning a blind eye? Why weren't the scholars speaking out against clitoridectomy, which had made its way to Gaza while the Strip was under Egyptian rule?

"It is a sensitive subject. Some people say it makes women calmer. But of course Islam is against it. Every part of the body that is created has a function. It's like tonsils: only if it is threatening health should you remove it; if it is not threatening, leave it be. Perhaps the women preachers are preaching against it. Of course, we don't have such operations here. In Egypt, but not here."

"Among the older women . . ." Asya began, but Ahmad interrupted. "Not here. Never among Palestinians." Asya was silent. The night before, she had told me that her mother's clitoris had been removed.

"This is an Eastern society," he continued. "There are many things to do with women in Eastern societies that are not correct according to Islam. But it takes time to change them. First we must get an Islamic state. All the disasters in the world are from not adopting Islam. When Islam is adopted, all will be right."

When Ahmad excused himself for a moment to speak with a colleague, Asya told me she wanted to visit the lavatory on the women's campus. "I can go here, but I don't feel comfortable."

When Ahmad returned and found me by myself, he recoiled

from the doorway. "Where is Asya? It's forbidden to me to sit with you alone." We were hardly alone. The door to the office stood wide open, onto a passageway teeming with students.

"Even with the door open?" I asked.

"Yes, yes, I am sorry. You must bring Asya," he said, backing away down the corridor as if I had the plague. When Asya returned, we continued our discussion, turning to the role of women in politics. Ahmad was explaining that, while women can't lead a Muslim community, they have a duty to comment and protest to the leader if they feel he's astray.

"It's exactly the same as the role of women during family prayers," he said. "A woman can't lead her husband—or any man—at prayer, but if he makes a mistake—say he leaves something out—she must let him know by clapping her hands."

"Can't she just say the right words?"

"No, because her voice is alluring. She mustn't raise it."

Asya broke in. "Surely, if it is her family, she can raise her voice to say *'Subhan Allah.'* "

"No, no," he said. "She can't raise it at all. She may only clap. Women must be very careful of their voices. If someone comes to my house and asks for me, my wife may say, 'Yes, wait,' or 'He's not here.' Very briefly, very formally. She must not speak in a delicate tone. This is from the Koran. Things begun with a few words will continue to other things."

I left Gaza that night and drove, the next day, out through the stony hills and olive groves of the West Bank, to meet with some women professors from a very different Palestinian university, Birzeit.

These women were less than a generation removed from Asya—women in their late thirties and early forties who could have been her older sisters. But something had happened in the years that separated her education from theirs, and the gulf, widening between them, seemed almost unbridgeable. Yet the women professors at Birzeit, while acknowledging the problem, seemed to me to be in deep denial about its extent.

"The trouble is, these people don't understand their own culture," said Islah Gad, sipping fresh orange juice after a day's teaching. We sat in the sunroom of her house, a huge, Ottoman-style stone building with a portico and domed ceilings. Islah's eyes drifted to the garden, where carefully tended fruit trees blossomed in the red soil. She was watching a small tortoise make its uncertain way through the furrows of plowed earth. She had noticed the creature on the roadway as she drove back from the university and had rescued it from being splattered under the wheels of a car.

Islah had grown up in Egypt and met her husband, a prominent Palestinian activist, at university there. She had returned with him to El Bireh, the West Bank village where his father was mayor until the Israelis deported him as a PLO activist. "Israelis did a lot to uproot traditional Palestinian culture here, but not as much as the Islamic movements are doing," she said. She ticked off the problems on her long, elegant fingers. First, there was the issue Hamas had made of traditional Palestinian dress—the beautiful long black or maroon caftans that Palestinian women had always worn, elaborately embroidered in cross-stitch in the front and at the hem, twinned with a delicate white scarf wrapped around the hair. "This is Islamic dress—but not to them. According to them, the colors in the embroidery are haram. Where in the Koran does it say so? A thousand Palestinian women are earning their bread making those dresses. But they don't think of that. They accuse leftists of having imported ideas. But all of their ideas are imported. At the Birzeit book fair this year I counted a hundred books on women and Islam—all from Egypt and Saudi Arabia."

At Birzeit, the Palestinians' most liberal and secular college, Islamic movements such as Hamas and Jihad had made less headway than at any other school, but still their influence was being felt. "They are like mushrooms," said Lily Feidy, one of Islah's colleagues. "They grow up in certain conditions, and then when the conditions change, they die out. Right now, their resurgence is a sign of pessimism. Because people are desperate, they are resorting to the supernatural."

Lily Feidy, who taught linguistics at Birzeit, had never set foot on the campus of the Gaza Islamic University. "I can't go there because I won't put on the veil. And anyway, I'm not interested in sitting and arguing with them. What was true fourteen hundred years ago is not true now. I'm sorry, but we're not living in the desert anymore; we're not living in tents."

Islah Gad, for her part, welcomed the chance to argue her case. "It's easy to break their logic," she said. "At a debate we had on coeducation, the Hamas boys were saying coeducation is haram—that we must close the coed schools. I said to them, 'Wait: in all our villages, the schools are coed. The villagers can't afford to build two schools. So what will happen in your scenario? All the girls will have to stay away from school. Is that what you want?' They of course said, 'No, no—we didn't think about the expense of new schools.' So I said to them, 'Go, read your own reality. Forget these prefab ideas from Saudi Arabia.' "

Both Islah and Lily seemed to be unwilling to accept that the rising Islamic tide could pose a threat to their own cherished liberal views. To me, their analysis seemed wishful. I heard it a lot from the educated women of their generation—women like Jordan's Leila Sharaf, who had grown up in the heady days of the Arab nationalist movement, when the charismatic figures were all secular leftists who urged women's emancipation. For these women, Hamas's view of women was laughable. And since they couldn't hear the appeal of such views themselves, they were deaf to the appeal they held for their students.

Islamic movements were on the ascendant in almost every university in the Middle East. And the faculties in which they were most heavily represented were the bastions of the most gifted—the medical schools, the engineering departments. The students who were hearing the Islamic call included the students with the most options, not just the desperate cases: the Sahars and the Asyas, with the scholarships to Harvard and London. They were the elites of the next decade: the people who would shape their nations' futures.

A decade or two earlier, these same gifted intellectuals would have been Arab nationalists, but that idea had failed to deliver anything but military defeats and crumbling economies. To an outsider, it was hard to imagine this new "big idea" doing any better. But the return to roots and the rejection of outside influence is always an attractive notion; I had felt its pull myself as an Australian adolescent, living in the shadow of United States influence and watching my country march lockstep into the quagmire of Vietnam. For intelligent young Muslims facing futures limited by the failures of so many imported ideologies, Islam's lure was its very homegrownness. Sahar had said it from the beginning: "Why not try something of our own?"

What worried me most was that the Islam taking hold in so many of the universities wasn't their own; not the tolerant tradition of Egypt nor the progressive practices of Palestinians, but rather the warped interpretation promoted by the wealth of the Saudis. I hated to think of a generation squandering its talent in the service of that repressive creed.

When my Saudi friend took me into the sand dunes north of Riyadh to meet his uncle, I'd assumed that the older man was a relic of a passing era, whose values would erode as surely as the old sand-castle fortresses we'd passed along the highway.

My friend seemed to have traveled such a vast distance in the span of half a lifetime. Born under a palm tree on his uncle's farm, he'd been carried home to his father's house by camelback. Twenty-five years later he crossed the Atlantic by Concorde. Educated at the best colleges in the United States, dividing his professional life between London, Washington and Riyadh, he had an iconoclastic intellect that reveled in exposing cant and upending orthodoxy.

It seemed clear to me that he was the future: his uncle, with the sad story of the sequestered, school-deprived daughters, was the past. It took me awhile to realize that it wasn't as clear as I thought.

My friend was more comfortable critiquing the oddities of OPEC or lamenting the dominance of the Levantine voice in Arabic literature than he was in discussing his personal life. Once, when I pestered him, he described in a slightly self-deprecating way how he'd returned from his liberated life in the West to marry a Saudi bride he "managed to see" just once before their wedding. He never took her with him on his business trips and never offered to introduce me to her when I was in Saudi Arabia. He had daughters, who clearly delighted him, although he never spoke of them unless I asked after them.

How, I asked him one night over dinner in London, was he planning to educate them? He looked down into his plate of pasta and played with his fork. "I will raise them as Saudi women. I won't make the mistake some people make, of bringing them up half here and half there, so that they don't know who they are," he said.

"But what if one of them is a gifted physicist or mathematician?" I asked. "What if she needs to go abroad to study?" I thought he would say, "Well, in that case, of course, she'll study at Harvard, or Princeton, or Cambridge." But he didn't say that at all.

Instead, he sighed. It was a long, deep sigh that reminded me of his uncle when I'd asked him about women driving.

"That," he said, "would be a problem. And I would have to solve it when it happened." It was only then that I realized the distance between uncle and nephew wasn't nearly as great as I'd assumed.

Like most Westerners, I always imagined the future as an inevitably brighter place, where a kind of moral geology will have eroded the cruel edges of past and present wrongs. But in Gaza and Saudi Arabia, what I saw gave me a different view.

From there, the future is a place that looks darker every day.

Chapter 9

RISKY BUSINESS

"I suffer not the work of any worker, male or female, to be lost."

THE KORAN
THE FAMILY OF IMRAN

At the office of the *Arab News* in Jeddah, a reporter named Faiza Ambah had a cartoon tacked to the bulletin board over her desk. "Behold the turtle," said the caption under a whimsical drawing of the creature. "He makes progress only when he sticks out his neck." Every now and then Faiza would uncoil from a hunched position over her keyboard and tug pensively at the black chiffon scarf tied around her face.

Faiza was sticking her own neck out. By Saudi standards, her articles were daring. In the aftermath of the Kuwait invasion, she probed the new mood of Saudi women and the delicate question of press censorship. But the most daring thing she did was to come to work at all. Even cloaked and veiled, she ran a risk every day she came to the newspaper's unsegregated office, where men worked in cubicles alongside her. "When the editor hired me, I think the idea was that I'd work at home: do my reporting by phone and file my copy electronically," she said. "But a reporter can't work like that. You have to see what's going on in the world."

At the end of the day, when she'd filed her article, she would adjust her scarf and abaya and head for the carpark. There, because Saudi law banned her from driving, her Yemeni chauffeur waited to take her home. The first time I met Faiza, she berated me for an article I'd written about the difficulties faced by Saudi women. She was proud of her achievements and those of her friends, who worked as doctors or ran their own companies. She felt I hadn't paid enough attention to the Saudi women who *were* working and making a difference in the society.

What women like Faiza and her friends were doing was simply reclaiming the ground lost in the centuries since the death of the prophet. Every Saudi knew that Muhammad's first wife, Khadija, had run an international trading company. Sawda, his second wife, had been famous for her leatherwork, which she sold to help support the household. Fatima, the prophet's daughter, had labored at spinning until her hands bled, alternating days at work and at study. When she worked, she gave her slave girl time off to study, insisting that everyone had a right to learn.

Faiza was the most visible of the handful of working Saudi women because her name appeared so often in the newspaper. There were a few other Saudi women journalists, but Faiza was the only one I knew who risked working in her newspaper's office. The risk was that the *mutawain*—religious police from the Committee for the Promotion of Virtue and the Prevention of Vice—would one day burst into the office and discover her breaking the rules on segregation. The mutawain are the loose cannons of the Saudi justice system; fanatical volunteers who patrol the streets and shopping malls yelling at people. Women with uncovered faces are one target; men dawdling over closing their shops at prayer time are another. Some mutawain wielded long canes with which to whip offenders. The government didn't encourage the mutawain's excesses, but it didn't rein them in, either. The Saudi ruling family was terrified of a fundamentalist upsurge that would sweep it from power in the way the Iranians had disposed of the shah. So it bought off the mutawain with fleets of fancy cars to use in its patrols, and with a hands-off policy toward its activities. As a result, the mutawain were fearless, even abusing an al-Saud princess when they caught her walking with a maid who wasn't wearing a face veil.

Perhaps the most humiliating thing about the mutawain was that, apart from abusing women in the streets, they didn't deign to deal with them directly regarding so-called "offenses." If a woman transgressed a rule of dress or segregation, the mutawain would take the matter up with her husband, father or brother—the "responsible male" deemed to be in charge of her—in the manner of a school principal dealing with a recalcitrant child. Women of all ages are infantilized by the Saudi system. A woman, no matter how old, has to be able to show a signed permission from her husband, son or grandson before she is free to travel, even inside her own country.

Once, Faiza left her permission behind in Cairo. Her husband was traveling out of the country and was unreachable. She was due to travel herself, but without her permit, she was trapped in Jeddah. "I was tearing my hair out," she said. Her father couldn't help her because, once a woman marries, only her husband's word counts with the Saudi authorities. In the end, she had to wait for a cousin to travel to Cairo and collect the document. Such laws can be even more humiliating for older women. A widowed grandmother, for example, may have to rely on the permission of a grandson if he is her closest male relative.

Partly because of the risk of such humiliation, few Saudi women work outside the home. In 1986 women made up only four percent of the paid work force. Mostly, the small number reflected a lack of jobs open to women. In the Saudi government, even jobs directly concerned with women's affairs were held by men. At United Nations International Women's Year conference in Mexico City in 1975 and the Decade for Women conference in Nairobi in 1985, the Saudi Arabian "women's delegation" was entirely composed of men.

But even in fields where women could work, some husbands were reluctant to let them. Faiza's husband, a Lebanese, was proud of her accomplishments. And some Saudi husbands felt the same. But often there was tension between pride in a wife's achievements and apprehension about where her work might lead her. One businessman bragged of his wife's graduation from medical school, then told me he hoped she would go on to specialize in surgery, "so her patients will be unconscious when she touches them."

The issue of working wives came up frequently in Saudi newspapers, especially on the religion pages. "What are the conditions relating to a wife going out to work? Is this permitted under Islam, and if so, under which circumstances?" asked "Working Wife, Jeddah" in a letter to the *Saudi Gazette*'s religious editor. "There are legal and moral rights that become consequential on marriage," responded the editor. "Because of their different physiological structures and biological functions, each sex is assigned a role to play in the family. . . . It is the husband who is supposed to provide for the family. If he cannot gain enough to support the family, or if his income is too low to provide for a relatively acceptable standard of living, and provided the wife is willing, both of them may work for gain. However:

"1. The husband has the right to terminate a wife's working whenever he deems it necessary;

"2. He has the right to object to any job if he feels that it would expose his wife to any harm, seduction or humiliation;

"3. The wife has the right to discontinue working whenever she pleases."

Once, flying to Saudi Arabia, I'd sat next to a Saudi who had been grappling for a year with the issue of what kind of job might be appropriate for his wife. His own business was trading, and he became increasingly edgy when our plane approached Jeddah. As we circled for landing, he mopped his brow with a large white handkerchief. He was worried about the underwear in his luggage. "More than two hundred brassieres," he whispered. "I bought them in London, from Marks and Spencer. All made in Israel." Saudi Arabia enforced a boycott on goods from the land it referred to as "the Zionist entity." So the night before, in his London hotel, he had sat up late with a thick marker pen, writing Saudi-riyal prices over the offending labels to make the country of origin illegible. "But by the end I was very tired," he said. "If I missed one, and customs sees it, I will be in big trouble." He swabbed again at his brow. "What can I do? I'm a trader, and these are the brassieres that Saudi women like to buy."

Saudi customs searches were notorious. One American who'd gone to work there had had his five-generation family Bible ripped up in front of him, because it flouted the kingdom's ban on non-Muslim religious items. The Saudis took the ban on other religions' symbols to such an extreme that the plane in which we were flying had just been repainted, along with the rest of the Saudia Airlines fleet, following a fundamentalist's complaint that the space between the *s* and the *a* in the previous Saudia logo had formed the shape of a Christian cross.

I thought I had purged my luggage of anything that could be construed, or misconstrued, as religious. But at the customs desk in Jeddah the grim young inspector scowled as he plucked two pieces of contraband from my bag: a dry reference work titled *Political Dictionary of the Arab World* and a book about early explorers in Arabia called *Passionate Pilgrims*. He objected to the first because the word "political" in the title made it potentially seditious; the second because the word "passionate" had pornographic potential, while the word "pilgrims" might have referred to religion.

The trader, Mohamed, had been luckier. I saw him in the arrival hall, grinning broadly. The illicit bras had passed inspection. To celebrate, he said, I should come to lunch the next day and meet his wife, Adela.

Mohamed shared a small apartment building with his extended family: father and mother on the ground floor; brothers, their wives and children filling the flats above. Even in Saudi Arabia's modern cities, families still followed the tribal patterns of the desert. Saudi men, when they married, brought their wives into their parents' home. Rich families managed this in rambling walled compounds with several villas arranged around a garden. Poorer families built slab houses that grew by a floor every time a son took a wife. As a result, Saudi cities seemed dotted with unfinished buildings. Tufts of steel reinforcing bars stuck out of the flat roofs as if the houses had been given punk haircuts.

To me, with family scattered on three continents, having everyone together in one building seemed enviable. But Mohamed had begun to find it stifling. When we climbed the stairs to his flat, doors opened on every floor, as brothers and tiny nieces and nephews peered out to see who Mohamed was bringing home. To get some privacy, he'd started to build a new house, just for himself, Adela and their three children. But he didn't know if he'd be able to move into it. "It's difficult to convince my father that moving away is a good idea," he sighed. Mohamed was thirty-five years old, but his father's word was still law.

Like most Saudis, Mohamed worked from 7 A.M. until one in the afternoon, then returned to his business for a few hours in the evening. Schools and offices closed during the heat of the day, and families gathered to take lunch together. Mohamed and Adela ate at a table, Western style, instead of spreading a cloth on the floor in the traditional Arabian way. They served an array of Arabian specialties —steaming bowls of rice, braised lamb in saffron gravy, skewers of grilled chicken—and a Western-style plate of french fries. After lunch the family sprawled in front of the TV, flipping past the heavily religious Saudi stations to pick up the wobbly signal from Egypt, with its racier fare of movies and variety shows.

Adela had been just sixteen years old and still at school when she married Mohamed. She completed a sociology degree while having her children. "Most of the women in the course were doing the same," she said. Many Saudi schools provide day-care centers and nurseries for their students' children. Exams can be rescheduled to accommodate the arrival of a baby. After university, when her two sons and daughter had all started school, Adela became miserable. "There was just this terrible boredom every morning once the kids left," she said. In the past, she would simply have had more children. In rural areas, many Saudi women still reproduced to their utmost capability. One British doctor, on an eighteen-month posting to a Jeddah hospital, thought his interpreter had failed him during an ante-natal checkup on a twenty-eight-year-old Bedouin. "I asked her when she'd had her last period, and she said, 'What's a period?' It turned out she'd never had one. She'd been married at twelve, before her menarche, and had been pregnant or lactating ever since."

But, for the majority of urban Saudis such as Adela and Mohamed, the tribal imperative for a huge family no longer applied. So more and more educated women were competing for the few Islamically sanctioned jobs in medicine, education or women's banks. The banks, run by Saudi women managers and staff, had opened in 1980 because, although the Koran gives women control of their own wealth, Saudi segregation rules were denying them that control by effectively banning their entry to banks used by men. Even though daughters inherit only half as much as sons, in post-oil Saudi Arabia that often comes to a fortune. The new banks were meticulously segregated, down to women auditors to oversee the accounts of the female branches and guards posted at the door to see that men didn't enter by mistake. Usually a guard was married to one of the women employees inside, so that if documents had to be delivered he could deal with his wife rather than risking even that slight contact taking place between unmarried members of the opposite sex.

Medicine, the only career in which segregation isn't enforced, is under constant attack by fundamentalists, who object to women doctors treating male patients. Their campaign has been unsuccessful so far because the government has been able to show that there aren't enough Saudi men in medicine yet to handle the demand.

There had been an opening at the Ministry of Health for which Adela was qualified, but Mohamed had been against it because it involved some contact with men. "She would have had to keep her headscarf on, never laugh, never smile—if she smiles at a man he will think, 'Ah, she loves me,'" Mohamed explained. As he sat on the sofa flipping the TV channel selector, he paused for a minute on a Saudi channel where a woman announcer, her hair carefully veiled, was reading the news. "This is new," he said. The television had had women presenters before, but rarely a Saudi. What if Adela wanted to be a news reader? I asked. "She would never agree to be seen in public like that, and I wouldn't permit it," Mohamed said firmly. Soon Adela would start work in the only job she could find that both she and Mohamed deemed suitable: a clerical position in a girls' school. The job wasn't up to her qualifications, "but the hours are good, and it is better than sleeping all day," she said. Without a job, any job, Adela had little to fill her empty hours besides TV, videos and women's tea parties. There were no theaters or cinemas in Saudi Arabia, and she couldn't go shopping alone without risking stares and harassment.

As the afternoon turned to evening, Mohamed suggested a drive along Jeddah's seaside. Before Adela stepped outside, she tied her hair back in a large black scarf, wrapped a small piece of black cloth around her face like a baddie in a Western, leaving just her eyes exposed, then slipped an abaya on top of everything, covering her colorful floor-length dress. The two of us sat in the back seat of the car with the children, with Mohamed and his uncle up front. All along the Red Sea shore, clumps of white-robed men sat just a little apart from clusters of women, their black cloaks billowing in the hot sea breeze as they arranged their evening picnics.

We parked and strolled along the waterfront, the white pavement throwing out the day's stored heat. As the sun eased into the sea, the city behind us exploded in a cacophony of calls to evening prayer. Mohamed reached into the trunk of his car for prayer mats. He and his uncle lined up, raised their palms to God, and bowed toward the nearby city of Mecca. Adela didn't join them, explaining that Saudi women usually didn't pray in public. As we waited, she groped for a tissue, lifting her black veil to wipe the sweat-drenched face beneath. Nevertheless, Adela seemed to be enjoying this modest outing. It was one of the few things she and Mohamed still could do together. A few months earlier they'd been able to take the children to an amusement park, or skating at a rink where dense white plastic substituted for ice. But both places had come under pressure from the religious establishment and now offered only segregated men's and women's hours that made family visits impossible.

Some Saudi businessmen were fed up with segregation's effects on their companies. Hussein Abudawood, whose factories produced Clorox bleach in Saudi Arabia, had wanted to do some Western-style market research to see how Saudi households did their laundry. "Obviously, I couldn't send male market researchers to talk to women. But I couldn't send Saudi women, either, because they might run into the men of the household. And how do I find enough Arabic-speaking women here who aren't Saudi?" He'd eventually scraped together a few Egyptian and Lebanese interviewers, who'd had a terrible time explaining themselves in a land where strangers just don't come to the door. "Most places have a guard at the gate with instructions not to admit anyone who doesn't have an appointment," he said.

Hussein found the whole system riddled with contradictions. "If a Saudi woman wants a new bra and panties she has to discuss it over the counter in a shop staffed by a bunch of guys from India. Yet if she's a businesswoman who needs to file a document at a government ministry, she can't set foot in there—she has to send a man." Hussein had been part of a group of businessmen asked to comment on a draft of a Ministry of Development economic plan. He had taken issue with a line in the draft that stated that the government would promote women working according to Islamic rules. "I got up and said, 'Here's half a line about women in a thirty-six-page development plan and you have to put 'according to Islamic rules.' What about the rest of the thirty-six pages? You mean the rest of it *isn't* according to Islamic rules? Are you just trying to satisfy the extremists?' "

The extremists were almost impossible to satisfy. Even segregated workplaces were at risk. Saudi Cable Company, the kingdom's biggest industrial concern, had floated a proposal to build a factory where every job, from production line to senior management, would be filled by women. In a country with an acute labor shortage, I thought such a plan would be hailed for its initiative. But when I went to see the official in charge of the project, he begged me not to write about it. "We have already had too much attention," he said. He worried that the project would be scuttled if the fundamentalists started a campaign decrying it for luring women from their homes. However, he did introduce me to his wife, Basilah, who ran the magnificent Dar al Fikr girls' school.

After showing me the school, Basilah invited me to her home for afternoon tea. The pale stone villa, with its floodlit pool, Persian carpets and elegant furnishings, made it clear that her job wasn't a case of "financial necessity," such as the *Saudi Gazette*'s religious editor would have approved. "I didn't work when I first got married," she said. "I would spend most of the day in bed, then when Fawaz would get home tired from a hard day's work I'd be so bored I'd insist he take me out to the shopping mall. After a while we both decided the situation was crazy, that I should be doing something with my life that would make some kind of contribution."

Basilah had invited a woman friend who helped her mother run a successful construction company to join us for tea. When her father died, she and her mother had expected his male relations to run the business and provide for her and her children. But they were lazy and incompetent, and it seemed that everything her father had worked for was going to be destroyed. "Finally my mother took over," the woman explained. "She went to the Ministry of Construction with the papers that needed official approval. No woman had been in there before. The officials ordered her out. She refused to go. She sat there, and sat there, until they were forced to deal with her. She turned out to be a very good manager, and she saved the business."

As maids glided in and out with glasses of tea and a dazzling array of French cakes and pastries, conversation turned to how my husband felt about all the traveling I had to do for my job. I told Basilah that neither of us liked being apart so much but that, as a journalist himself, he understood the job's demands. Then, bragging a little, I told her how he'd rearranged his own career to accommodate mine. "When my newspaper offered me the Middle East post," I said, "he gave up his own job so I could accept it." I had expected Basilah to be surprised; Tony and I were used to the automatic assumption in the Middle East that he was the one whose job had brought us there. But the look on Basilah's face was beyond surprise. She looked utterly dismayed, as if I'd just admitted that my husband had committed mass murder. She fussed with her tea glass, cleared her throat and changed the subject.

It was hard to get information on women who worked in jobs outside the relatively safe spheres of girls' education, women's banking and medicine. When I asked the Ministry of Information for help, I was stonewalled. So I tried various other contacts. "Don't even touch this subject unless what you plan to write is a hundred percent positive," warned a Lebanese businessman in Jeddah. When I indicated that was unlikely, he refused to arrange any introductions. I'd heard of women in Jeddah and Riyadh who were the bosses of businesses as diverse as photography studios, clothing manufacture and computer training schools. I thought the Chamber of Commerce might be able to give me some leads. "No problem," said a helpful official, "I'll set you up some appointments."

The next day he told me to be at the administrative office at Jeddah airport at 2 P.M. I thought he'd found a woman executive for me to talk to there. But when I arrived I found I'd been scheduled for a mind-numbing "official tour" that had absolutely nothing to do with women. I was there for hours, being shown videos, walked through computer rooms and deluged with official statistics—a 625% increase in passenger traffic between 1975 and 1988, an 870% rise in cargo traffic, a terminal the size of eighty football fields just for pilgrims making the Hajj, roofed with Teflon-coated fiberglass to deflect the heat. There was no polite way to cut the tour short. Developing countries always complain that reporters don't write about their achievements; that we focus on colorful tribal traditions and neglect technological progress. Still, I was irritated with the Chamber of Commerce for wasting my time and the time of the airport officials.

As it happened, there was a part of the shining modern airport that had relevance to my story on the status of women in Saudi Arabia. But it wasn't part of the tour. I didn't see it until I was leaving the country, two weeks later. While I was waiting in the departure lounge I had to use the women's toilet. I walked past the polished glass and gleaming chrome of the public areas and pushed on the blond wood door marked by a stylized drawing of a veiled head.

Inside, I gagged. The floor was awash with excrement. Blocked toilet bowls brimmed with sewage. The place looked as if it hadn't been cleaned in weeks. Nobody had noticed, because nobody who mattered ever went in there.

Saudi Arabia is the extreme. Why dwell on the extreme, when it would be just as easy to write about a Muslim country such as Turkey, led by a woman, where one in six judges is a woman, and one in every thirty private companies has a woman manager?

I think it important to look in detail at Saudi Arabia's grim reality because this is the kind of sterile, segregated world that Hamas in Israel, most mujahedin factions in Afghanistan, many radicals in Egypt and the Islamic Salvation Front in Algeria are calling for, right now, for their countries and for the entire Islamic world. None of these groups is saying, "Let's recreate Turkey, and separate church and state." Instead, what they want is Saudi-style, theocratically enforced repression of women, cloaked in vapid clichés about a woman's place being the paradise of her home.

In the vast majority of Muslim countries, barriers to women's employment have fallen so far in the last fifty years that it seems it would be impossible to reerect them, even if hard-line fundamentalist governments one day came to power. But under the surface there is often ambivalence about women at work that makes their position vulnerable.

In Egypt women are everywhere in the work force: in the fields, as they always have been, sowing and planting; and sitting on city sidewalks, selling their produce. But they are also in positions that would have been unthinkable in the first half of the century, when only the poorest and most wretched families subjected their women to the "indignity" of work outside the home. Egyptian women are doctors, filmmakers, politicians, economists, academics, engineers. Mostly they are public servants, cogs in the country's bloated bureaucracy. Now, it is almost unthinkable that a young Egyptian woman won't go to work, at least until she marries. Often she will find the man she will marry among her coworkers.

It was President Nasser who made way for women in the government, promising a job to any Egyptian who got a college degree. Now, many an educated, lower-middle-class woman finds work as a *muwazzaf,* a government employee, typing, filing or otherwise pushing paper six days a week, from about eight in the morning to two in the afternoon. The size of the bureaucracy means that most workers are underemployed, and most, men and women, pass the workday gossiping and sipping endless cups of sugary tea. While the pay is pitiful—less than $40 a month—the money gives the women at least a small degree of discretion in spending and the prestige that comes from contributing to the family budget.

Most of the young, unmarried women I knew enjoyed the freedom of a salary and the challenge of even an undemanding workplace. But my married friends often saw things differently. Often, the job itself was a respite, wedged with great difficulty between hours of backbreaking household labor.

An afternoon I spent with a recently married woman went like this. After commuting for about an hour and a half on a bus so packed that three or four passengers hung out the door with just one foot each on the step, she elbowed her way off at a stop about half a mile from her apartment and stood in line for twenty minutes at a government food store, to get the lower-priced food available there. She hauled the groceries home to a cold-water kitchen with no fridge, and immediately made tea for her husband, who'd arrived home from work and plopped on the sofa to chat with his father and a young nephew. Next she climbed the stairs to the pigeon coops she kept on the roof of the apartment building, fed yesterday's leftover bread to the birds, then chose the two plumpest and wrung their necks on the spot.

She plucked the birds, gutted and cooked them, boiled cracked wheat and noodles for the stuffing, served the meal to the men, who seemed a bit grumpy to be kept waiting so late to eat; made and served more tea, scoured the cooking pans and plates, swept the ubiq-uitous Cairo dust from the floors and furniture, scrubbed everyone's clothes by hand and left them in a bucket to hang out on the roof before she left for work the next morning; set some lentils to soak for the next day's meal, finally sat down, with some sewing on her lap, at about 9 P.M., only to jump up ten minutes later to make another round of tea for some neighbors who'd popped in. There were only two unusual things about the woman's situation; she didn't have other women in the house—a sister-in-law or mother-in-law—to help her with the chores, and she didn't yet have children to add to her responsibilities.

While women now share the economic burden of their families, very few Egyptian men are prepared to share the housework. To women run ragged by the routine of rushing home from work to have a large meal ready for a demanding family, the fundamentalists' message of women's place being in the home sometimes has some appeal.

Husbands, too, hear that message. Mostly raised by women who didn't work outside the home, they are used to a household where their shirts are ironed, the floors swept, the food elaborately prepared and always ready. Now, a young man might meet his bride as a coworker in his office. Before their marriage, he enjoyed the chance to admire her beauty, share a joke and gossip with her. But once she is his wife, he resents the fact that other men in the office have the pleasure of her company. If she is not already veiled, he may begin pressuring her to wear hijab.

When home life with a working wife turns out to be less salubrious than with the nonworking women of his youth, he doesn't think of lending a hand with the chores, for he has never seen a man do such a thing. Instead, he curses the government for a ruined economy that makes his wife's salary a necessity. And when he hears an imam or sheik preaching of a woman's place, and promising better times under an Islamic regime, he eyes the pile of rumpled laundry, the dusty floor and the simple lunch his exhausted wife has slapped together, and wonders whether such a cause might not be worth supporting.

To see what happens if he takes the next step and joins the revolutionaries, it is necessary to look at Iran.

Even when a revolution succeeds, it doesn't always achieve everything its extremists have envisioned. It is one thing to hold tenaciously, as Saudi Arabia does, to traditions that have existed unchanged for centuries. It is another thing altogether to reimpose such traditions after change has already reshaped a culture.

Since the 1920s, Iran's Pahlavi rulers had tried to Westernize their nation, sometimes by force, scrapping thousands of years of traditional separation of men and women. By the time the Iranian revolutionaries threw out the shah in 1979, there were male hairstylists for women, male tailors fitting women's gowns, male teachers in girls' classrooms.

The extremists set out to end all that, telling male gynecologists that they should find another area of medicine, attempting to install curtains to divide university lecture halls into male and female sections, and banning male barbers from touching female heads.

Apart from the barbers, very little of it worked. What the extremists hadn't realized was that, when it came to sex segregation, Khomeini wasn't entirely with them. Khomeini, always a literalist, read the words of the Koran and the hadith and didn't extrapolate from them. When he read that the prophet's wives were to remain in their houses, he took that to mean the prophet's wives, and only the prophet's wives. Other Muslim women had roles to play outside their houses, and he encouraged them. From the beginning he encouraged women to come into the streets to demonstrate and praised their role as revolutionaries, fighting in the streets side by side with the men.

To him, the rules were clear: unrelated men and women mustn't be alone together; they mustn't touch each other, except in medical situations; and women must wear hijab. Obviously, since hairdressers touched their clients and saw them out of hijab, there would be no more male staff in salons serving women. The same went for gym instructors whose students worked out in athletic gear, and reporters who covered women's activities where hijab wasn't worn.

But that didn't mean that such activities should cease. What happened instead was a sudden flowering of job opportunities for women. The prohibition on men and women being alone created a demand for women driving instructors. In the media, the need for women to cover certain women's sports and other segregated events opened jobs for producers, directors, reporters and sound recordists.

Since the hadith made it clear that the prophet had approved of women tending men's war wounds, there was to be no segregation when it came to medicine. But since the new Islamic atmosphere made many women prefer to be seen by women doctors, there was an upsurge in demand for more women's places in medical school. Nurse-midwives saw their status rise. While schools were quickly segregated to protect the impressionable young, the idea of curtaining off university classrooms was abandoned in most places. Since the universities were to be thoroughly Islamic, with admission requiring a reference from the would-be student's local mosque, there was no need to physically separate these devout youngsters, who automatically separated themselves. In lectures, men sat on one side of the room, women on the other. Only the placement of the professor's podium posed problems. In some lecture rooms, builders bolted it to the floor on the men's side of the room, on the obsolete premise that professors were all male. That left the growing number of women professors standing on the women's side for the sake of the new proprieties, but having nowhere to rest their notes.

At the university in the southern city of Awaz, I met a young student who had benefited from the postrevolutionary changes. She was studying medicine, living in a dormitory far from her extremely religious rural family. Her parents, she said, would never have permitted her to go to university under the shah, or to live away from home, or to work in a hospital. But now they saw the universities and the hospitals as part of the Islamic system, and therefore safe places for their daughter. Away from home, she had the freedom to meet men, albeit in very controlled circumstances, and had recently found the one she wanted to marry. Her parents, to her astonishment, had accepted her choice, making her the first woman in her family's history to marry for love.

In the theocratic Iranian government women have risen to the ranks of deputy ministers, and at each election Rafsanjani has called on voters to return more women to the Parliament. In business, I met a woman running a valve factory and another heading a trucking company. Nasi Ravandoost, who ran the factory, said she had no problems getting on with her business inside Iran. "My problems are all created outside," she said. Traveling to buy parts was often complicated by embargoes and visa obstacles. The woman who ran the trucking concern said that success was a matter of common sense and tact, just as it was in business anywhere. "Obviously, I don't go into the Transport Ministry wearing this," she said, fingering the floral silk outfit she'd worn to an evening party in North Tehran.

By now, women have so solidified their place in postrevolutionary society that some of them are outspokenly criticizing it. At the offices of the satirical magazine *Golagha,* some of the sharpest political cartoons are penned by a woman. But even more tellingly, in the fall 1991 issue of the *Iranian Journal for International Affairs,* Iran's showpiece foreign policy publication, an assistant professor of anthropology named Fatemeh Givechian wrote a paper that criticized the lingering remnants of the policy of sex segregation.

"No doubt," she wrote, the policy led to "more awareness of one's own gender, but not necessarily any increase in one's knowledge of the opposite gender. Sex segregation to this extent is not natural. . . . There will emerge a dual society of male and female stranger to one another and unaware of each other's anxieties."

Chapter 10

POLITICS, WITH AND WITHOUT A VOTE

> "Say, O God, possessor of all
> sovereignty, you give sovereignty to
> whom you wish and take sovereignty
> from whom you wish."
>
> THE KORAN
> CHAPTER OF THE FAMILY OF IMRAN

A year after the Gulf War, in the mountains and valleys of Iraqi Kurdistan, the lines of women seemed to stretch forever. Spring sunbeams glinted on sparkling dresses of silver and gold. They had worn their best, because this was a day of celebration. For the first time in their lives, the women of Kurdistan were lining up to vote for their own representatives.

A year earlier, during the Kurdish uprising that followed the end of the war, I had seen similar sparkling, bright-colored dresses torn and discarded in a dusty pile by a door to a prefab hut on the grounds of an Iraqi prison. A stained mattress lay inside the hut.

Kurdish women had been brought to this place, stripped naked and raped. For some, the rape had been part of the regime of torture they experienced as political prisoners. Others had been raped as a means of torturing their imprisoned fathers, brothers or husbands. The idea was to break the spirit of the men by destroying their honor through the violation of the bodies of their women. The procedure was so routine that the bureaucrats of the prison had made up an index card for one of the employees, a Mr. Aziz Saleh Ahmad. Neatly and methodically, in the bottom left-hand corner, it listed his profession, *Fighter in the Popular Army*, and his "Activity," *Violation of*

Women's Honor. Aziz Saleh Ahmad was, in other words, employed as a rapist at the prison. Saddam Hussein had called his campaign against the Kurds the Anfal, after a chapter of the Koran which speaks of the spoils of holy war. It was hard to imagine a more perverse appropriation of religion.

For most of their lives, this had been the meaning of politics for the women of Kurdistan: a dangerous and possibly deadly activity that led to places like the stained mattress, or the airless, feces-smeared cells tunneled through the earth beneath it. To me, it seemed like a miracle that the meaning had changed, in one short year, to something so different as lines of smiling women, lining up to vote. Even more surprising were the names of the women on the ballot.

The road to political power is full of obstacles for women in most Muslim societies. In countries such as Kuwait, women have yet to win the right to vote, much less govern. And even where the system is supposedly open to women, claiming a place in it often means standing up to abuse and the threat of physical violence. In Jordan's 1993 election, one woman candidate had to fight for the right to even speak at a rally, because Muslim extremists objected to the sound of a female voice at a mixed gathering.

In 1994, women led three Muslim countries. Yet often their place at the top has little effect on the lives of women at the bottom. As Tansu Ciller turned her attention to remaking Turkey's economy, young Turkish women caught socializing with men in rural areas were being forced to undergo "virginity checks" at local police stations. As Bangladesh's Begum Khaleda Zia became the first Muslim woman head of state to address the U. N. General Assembly in 1993, extremists were using death threats to attempt to silence a Bangladeshi woman writer who criticized aspects of Islam. In her first term in office, Pakistan's Benazir Bhutto let stand rape laws that punished the victim as a "fornicator" and let the rapist go free. On her return to power in 1993, it seemed that she might do better, promising to set up all-women police stations and appoint women judges.

Part of the difficulty for women leaders in Muslim countries is that their own position is often so tenuous and the risk of a backlash always a threat. In Turkey, signs of resentment of Ciller's sex surfaced at a conference in August 1993 for former Prime Minister Mesyut Yilmaz when delegates began chanting "*Mesyut koltuga, Tansu mutfaga* [Mesyut back to power and Tansu back to the kitchen]."

Muslim women politicians tend to be a special breed. On election day in Kurdistan in May 1992, one woman candidate, Hero Ahmed, didn't wear a sparkling dress. She wore the same earth-toned baggy pants and sashed shirt she'd worn since 1979, when she went to the mountains to join the Pesh Merga, the Kurdish guerrillas whose name means We Who Face Death. During her twelve years in the mountains Hero, a psychologist, learned to use an assault rifle and an antiaircraft gun. But mostly she shot film. Her most famous clip shows clouds of gas rising over the village of Yak Sammer in 1988— one of the few pieces of film known to exist of an Iraqi poison gas attack.

On election day, women stood in line all day to vote for her. Some, illiterate, had never held a pen before. At the end of the count, seven women, including Hero, had been elected to the hundred-and-five-seat Parliament.

What happened next followed a pattern that has repeated itself in almost every Islamic state where women have won a political voice. Almost always, women politicians try to reform the inequitable personal status laws that govern marriage, divorce, child custody and property. In Kurdistan, the women parliamentarians began to campaign for reform of laws based on sharia that deprived them of equal rights with men. Among their demands: outlawing polygamy, except in the case of a woman's mental illness, and changing inheritance laws so that daughters receive an equal share of a parent's estate, instead of half the share allotted to sons.

Hero thought the Parliament would probably pass the anti-polygamy law. In the Koran, polygamy is presented as an option for men, not as a requirement. In seventh-century Arabian society, there had been no restriction on how many wives a man could take. The Koran, in stipulating four as a maximum, was setting limits, not giving license. A close reading of the text suggests that monogamy is preferred. "If you shall not be able to deal justly, [take] only one" the Koran says, then later states: "You are never able to be fair and just between women even if that is your ardent desire."

The issue of polygamy is analogous to that of slavery, which was gradually banned in Islamic countries. Saudi Arabia was among the last to legislate against it in 1962, when the government bought the freedom of all the slaves in the kingdom at three times the going rate. As with polygamy, the wording of the Koran permits, but discourages, slavery. Muhammad's sunnah included the freeing of many of his war-captive slaves. Because freeing slaves is extolled as the act of a good Muslim, most Muslims now accept that conditions have changed enough since the seventh century to allow them to legislate against a practice that the prophet probably would have chosen to ban outright, if his own times had allowed. Polygamy is already on the decline throughout the Islamic world, and many Muslim scholars see no religious obstacle to a legal ban on the practice.

For the Kurdish Parliament, the difficulties would come with demands for change in things that the Koran doesn't present as optional, such as the division of an estate to give sons double the share of daughters.

The Koran sets out the formula for inheritance as an instruction which all believers must follow. In seventh-century Arabia the Koran's formula was a giant leap forward for women, who up until then had usually been considered as chattels to be inherited, rather than as heirs and property owners in their own right. Most European women had to wait another twelve centuries to catch up to the rights the Koran granted Muslim women. In England it wasn't until 1870 that the Married Women's Property Acts finally abolished the rule that put all a woman's wealth under her husband's control on marriage.

Today, Muslim authorities defend the unequal division of inheritance by pointing out that the Koran requires men to support their wives and children, whereas women are allowed to keep their wealth entirely for their own use. In practice, of course, it rarely works that way. Hero headed the Kurdish chapter of Save the Children, an organization whose research has proved repeatedly that money in women's hands benefits families much more than money flowing to men.

I went to visit Hero in January 1993, as Parliament got ready to debate the women's platform. Her office was a small room in a large house that had once belonged to one of Saddam Hussein's top officials. Hero had stripped the room of furniture and tried to recreate the mood of a traditional Kurdish mountain dwelling. Kurdish kilims and cushions covered the floor. Climbing plants wound their way up the walls and over the rafters. Near the ceiling, a squirrel darted in and out of a small knitted pouch that dangled from a beam.

To Hero, legislation was only a beginning. "I don't believe some habits and ways of thinking can be changed by making a new set of rules," she said. "It needs time, publicity, education; first to make people understand it, then, gradually, to get them to accept it."

At that time, members of a committee formed by the women parliamentarians were traveling Kurdistan, trying to raise support for the law reforms. They visited women in towns and remote villages, carrying a petition in favor of reform. In August 1992, the petition carried 3,000 names. A year later, 30,000 had signed.

In principle, the support of ten parliamentarians is all that is required for a proposed law reform to be put to a vote by legislators. By September 1993, thirty-five MPs had signed the proposals. But still the reforms languished. Timid MPs said it was necessary to wait for what they called the "right" time to present them.

It wasn't clear when that "right" time might be. And by the summer of 1994, it seemed it might not come at all. By then, the Kurdish parliament had collapsed amid bitter fighting between the two main Kurdish parties. It seemed unlikely that any meaningful change would come from there.

Even if it had, legislative reform of sharia-based law has rarely been a lasting success. Tunisia in 1956 replaced its Koranic law with a unified code for Muslims, Christians and Jews that banned polygamy and repudiation, and gave women equal pay and equal rights in divorce. But the law was so far ahead of public attitudes that it never succeeded in creating deep change. To walk the streets in Tunis today is to be transported to a planet where women barely exist. Apart from a few foreign tourists, women aren't seen in public places.

In Iran the shah's laws banning polygamy and child marriage were overturned after the revolution. In Egypt, the birthplace of the modern Arab feminist movement, legal reform had a mixed history. In 1919 veiled women marched through the streets of Cairo to protest British colonial rule. In 1956, with British rule banished, Egyptian President Gamal Abdel Nasser granted women the vote. But until 1979 restrictive personal status laws prohibited a woman leaving her husband's house without his permission or a court order.

In his novel, *Palace Walk*, Egypt's Nobel Prize-winning novelist Naguib Mahfouz writes movingly of Amina, who leaves her house just once in twenty-five years of marriage to visit a nearby mosque. When her husband learns she has defied him and gone out, he orders her from the house: "His command fell on her head like a fatal blow. She was dumbfounded and did not utter a word. She could not move . . . she had entertained many kinds of fears: that he might pour out his anger on her and deafen her with his shouts and curses. She had not even ruled out physical violence, but the idea of being evicted had never troubled her. She had lived with him for twenty-five years and could not imagine that anything could separate them or pluck her from this house of which she had become an inseparable part."

Perhaps even worse than the threat of banishment, though, was the law of Bait el Taa, or House of Obedience. This law empowered a husband to compel an estranged or runaway wife to return home and have sex with him, no matter how great her hatred or aversion. If necessary, the police could be called to drag a woman back to her husband's house. Other laws meant Egyptian women could be divorced without even knowing it. Polygamous husbands weren't legally required to tell their wives about one another. Some found out only on the death of the husband, when a "new" family showed up to claim a share of the estate.

Gradually, Egyptian women worked their way into politics. In 1962, Hakmet Abu Zeid became the first woman in the cabinet, in the post of social affairs minister. But it wasn't until 1978, backed by the president's wife, Jehan Sadat, that her successor, Aisha Rateb, began a sustained campaign for reform of the personal status laws. They were mild reforms, calling for a husband to inform a wife of divorce, or of his intention to take another wife. If he married another, the first wife had the right to divorce him within twelve months. The reforms also gave divorced women custody of children at least until age ten for boys and twelve for girls, extendable, by court order, to fifteen and marriage. There was to be fairer alimony; the right of a wife with children to retain the family home; and the right of appeal to a court against a husband's enforcement of Bait el Taa.

But despite their mildness, the reforms immediately provoked cries of "Islam's Laws not Jehan's Laws." Radical sheiks branded Jehan Sadat and Aisha Rateb atheists and enemies of the family. Rioting broke out at Al Azhar, the ancient Islamic university. "One, two, three, four!" screamed the male students. "We want one, two, three, four wives!" In fact, the laws hadn't challenged the right to polygamy or unilateral divorce. They hadn't even mentioned clitoridectomy.

In 1979, Anwar Sadat enacted the laws by presidential decree, during a parliamentary recess. He also set up new quotas aimed at raising the number of women in government. But opponents continued the battle in court. In 1985 they succeeded in having "Jehan's Laws" struck down. Now the fight has widened, with fundamentalists seeking to overthrow Egypt's government in favor of what they say is a pure Islamic system. And that system is at odds with all forms of government that currently exist, including Western democracy.

In its ideal form, the Islamic state isn't a nation in any modern sense of the word. It has no borders. It would be a political and religious union of all Muslims, modeled on the community Muhammad set up in Medina. There would be no political parties, just a single, unified Islamic *ummah*, or community. At its head would be a *caliph*, literally, successor, who would follow in the footsteps of the prophet Muhammad as the Muslims' leading political and religious authority.

The caliph must be a man, for part of his duty is leading community prayers, and a woman isn't allowed to lead men at prayer lest the sound of her voice arouse carnal rather than spiritual thoughts. The caliph should be chosen by the distinguished members of the community and ideally would be someone who serves reluctantly rather than one who puts himself forward for election.

Under the caliph are legislative and judicial branches of government: a *majlis as shura,* which resembles a parliament in some ways, although its role is more advisory than legislative; a council of experts who serve as the caliph's close advisers; and the qadis, or judges, who according to most sources also must be men, since women are considered too emotional to sit in judgment.

The laws of the Islamic state would be derived first from the Koran. But since only about six hundred of its six thousand verses are concerned with law, and only about eighty of these deal directly with crime, punishments, contracts and family law, other sources also have to be consulted. The hadith fills many gaps. A third source of legislation, on matters not touched on in either Koran or hadith, are practices decided upon by the unanimous agreement of the Islamic community, for Muhammad is believed to have stated that "my community will not agree upon an error."

While Muslims may vote for their representatives in an ideal Islamic state, the system can't be a democracy in the sense of tolerating competing ideologies, for no earthly ideology—even if supported by the will of the majority—can ever be allowed to overrule the divine laws of the Koran. When the Algerian government called off elections that looked likely to bring an Islamic government to power in 1992, it did so on the basis that the Islamicists, once democratically elected, would then dismantle Algerian democratic institutions. Members of the main Islamic party, the Islamic Salvation Front, even joked that their slogan was: "One man, one vote. Once."

How women would participate in an ideal Islamic state is a matter of debate. While they can't be caliph or qadi, the history of the community at Medina shows women taking part in key decisions and being present at discussions of policy. Women often argued with Muhammad and the caliphs who followed him, and sometimes their opinions proved decisive.

Yet at the Islamic University of Gaza women students get a decidedly dimmer view of their likely role in a future Islamic state. "Politics needs a certain mental ability," explained Ahmad Saati, the university's spokesman. "Very few women have this kind of mind." I found his answer odd, seeing that the most prominent Palestinian political figure at that moment was Hanan Ashrawi, the Palestinian spokeswoman at peace talks in Washington.

"Ask Ashrawi's husband. Ask her children," Ahmad Saati responded. "If she is a good wife, and a good mother, and a good sister —if she is perfectly fulfilling all those roles, and then has some ability to participate beyond that, fine, she is welcome in politics. But if her husband and children are suffering from her absence or her preoccupation with politics, then this is not Islam." It was widely known that Hanan's husband cared for their two daughters in her absence, was comfortable in the kitchen and proud of his wife's work. Ahmad Saati neither understood nor approved of any of this. "How," he asked contemptuously, "can I build homes for others when my own home is falling down?"

In Iran, which has tried to model many of its political institutions on those of the original Islamic community, women's political participation has been encouraged since the demonstrations that brought the revolution. There are women in the Parliament, and some women have risen to as high rank as deputy ministers.

After its revolution, Iran nodded once in the direction of democracy by holding a referendum asking the question: Islamic Republic, yes or no? An overwhelming "yes" opened the way for a ban on political parties and a prohibition on anyone standing for office who didn't support the goals of the Islamic revolution. In Iran everyone over the age of sixteen has the vote. Since voting is considered a religious duty, turnout is high. But the choice of candidates is strictly limited to those acceptable to the theocracy.

Marziyeh Dabbagh, one of four women elected to Iran's first postrevolutionary Parliament, is typical of politicians likely to succeed in the Iranian system. With a hunched asymmetry caused by severe beatings, she looks much older than her fifty-three years. Her wrists bear a bracelet of scars from cigarette burns, inflicted in the jails of the shah's secret police. Before the revolution Marziyeh used her father's book business as a front for arms smuggling and bomb making. When the police tracked her down and tried to torture information from her, they forced electrodes into her vagina, causing an infection so severe, she says, that "the Savak chief wouldn't come into my cell for the smell." In a final effort to extract a confession, the police tortured her twelve-year-old daughter. But even that failed. "When I heard my daughter screaming," she said, "I recited the Koran."

Marziyeh would probably have died in the Savak prison if a woman relative hadn't agreed to take her place while Marziyeh crept out disguised in the woman's chador. When she recovered her health, she went back to smuggling arms and training commandos from bases in Lebanon. During Khomeini's Paris exile, she became chief of his household security. She told me she'd never quite forgiven the press for making her miss Khomeini's historic flight home in 1979. The day before, a French reporter had tried to get a scoop by climbing into the ayatollah's house over a back wall. "I tackled him, and sprained my ankle," she confided. When she did get home, she found her military skills in heavy demand. For six months she commanded a Revolutionary Guards corps in her hometown of Hamdan. The men, she said, had no problems taking orders from a woman: "I knew how to shoot, and they didn't."

After her election to Parliament, she became one of Khomeini's two envoys to Mikhail Gorbachev when Iran restored relations with the Soviet Union. When Gorbachev extended his hand in greeting, she remembers a moment of alarm. Muslim women aren't allowed to touch unrelated men, but she didn't want to insult the Soviet leader at such a sensitive diplomatic moment. She solved the problem by sticking out her hand wrapped in her chador.

In Parliament, Marziyeh generally voted with the hard-liners on matters of foreign policy and economic reform. But she always supported initiatives for women, such as easing access to pensions, improving benefits for single mothers and ending discrimination in the distribution of foreign-study scholarships.

It seemed ironic that women like Marziyeh could get elected in hard-line Iran, while women in much more moderate Islamic countries often got nowhere. In Jordan women got the vote in 1973. Unfortunately, since Parliament was suspended in 1967, they didn't get a chance to exercise it until King Hussein finally called elections in 1989. Toujan Faisal, a forty-one-year-old TV presenter, thought she had a good chance of winning a seat. A year earlier, Toujan had been made moderator of a new chat show called "Women's Issues," which dealt each week with a particular topic of special concern to women. It had quickly become the most controversial TV show in Jordan's history. One program that deplored the high incidence of wife beating drew hundreds of letters from angry men, who insisted that beating their wives was a God-given right.

For Muslim feminists, few issues are more sensitive. "Good women are the obedient," says the Koran. "As for those from whom ye fear rebellion, admonish them and banish them to beds apart, and scourge them." Muslim feminists argue that "scourge" is only one of the possible translations for the word used in the Koran, *dharaba*. They say the word can also be translated as "strike with a feather." In the context of the Koran, which elsewhere urges gentle treatment of women, they argue, it is illogical to accept that the word is being used in its severest definition. The passage, they say, is meant to be read as a series of steps: first, admonish them; if that fails, withdraw sex; as a last resort, hit them lightly. No Muslim emulating Muhammad would ever go as far as the third step. While the prophet is known to have deprived his wives of sex as a punishment, there is no evidence that he ever raised a hand against them. One hadith records Muhammad telling his followers: "Some of your wives came to me complaining that their husbands have been beating them. I swear by Allah those are not the best among you." Toujan delved deep into the hadith to make her case for an end to domestic violence. But a literal reading of the Koran clearly sanctions beatings, and the men who attacked her were quick to brand her a heretic.

When the television station canceled her program after nearly a year of threats, Toujan decided to run for election. Part of her platform was reform of family law to give women more rights. Fundamentalists answered her candidacy by bringing charges against her in religious court, accusing her of apostasy. While the Koran prescribes death to apostates, Jordan doesn't sanction such executions. Still, if convicted, Toujan faced dissolution of her marriage and loss of custody of her children. Unsatisfied by that, her accusers also called for the lifting of penalties on any Muslim who chose to assassinate her. At her court appearances, Toujan had to be protected by the police from hordes of yelling zealots.

"I started getting calls in the middle of the night, women as well as men screaming at me," she said. "They promised I would die." Toujan was forced to campaign surrounded by volunteer bodyguards. Her husband, a gynecologist, had to close his clinic because of the intense harassment. In the election, Toujan finished third out of six candidates. Her seat was one of only two where electoral officers found evidence of serious irregularities, possibly fraud. No woman candidate won a seat in Parliament. The Islamicists ended up as the dominant faction, with twenty seats going to the Islamic Brotherhood and another dozen to independent Muslim hard-liners.

Immediately the Islamic bloc began campaigning for segregated schools, a ban on alcohol and an end to interest payments. In Parliament they introduced debates over issues as trivial as outlawing male hairdressers for women. When some were appointed ministers, the ministries they controlled became difficult places for women workers. Some were pressured to cover their hair; others, especially married women, were urged to resign to open jobs for unemployed men.

Soon Toujan had a steady stream of women turning up at the door of her small flat. "Most of them came to say how sorry they were that they hadn't taken the election more seriously," she said. Jordan's moderates, the wealthy and well educated, had been cynical about the election and hadn't believed that Jordan's king actually intended to give the Parliament real power. They'd used election day as a holiday, heading for the beach at Aqaba or on a shopping trip to Damascus, and hadn't bothered to vote. "All of them say they'll vote next time," said Toujan. "I just hope that by then it isn't too late."

When Jordanians went back to the polls in November 1993, more than sixty percent of the electorate voted, up from forty-one percent in 1989. The extra votes were enough to throw out almost half the fundamentalists and put Toujan into Parliament as Jordan's first elected woman representative.

The outcome rested in part on a nudge from King Hussein, who ordered subtle changes in voting rules to lessen the fundamentalists' advantage in urban areas, where their following was strongest. In a speech just before lifting a ban on mass rallies, Hussein warned those who "climb the pulpits . . . to fear God in what they say." The king's deftness lay in containing fundamentalist influence without excluding it from the political process and driving it underground, as had happened in Algeria.

But even without the electoral changes, Toujan's support had swelled. Many Jordanians admired her courage throughout a campaign in which extremists once again declared it a religious duty "to shed her blood." A competing candidate in Amman ran on a platform promising "to wrest women's constitutional rights" away from them.

"I did it by being myself, and it worked," said Toujan, ecstatic about her victory. Other women candidates didn't fare so well. Nadia Bouchnaq, a fifty-year-old with a record of three decades of social service, was stoned after leaving debates in which fundamentalists asked that a male answer questions directed to her, on the grounds that a woman's voice is too alluring to be heard in mixed company. Nadia greeted her loss philosophically. "There will come a time when people will get used to having women in Parliament," she said.

Toujan certainly aimed to make it so, and not by treading softly. Her first goal as a legislator was a modest but telling reform of one of the many laws that belittle women. She sought to change an old travel regulation that required wives to seek their husbands' permission before leaving the country. She also wanted to alter women's passports that list them as 'wife of,' 'widow of,' or 'divorcee of' a husband or ex-husband, rather than giving them the dignity of their own names.

It is still too early to know what Toujan will be able to accomplish in Parliament. But the extremists know she has already achieved something vastly significant just by being there, in place of one of those who tried every means to destroy her.

In some Islamic countries, even the idea of women politicians remains a distant dream. In Kuwait it was women, during the seven-month Iraqi occupation, who faced Iraqi bullets, demonstrating for the return of the emir. Women kept the small resistance movement alive, smuggling weapons and food, hiding foreigners and fighters. But when the emir came back, he showed his appreciation by declining to let them vote in the 1992 parliamentary election.

Before the invasion a medical student named Areej al-Khateeb did her political organizing from the car phone in her gold Mercedes sports car. The Iraqis stole the car, complete with its "I Love Democracy" bumper stickers. While Areej's socialist parents didn't care about Kuwait's traditional view of women, Areej herself trod a careful path, tempering her own feminist views with a keen sense of how far she could go and still be listened to by a wide range of her fellow university students. To conform to Kuwaiti traditions of separating the sexes, she organized separate rooms for women at political gatherings, with audio hookups so they could listen to the debate.

Across the border in Saudi Arabia, even the notion of a debate is anathema. Saudi Arabia has virtually no political culture. "We don't need democracy, we have our own 'desert democracy,'" explained Nabila al-Bassam, a Saudi woman who ran her own clothing and gift store in Dhahran. What she was referring to was an ancient desert tradition known as the *majlis*, weekly gatherings hosted by members of the ruling family, where any of their subjects were free to present petitions or air grievances. In fact, the majlis was an intensely feudal scene, with respectful subjects waiting humbly for a few seconds' opportunity to whisper in their prince's ear.

Nabila told me of a friend who had recently petitioned King Fahd's wife to allow the legal import of hair-salon equipment. Technically, hairdressing salons were banned in Saudi Arabia, where the religious establishment frowned on anything that drew women from their houses. In fact, thriving salons owned by prominent Saudis and staffed by Filipina or Syrian beauticians did a roaring trade. "My friend is tired of having to run her business in secret," Nabila said. But so far she had received no response to her petition. "Petitions *do* work," said Nabila. "But in this society you have to do things on a friendly basis, like a family. You can ask for things, but you can't just reach out and take things as if it's your right." A rejected petitioner had no choice but to accept the al-Sauds' decision. With no free press and no way to mobilize public opinion, the al-Sauds ruled as they liked.

If there was one thing that Saudi women were prepared to criticize about their lot, it was the ban that prevented them from driving. During the Gulf War the sight of pony-tailed American servicewomen driving trucks and Humvees on Saudi Arabian roads invigorated a long-simmering debate on the issue. The Americans weren't the only women drivers the war had brought. Many Kuwaiti women, fleeing the Iraqi invasion, had arrived in Saudi Arabia unveiled, at the wheel of the family Mercedes.

By October 1990, articles about Saudi women seeking the right to drive had begun appearing in the heavily censored press. Women quoted in these articles said they'd been alarmed to realize that they wouldn't have been able to transport their children to safety as the Kuwaiti women had done. Some raised economic issues, calculating that twenty percent of average Saudi family income was spent on drivers, who had to be fed and housed as well as paid a salary. Saudi Arabia had 300,000 full-time private chauffeurs—a staggering number, but still far short of providing a driver for every Saudi woman who needed mobility. Women without their own drivers could get around only at the whim of husbands and sons. Some proponents of allowing women to drive played the Islam card, pointing out how undesirable it was for a woman to be forced to have a strange man as part of her household, and to drive around alone with him.

On a Tuesday afternoon in early November, forty-seven women, driven by their chauffeurs, converged on the parking lot of the Al Tamimi supermarket in downtown Riyadh. There, they dismissed their drivers. About a quarter then slid into the drivers' seats of their cars, the rest taking their places as passengers. They drove off in convoy down the busy thoroughfare. A few blocks later, the cane-wielding *mutawain* of the Committee for the Promotion of Virtue and the Prevention of Vice stopped the cars at intersections, ordering the women out of the drivers' seats. Soon, regular police arrived, and the women asked them to see that they weren't taken off to the mutawain headquarters. There was a scuffle between the mutawain, who yelled that the women had committed a religious crime, and the traffic police, who said the matter was their affair. In the end, the police drove the women's cars to police headquarters with a mutawa in the passenger seat and the women in the back.

The women who had taken part in the demonstration were all from what Saudis call "good families"—wealthy, prominent clans with close ties to the ruling al-Saud dynasty. All the women who actually drove were mature professionals who had international drivers' licenses they'd acquired overseas. Many of them were from the faculty of the women's branch of Riyadh's university, such as Fatin al-Zamil, a professor of medicine. Others were women of achievement such as Aisha al-Mana, who had a doctorate in sociology from the University of Colorado and headed a consortium of women-owned businesses from fashion to computer-training centers. Even though some of these women didn't normally veil their faces, for the demonstration all wore the covering that leaves only eyes exposed.

Before the demonstration, the women had sent a petition to the governor of Riyadh, Prince Salman bin Abdul Aziz, who was thought to be a fairly progressive member of the ruling family. The petition begged King Fahd to open his "paternal heart" to what they termed their "humane demand" to drive. They argued that women of the prophet's era had ridden camels, the main mode of transportation of their day. The evidence, they wrote in their petition, was there in Islam, "such is the greatness of the teacher of humanity and the master of men in leaving lessons that are as clear as the sunlight to dispel the darkness of ignorance."

While the women were held at the police station, Prince Salman summoned a group of prominent religious and legal experts to discuss what they had done. The legal scholars concluded that no civil violations had occurred, since the women all had international drivers' licenses recognized by Saudi law. The religious representatives found that no moral issues were at stake, since the women were veiled and the Koran says nothing that could be construed as forbidding an act such as driving. The women were released.

In Jeddah and Dhahran, women gathered to plan parallel demonstrations, encouraged by what they saw as tacit support from the ruling family. But then came the backlash.

Word of the demonstration spread quickly, despite a total blackout of coverage in the Saudi media. When the women who had taken part arrived for work the next day at the university, they expected to be greeted as heroines by their all-women students. Instead, some found their office doors daubed with graffiti, criticizing them as un-Islamic. Others found their classes boycotted by large numbers of conservative students. Soon denunciations spewed from the mosques. Leaflets flooded the streets. Under a heading "Names of the Promoters of Vice and Lasciviousness," the demonstration participants were listed, along with their phone numbers, and a designation of either "American secularist," or "communist" after each name. "These Are the Roots of Calamity," the leaflets shrieked. "Uproot them! Uproot them! Uproot them! Purify the Land of Monotheism." Predictably, the women's phones began ringing off the hook with abusive calls. If their husbands answered, they were told to divorce their whorish wives, or berated for being unable to control them.

The royal family immediately caved in to the extremists' pressures. Prince Salman's committee's findings were quickly buried. Instead, the government suspended the women from their jobs and confiscated their passports. The security police also arrested a prominent, well-connected Saudi man accused of leaking word of the protest to a British film crew. He was given a grueling interrogation, including a beating, and thrown in jail for several weeks.

The ruling family could have stood by the women on Islamic grounds. What the extremists were doing was entirely contrary to the Koran, which excoriates anyone who impugns a woman's reputation and sentences them to eighty lashes.

But a week after the demonstration Prince Naif bin Abdul Aziz, the interior minister, joined the slanderers. At a meeting in Mecca he denounced the demonstration as "a stupid act" and said some of the women involved were raised outside Saudi Arabia and "not brought up in an Islamic home." He then read out a new *fatwa,* or ruling with the force of law, from Saudi Arabia's leading sheik, Abdul Aziz bin Baz, stating that women driving contradicted "Islamic traditions followed by Saudi citizens." If driving hadn't been illegal before, it was now. Naif's remarks got front-page coverage, the first mention of the driving demonstration that had appeared in the Saudi press.

Although I had been in touch with some of the women drivers before the demonstration, none of them would take my calls afterward. They all had been warned that any contact with foreign media would lead to rearrest. All were sure that their phones were tapped and their homes watched. I did get a sad letter, signed simply "A proud Saudi woman" detailing the "witch hunt" under way. "Fanatics," she wrote, "are forcing students to sign petitions denouncing the women." They were "using this incident to demonstrate their strength and foment antiliberal, antigovernment and anti-American feelings." Another woman sent me a simple message: "I did it because I want my granddaughters to be able to say I was there."

I also talked to a relative of one of the women who'd taken part. "I encouraged her," he said sadly. "I thought the time was right. Now the cause has been set back ten years—buried under twenty tons of concrete. It's so easy for people like me"—a diplomat's son raised abroad and educated in America—"to be totally off base about this country and what it is ready to accept."

Chapter 11

MUSLIM WOMEN'S GAMES

"O true believers, forbid not the good things which God has allowed you; but transgress not, for God loveth not the transgressors."

THE KORAN
THE CHAPTER OF THE TABLE

As the torchbearer at the opening ceremony of the first Islamic Women's Games entered the arena, ten thousand spectators burst into a deafening cheer. Her stride long and rhythmic, the athlete loped around the track as the torch flames licked the air above her hooded head.

High in the stands, among the crowd, her father almost burst with pride. The torchbearer, eighteen-year-old Padideh Bolourizadeh, had been an Iranian track star since she was seven. But this was the first time her father had ever seen her run.

He was able to watch because Padideh was wearing the world's first track suit-hijab. The suit's white hood concealed every wisp of hair, and a black, ankle-length tunic slid under a long jersey and flapped around the ankles of her sweatpants.

At the center of the arena, all-women sports teams from ten Muslim countries lined up behind their national flags. Every now and then, among the contingents from Syria and Turkmenistan, it was possible to notice a surreptitious hand fiddling with an unfamiliar headscarf.

The next day, when the contests began in earnest, the athletes stripped down to their more familiar Lycra shorts and skimpy singlets. At the basketball stadium, as the captain of the Iranian team sprinted down the court past the Azerbaijanis to slamdunk the ball, ecstatic women spectators packing the stands raised a roar that would have drowned out a Metrodome crowd at a Twins' World Series game. Outside the stadium door, armed policemen paced the sidewalk, to make sure no men entered. Inside, high on the stadium wall, a larger-than-life-sized portrait of Khomeini gazed down on the sweaty, shorts-clad women athletes. In art, if not in life, his craggy countenance gave just the merest hint of a smile.

I had heard about the first Islamic Women's Games in early February 1993, when Mary Glen Haig, a British representative of the International Olympic Committee, phoned me at home in London to get advice about what a Western woman should pack for a trip to Tehran. The International Olympic Committee, she said, had been invited to observe the games and she—a former Olympic fencing champion—was to be the observer.

A few days later, having wangled an invitation of my own, I went looking for her among the contestants and spectators at the track and field stadium, to see what she was making of the events so far. Someone pointed me to an official table, where a black-hooded woman sat alongside a sporty, svelte figure with bobbed blond hair, a denim jacket over a Liberty-print shirt, blue jeans and Asics athletic shoes. I'd explained on the phone that it wasn't necessary to wear hijab at all-women gatherings, but I was surprised that she'd dressed so casually. I wandered over and introduced myself. The blonde smiled and held out her hand. "Faezeh Hashemi," she said. "Vice-president of the *Iranian* Olympic Committee. This," she said, indicating the woman in the black hood, "is our British guest from the International Committee."

Faezeh Hashemi was President Hashemi Rafsanjani's thirty-year-old daughter and the brains behind the first Islamic Women's Games. Women's sports had practically disappeared after the Islamic revolution, when the mullahs put an abrupt end to the mixed training and competition that had taken place under the shah. The idea of girls, in revealing athletic gear, training alongside boys had turned many religious Iranians against sports, especially for women.

"There is no fun in Islam," Khomeini had told his flock in a radio sermon in 1979. During his lifetime the city of Tehran reflected his opinion. A combination of an economically ruinous war with Iraq and the eagle eyes of Islamic zealots turned the city into a gray place of sandbagged buildings and circumspect citizens. All the old prerevolutionary night spots were gone. Even the Hiltons and the Kentucky Fried Chicken joints were changed utterly. Terrible hybrids had been born, such as the former Intercontinental Hotel on the former Los Angeles Boulevard, which had become the Flower of Martyrdom Hotel on Hijab Street, where mold bloomed in the bathrooms and a sign saying "Down With U.S.A." loomed in the lobby.

And yet even Khomeini hadn't been entirely oblivious to the need for bodily fitness. His own daily routine included a walk—round and round the courtyard of his house.

The wealthy, landowning Rafsanjani clan had taken a much more freewheeling approach to exercise, even having a little unmullah-like fun. In the privacy of their own family compound, Rafsanjani's two daughters and three sons swam, bicycled, played table tennis and volley ball. Before the duties of the presidency took up all his time, Rafsanjani himself often joined his kids in the pool or at table tennis.

After the 1979 revolution most of Iran's sports facilities had simply been handed over to men. The government set up an important-sounding "Directorate of Women's Sports Affairs" in 1980, but it remained nothing but a name until 1985, when an odd alliance of Iranian women began a patient campaign to get women's sports back on the agenda. Some of the activists were Iran's former women athletes—a few of them Olympic-class competitors—who had been forced out of sportswear and into hijab. Athletes who hadn't gone into exile eventually adopted an "if you can't beat 'em, join 'em," philosophy, and reached out to women's groups within the religious establishment for help. It was Faezeh Hashemi, who could speak the language of the radical mullahs, who proved their best ally. Faezeh had many assets, including her father's backing. As a master's degree student in management at the University of Tehran, she knew a lot about manipulating organizations.

Like most religious women who wanted to get something done, she built the foundations of her case on the prophet's hadith. Muhammad is on the record as recommending that Muslims have "strong bodies." He also said: "You shall excel in all respects if you are the believers." Faezeh argued that sports should be part of the search for excellence, and that these recommendations applied equally to women and men. Women, as the lynchpins of the Islamic family, needed the physical and mental benefits that sports could provide. Fine, the conservatives responded; let them follow a program of exercise in the privacy of their homes. Faezeh responded that women and girls shouldn't be robbed of the social benefits of teamwork and competition.

The prophet is said to have praised three sports in particular: swimming, archery and horseback riding. Since the hadith, "Teach your children swimming and archery," used the Arabic word *awalaad*, which may be translated either as "sons" or "children," and not the more specific *awalaad wa binaat*—sons and daughters—some strict parents argued that only sons were meant to take part in such pursuits. But archery's modern equivalent, pistol or rifle shooting, was a useful skill in a revolutionary country recently at war and was one of the few sports that could be done in a chador. So shooting ranges were among the first sports facilities to welcome women, at first as members of civil defense militias, and later just as women looking for a hobby that would get them out of the house.

Faezeh argued that Iran's Islamic government could differentiate itself from the old shah regime by demonstrating that it was interested in "sports for all women," rather than the elite squad of top-flight athletes the shah had encouraged to show off amid the "corruption" of mixed international competitions. Her arguments led to the handing back of sports facilities for certain "women's hours" each week, and more emphasis on sports in girls' schools. Eventually Tehran's woodsy "Runners' Park" banned men three days a week, between eight and four, so women could jog without hijab.

Then Faezeh began to tackle the much more difficult question of international competition. Many Islamic countries kept their women out of international arenas: sometimes because of considerations of modesty, sometimes because of lack of money, and sometimes both. With tight sports budgets, countries such as Pakistan that had many Olympic-class women competitors sent none of them to the Barcelona Olympics. "The men, basically, are better than we, and the government selects those who are in with a chance," said Firhana Ayaz, a sports writer with the *Pakistan Observer*. But she also saw a growing Islamic influence behind such decisions. In Pakistan most women athletes played in modest costumes of loose, long T-shirts over long pants, but that was no longer seen as adequate in some circles. "Mullahs have been making an issue of field hockey lately, because you have to run and bend. And during the Olympics, none of the women's events were televised, because of pressure from the mullahs."

When Hassiba Boulmerka, the Algerian runner, won a gold medal for her country at the Barcelona Olympics, she made a moving speech about her victory, saying she was glad to show that a Muslim woman could achieve such things. But not all of the Islamic world cheered her triumph. In Algeria the main Muslim political party, the Islamic Salvation Front, denounced her from the mosques for running "half naked" in shorts and a vest, and forced her to leave the country to avoid harassment while she trained.

While some Iranians joined in branding Hassiba "a phony Muslim," Faezeh Hashemi saw the danger in such denunciations from Islamists who weren't offering any positive alternatives. Muslims, she said, should be happy if any Muslim sportswoman excelled. All Muslim countries had different traditions, she said, and it was up to Iran to demonstrate the superiority of a truly Islamic system. She argued that the "oppressors," meaning Western countries, used Muslim women's absence from the sports field as an example of women's inferior position in Islamic countries. "If Islamic countries can't come up with their own principles for women's competition," she said in one widely reported speech, "then the way dictated by Western oppressing countries will be imposed on us." Iran sent men's teams to international contests. Why not, she said, let those women who excelled in any of the five sports that could be done in hijab go too?

In September 1990 she won her point, and when the Iranian

team joined the march at the opening of the Asian Games in Beijing, six chador-clad women—the Iranian shooting team—led the way. One of them, an eighteen-year-old student named Elham Hashemi, managed to break the Iranian men's record.

By the Atlanta Olympics in 1996, Faezeh hoped to be able to send a squad of hijab-wearing equestrians as well. I doubted she'd win that one. It's quite possible to show-jump wearing a neck-hiding wimple under a riding helmet and a tunic covering the legs down to the tops of riding boots, but what if a rider fell off her horse and was photographed with limbs sprawled and, heaven forfend, scarf askew? Conservatives were already arguing against women archers being allowed to compete in front of men, because the motion of pulling back the bowstring was too revealing, even in a chador.

For most of Iran's women athletes—runners, swimmers, high jumpers—competing in hijab wasn't even a remote possibility. It was for them that Faezeh had come up with the notion of an alternative Olympics, the Islamic Women's Games, where women athletes from Muslim countries would gather in hijab for an opening ceremony that both men and women could attend. Afterward, the athletes would toss off their coverings and compete against each other with only women watching.

The paradox of her scheme was that the strict Muslim countries whose women could have benefited from the games' women-only environment had no women athletes to send. In Saudi Arabia and most of the Gulf States, there were no women's sporting organizations of any kind. Women's competition, even strictly segregated, didn't exist. Wealthy women who wanted to keep fit maintained well-equipped gyms in their homes and hired personal trainers. The rest led completely sedentary lives.

The countries that jumped at Iran's invitation were the former Soviet Muslim republics, whose women athletes had been trained in the Soviet sports juggernaut. None of them had ever veiled; few had cracked the binding on a Koran. But, with the collapse of the Soviet system, nominally Muslim republics such as Azerbaijan were strapped for cash for luxuries such as sports. "Our entire budget for this year is enough to send one athlete to one competition—so long as it's in Europe," sighed Alyev Mouslim, the Azerbaijani team manager. For him, an all-expenses-paid trip for a hundred and twenty women athletes—even if they had to veil and sit on a bus for the twenty-six-hour bus ride from Baku—was an offer too good to refuse.

As always with Iran, politics played a part. Iran was prepared to pay for big teams from the former Soviet republics because it was anxious to extend its influence there. But it balked at footing the bill for countries such as Sudan, that were already firmly in its orbit. So the cash-strapped Sudanese didn't send women to the games. Nor did countries such as Egypt, which had sour relations with the Iranian government. Others sent tiny teams as a good-will gesture. "We are here to say 'yes' to the Iranian system," said a diminutive table-tennis player from the five-woman Maldives squad. "But from a sports point of view, it's pointless for us," she said, shivering as a light snow fell outside Tehran's underheated table-tennis center. "We're from the equator. It's impossible to get warmed up in this place."

In the end, the former Soviet republics had the biggest teams, in every sense. Altogether, four republics sent 332 athletes, most of them tall, big-boned blondes who towered over the 51 women from the small squads sent by Malaysia, Syria, Pakistan, Maldive and Bangladesh.

Some of the women were national champions; one or two were Olympians. But for all but the shooting team in the 122-member Iranian squad, this chance at international competition was a first. Under their chadors, their faces shone as they marched into the 12,000-seat Azadi stadium.

During the games men were banished from the stands at all but the shooting range. At the swimming complex, schoolgirls filled the spectators' benches, peering down at the unfamiliar sight of Iranian lane judges uniformed in fetching purple miniskirts and acid-green T-shirts.

At the track stadium Padideh, the torchbearer, had shaken off her hijab in favor of black Lycra shorts and had literally risen to the occasion by adding nine centimeters to her personal best in the high jump. Her jump, at 1.67 meters, wasn't good enough to beat the Kyrgyzistan champion, but it broke the Iranian record, set before the revolution. That afternoon, back at the athletes' hotel, Padideh was ebullient. At heats for the 400-meter race, she had made the final four and was beginning to allow herself to hope that the next day might bring her a medal.

Although Padideh's mother had been a sportswoman during the days of the shah, Padideh had grown up knowing nothing but segregated sports. "This is nice for us," she said, waving a hand at the foyer full of women athletes. "Our way of thinking, our culture is this way," said Padideh. "It would be hard for us, now, to compete in front of men."

Official translators milled among the athletes, facilitating conversations. Each of them wore the usual Iranian attire—black hood and long tunic—but with a vivid, color-coded athletes' warmup jacket pulled incongruously on top. Indigo and acid green meant the translator spoke English; pink and chrome yellow, Russian; lime and sky blue, Arabic. As conversations bounced from Farsi to Urdu to English, the hotel lobby filled with a pleasant, feminine buzz. It reminded me of sports day at my all-girl high school.

But in one corner a group of men sat self-consciously, murmuring together in Russian, without the aid of the young women translators. Alyev Mouslim, the Azerbaijani team's administrator, sighed as he leaned against the wall, waiting for the elevator marked "Special for Men." He was finding it hard to manage athletes who disappeared early in the morning on women-only buses, bound for arenas he wasn't allowed to enter. "Actually," he said, "I don't have it so bad; I don't have to coach." The Kyrgyzistan volleyball coach had had to wait outside during his team's matches for one of the women to grab a scarf and come out to tell him what was happening so he could make decisions on tactics. Alyev shrugged. "If we can play chess without seeing the board, why not this, too?"

I wondered if he was bored, being unable to go to the matches. "Not at all," he said. "I have my hands full with all the problems my team is having acclimating to these regulations." Some of the women had fallen foul of the Iranians because their big floral scarves kept slipping off. "It seems like the biggest fault here is if anybody sees your hair. But if God doesn't like this, why did he give you eyes?" Others resented the rule against women going out alone to tour the city between their events. The Iranian officials were taking a hyper-protective attitude toward their women guests, insisting that they travel only on official buses, and only with an official translator along. As someone who had wandered the streets of Tehran at all hours unmolested, I thought the rule silly, and likely to give the wrong impression. For a woman alone, Tehran was one of the safest cities in the world.

Murshida Mustakim thought the rule was pretty stupid, too. She had stunned one of the gun-toting male Revolutionary Guards who had tried to block her exit from the hotel. "I told him I was a retired superintendent of the Malaysian police force, and that I'd spent an entire career giving orders to boys like him," she said. "Then I told him to get out of my way." Murshida, a towering woman with the shoulders of a longshoreman, had come to Tehran as coach of the shooting team, who were all policewomen on the Malaysian force.

For her, trips to countries such as Iran and Saudi Arabia, which she'd visited as a pilgrim to Mecca, were like visits to the past. In her lifetime Malaysia had moved away from a doctrinaire approach to Islam. "When I was growing up, there was a lot of difficulty about girls being uncovered for sports," she said. While Malaysians' figure-hugging sarongs wouldn't have passed muster as hijab in Tehran, conservative Malays believed that their ankle length provided an essential degree of Muslim modesty. Murshida had been a hurdle racer. "I used to unwrap my sarong just before the starter's pistol, run the race in shorts, and then quickly retie the sarong at the finish line." These days, she said, most Malaysian Muslims were relaxed about their faith and accepted women's right to dress as they pleased and participate in society alongside men. But even her distant country hadn't been entirely immune to the Islamic revival, and many young women had started wearing long veils that covered the head and upper body. In one state, Kelantan, local voters had recently ushered in a fundamentalist mini-state, complete with "morals patrols" to catch unmarried couples dating.

I sat beside Murshida on the bus to one of the Iranians' official outings: a trip to the tomb of Ayatollah Khomeini. Most of the excursions had followed a similar theme: a visit to the Museum of Reversion and Admonition, a.k.a. the former shah's palace; a tour of an exhibition entitled "The Dignity and Prestige of Women in the Islamic System." Before the buses set off for the long drive to Khomeini's gold-domed shrine on the southern edge of the city, chador-wearing Iranian officials boarded, carrying boxes of Kleenex. At first I had the bizarre thought that they were arming us against the onrush of emotion we would no doubt feel at the sight of Khomeini's grave. But then I realized that what they were worried about was the lipstick that some of the non-Iranian athletes were wearing. Murshida politely took a proffered tissue and swiped at her glossy red lips. "Well," she said, "there'd be one good thing about staying here: I could save a fortune on makeup."

Not necessarily. At the final day of track events, makeup-less athletes and officials filed off the buses and past the guards at the stadium door. Inside, they shook off their hijab and raced for the women's changing room to powder noses and apply mascara. Everyone wanted to look her best for the videotaped record of the games that a camerawoman was making for later screening at women's gatherings all over Iran.

Padideh, the Iranian runner, sat by herself, nervously fingering worry beads as she waited for her shot at a medal in the 400 meters final. The night before, I'd commiserated with a Pakistani runner who had blown her heat and missed a chance at the final of her best event. It was a disaster for her, but by the next day she was already looking forward to another chance at the Asian Games, or the Pan-Pacifics, or one of half a dozen international contests she would attend in the following year or two.

For Padideh, everything rested on this one brief race. It would be four years before she had another chance at international competition. As she crouched at the starting line, her leggy, foallike figure looked frail alongside the muscular athletes from Turkmenistan, Kyrgyzistan and Azerbaijan. At the crack of the starter's pistol, she sped away, her long, loping stride keeping pace with that of her meatier competitors.

But it was a brief illusion of parity. A third of the way through the race, she had already fallen behind, and the strain of her initial effort showed in her face. For Padideh, training had to fit in between university classes, in the brief women's hours allowed at her nearby stadium. She had never worked out with weights or been trained by a professional coach. She fell across the finish line more than three seconds behind the winner and almost two seconds shy of the third-place runner. Collapsing on the ground, she grasped at her chest and gulped for air between sobs of pain and disappointment.

It was impossible to say whether Padideh could have been a champion in a different time and place, in a system that cared less for modesty and more for methodical training. But her time in the 400 meters, though nowhere near good enough to beat the competition, had shaved a remarkable eight seconds from her previous personal best.

At the farewell dinner after the games' closing ceremony, Padideh had regained her composure and spoke proudly of the bronze medal she'd helped win for the Iranian relay team. "Of course, I would have liked a medal of my own," she said, "and now I'll never get one." I reminded her that Pakistan and Azerbaijan had both talked of hosting an Islamic Women's Games in four years' time. Perhaps she would win her medal then.

She shook her head and gave a swift, sad smile. "No," she said, looking away. "Someone else maybe. For me, I think, it's just too late."

Chapter 12

A DIFFERENT DRUMMER

"O true believers, turn unto
God with a sincere repentance:
peradventure your God will do
away from you your evil deeds,
and will admit you into gardens,
through which rivers flow."

THE KORAN
THE CHAPTER OF BANNING

*S*oheir el-Babli, the doyen of the Cairo stage, seemed to
have it all. One of the biggest box-office draws in a city that has
always loved its performers, her starring role as "Attiya, the Terrorist
Woman," had been packing them in for a year at the 700-seat Misr
Art Theater.

Then, suddenly, as the play was about to begin its second season
in July 1993, she quit. She was, she said, renouncing show business
for good and adopting the Islamic veil.

Soheir's retirement was part of a wave of resignations by
women artists that had begun with Cairo's belly dancers back in the
late 1980s. Soon, dozens of singers and actresses also were hanging up
their spangles, wiping off their makeup, donning hijab and harangu-
ing their former audiences about the evils of the artists' world. By the
spring of 1992 the unthinkable had happened: the musicals with dancing that had enlivened the nightly celebrations of Ramadan were
banned as un-Islamic, depriving hundreds of artists of work.

But when Soheir resigned, the artists' world fought back. The
play's producer-director had already reworked the script for the second season to include references to the recent wave of terrorist bomb-
ings by Islamic extremists. To replace Soheir, he chose his own

twenty-two-year-old daughter, a student at American University in Cairo, whose only theatrical experience had been student productions.

At the play's reopening night, a who's who of the Egyptian artistic world turned out to show their support. It was the beginning of a backlash: for the first time, artists had stood up together in criticism of religiously motivated retirements and fundamentalist pressure on entertainment. A joke began making the rounds of Cairo: Who are the second-best-paid women in Egypt? The belly dancers, of course, because the Saudi tourists throw hundred-dollar bills beneath their feet when they dance. Who are the best paid? The dancers who've retired for Allah, of course, because the Saudi sheiks throw thousand-dollar bills into their bank accounts when they stop dancing.

The sudden veil-takings all tended to follow the same pattern. A famous woman performer would appear on the popular television program of Sheik Mohamed Sharawi, Egypt's equivalent of a televangelist. There she would denounce her former career as un-Islamic, take a veil from the aged sheik and put it on, with his blessing.

Cynical Egyptians believed the Saudis funded a special expense account for Sharawi to buy up women artists. "If it isn't for the money, why do it on television? Why not do it in private, with Allah for their witness?" asked Nawal Saadawi, Egypt's most outspoken feminist.

The newly veiled women certainly seemed to have plenty of cash. One of the first to veil, Shams al-Barudi, had spent a fortune buying the copyright to films in which she had appeared scantily dressed, including one particularly daring bathtub scene in which she'd appeared almost nude. She was determined, she said, that the films should never be shown again. She declined to comment on the source of the money she was using to buy the rights to her old films, but gossip in the Cairo movie business said it had been provided by a prominent clergyman.

Nawal Saadawi cynically pointed out that many of the women were past their prime as actresses or dancers anyway. "They know they're soon going to have to retire, so why not go out in a blaze of publicity? You've heard the joke on the streets: people are saying that these dancers were happy to make their fortune from sin in their youth. Now, in their old age, they want to share the pleasure of paradise with the poor."

But Nawal's own predicament provided another explanation for the rush to get behind the veil. As a psychiatrist and senior government health official in the 1960s, she had seen the physical and emotional effects of genital mutilation on Egyptian women. Her first book, *Women and Sex*, published in 1970, had been a condemnation of the distorted Islamic teaching she felt was responsible for ruining women's lives. Despite losing her job and spending three months in prison, she continued to write about taboo subjects in more than thirty books. She described the childhood trauma of her own clitoridectomy and how it had left her incapable of orgasm, wrote about the demand for prewedding hymen replacement in the surgical wards of Cairo, and exposed an epidemic of incest in Egyptian families.

In newspapers and public meetings she attacked powerful sheiks. On one of his television programs, Sheik Sharawi excoriated those who chose to lull themselves to sleep with Western classical music instead of the melodic drone of a Koran reading. A few days later extremist youths in Upper Egypt were arrested for storming a concert and breaking musical instruments. Nawal wrote a newspaper article asking why the government arrested the youths, and not Sharawi, whose ideas had inflamed them.

In the summer of 1992, Islamic Jihad put Nawal Saadawi on its death list, along with the writer Farag Foda. When Farag was shot dead outside his office, the Egyptian government that had often persecuted Nawal suddenly provided her with a round-the-clock military guard. Mindful that Sadat's assassin had been part of an extremist Islamic cell within the Egyptian army, Nawal found the presence outside her door of army conscripts rather less than reassuring. "I'm more afraid of them than I am of anyone else," she confided. In 1993 she went into exile, taking a post as a visiting professor at Duke University in America.

If authors were already targets, Nawal reasoned, it was only a matter of time before less political artists would come under direct attack. The dancers who renounced their profession often talked about the anxiety and fear that had been replaced by calm once they resigned from the stage. One famous dancer, Halah al-Safi, talked of a dream she'd had of walking by a mosque and feeling dread because she wasn't wearing the proper clothing. Suddenly, she said, a man in her dream took off his cloak and covered her. Nawal pointed out that it wasn't necessary to be a psychiatrist to interpret the fear in Halah's dream as a subconscious response to the pressure from religious extremists.

In 1993, Nawal's prediction was proved correct. When Farida Seif el Nasr decided to return to show business after having announced her retirement, an unknown assailant attempted to murder her with a volley of gunshots.

At my office, Sahar gloated over each new story of an artist's return to the veil. One morning she looked up from one of the local papers to read me an item about a famous dancer who had wanted to make the Hajj. The religious authorities had refused to give the woman the necessary papers unless she quit dancing. Sahar approved of their decision. "Why should she be able to go, spending money she earned sinning, and stand on the Plain of Arafat as though she's a good Muslim?" Sahar said.

But I was sorry to see Egypt's beautiful traditional dance being denigrated and threatened. I'd watched my first Egyptian dancer through a jet-lagged haze just after we arrived in Cairo, when a friend invited us to dinner at the Nile Hilton's nightclub. Egyptians keep late hours, and I struggled through dinner to keep my face from falling into my plate of stuffed pigeon. But once the dancing started I forgot all about fatigue.

Souhair Zaki swirled onto the stage along a pathway of sound. The slow rise and fall of the flute undulated in waves through her body. For the first time, the atonal Arabic music made sense to me. I could *see* it, weaving through space in elaborate arabesques. And I could see something else: the beauty of a woman's body that was neither young nor thin. Souhair Zaki was the most celebrated dancer in Cairo, but she hadn't seen thirty in a while. Flesh clung heavily to her hips. Her abdomen bulged like a ripe pear. I had never seen traditional oriental dance before, but I recognized every movement.

What she was doing with her body was what a woman's body *did*—
the natural movements of sex and childbirth. The dance drew the eye
to the hips and abdomen; the very center of the female body's womanliness.

As a girl I'd learned the profoundly unnatural movements of
Western ballet, whose aim was to make the body seem as insubstan-
tial as air. With its stress on elongation and fluttering extremities,
ballet denied womanliness, requiring adult dancers to retain the shape
of prepubescent girls. By the time I was fourteen the studio where I
did my classes was a miserable place, full of students who knew
they'd never be ballerinas. Their bodies had betrayed them by becoming too tall, too round, too womanly. I decided that, before I left
Egypt, I'd try to learn this other more ancient dance, whose every
movement celebrated a woman's body as it actually was.

Religious pressure had already forced Cairo's dancers to wear
one-piece costumes that didn't expose their bare midriffs. Anything
too revealing warranted a visit from a special squad known as the
"politeness police." Occasional items in the newspapers documented
raids on nightclubs where dancers' acts were too erotic or their costumes too revealing. One dancer in particular, Sahar Hamdi, was always being hauled to jail. Going through the newspapers, Sahar
would read me these items about her namesake, shaking her veiled
head in disapproval. Sahar Hamdi was the darling of the rich Saudi
tourists. Some nights she would dance on a stage covered by
banknotes and have her dance-weary feet bathed by the Saudis'
champagne. But by 1993 she too had supposedly seen the light and
was talking of retirement for the sake of religion.

Fundamentalists, impatient with the pace of artists' resignations,
wanted the government to ban belly dance at once, and for good. But
belly dancing was a big draw for the rich Arabs from the Persian Gulf
who poured into Cairo every summer. To accommodate both sides,
the government came up with one of its famous half measures: it
stopped issuing permits to new performers other than classical folk
artists but didn't ban the dance outright. When I decided to write a
story about the controversy, Sahar looked at the floor and said nothing. "Do you want me to find someone else to translate?" I asked. She
nodded. She didn't want to visit Cairo nightclubs or talk to dancers.

She had told me once that Souhair Zaki had danced at her parents' wedding. Now, Sahar felt that the way Souhair displayed her body was sinful.

But even Sahar wasn't all that comfortable with demands on the government to ban this and ban that. She felt religion was a personal matter that shouldn't be turned into political compulsion. The Islamic revolution she wanted would come through the gradual persúasion of people, not through force. That attitude had prevailed in Egypt and seemed to have served the country well. It was easy to buy alcohol in Cairo, but none of my Egyptian friends drank. Where Saudis had to be herded to prayers by religious police, Egyptians poured voluntarily into their mosques. Many had the dark, permanent bruise of the devout on their foreheads, acquired by a lifetime of touching the head to the ground in prayer.

If belly dance were banned, it would set a disturbing precedent and lead to increased clamor for further Islamic restrictions. To see how serious the new rules were, I went to visit Mahmoud Ramadan, an official with the Department of Artistic Inspection. Mahmoud had been the chief inspector of dancers, issuing permits to performers whose costumes and choreography weren't too risqué. "I had a wonderful job in those days," he sighed. He had seen performances by all of Egypt's leading artists. To him, the real stars had shone in the 1950s, when every Egyptian movie included a belly-dance sequence. The dancers had been idolized and paid up to three thousand pounds a night to perform onstage and at fancy weddings.

Now, Mahmoud was watching those women grow old, with no newcomers rising to replace them. "The next generation isn't as good, and after them, well . . ." His voice trailed off as he gestured at the empty desk in front of him.

The restrictions also threatened the band of women artisans who sewed the dancers' elaborate costumes. The most famous costumier in Egypt inhabited a tiny cubicle in the midst of the vast Khan el Khalili bazaar. Inside, a glittering profusion of glass beads and glossy fabrics spilled out of boxes stacked to the ceiling. Customers could leaf through a book of photographs showing possible designs—skirts embroidered with sunbursts in blazes of orange and gold or peacocks in indigo and aqua. An aged seamstress took the orders and the clients' measurements. "No Egyptians anymore," she lamented. That day her customers had been a Finn and a German. As I fingered beads and tried on belts, another woman entered. She spoke to the seamstress in heavily accented Arabic, full of guttural "ch" sounds. "Excuse me," I said in English. "Are you Israeli?"

"Yes," she said. "I came on the bus from Jerusalem today." Before the peace treaty between Egypt and Israel, she had to send European friends to buy her costumes for her. "They never fitted properly," she said. "Peace has been very good for my act." Not so good was the attention she was receiving back in Israel from fundamentalist Jews. Like their Muslim counterparts, they wanted belly dance banned. They were threatening to withdraw the kashrut certificate—the proof that food was prepared in accordance with Jewish law—from the hotels in which she performed. The daughter of Orthodox Jews herself, she had little patience with the rabbis. "This dance is part of our heritage," she said. "Moses's mother probably knew how to do it. We can't let these old men tell us we have to give it up."

Back home I unwrapped my purchase: a cheap practice outfit of skirt, belt and bra. As I looked at the costume, Sahar wandered out of the office and into the sitting room. I waited for the disapproving frown. Instead, she rubbed the transparent fabric of the skirt through her fingertips.

"How much did it cost?" she asked. I told her.

"Can you draw me a map of how to get to the store?"

"Why?" I asked, worried that she might be planning to have her fundamentalist friends picket the place, or worse.

"I want to buy a costume like this," she said. "I'm a wonderful dancer. I'll dance for my husband after we're married."

My own quest to become a wonderful dancer wasn't going so well. Egyptian girls acquired the ability to dance as naturally as the ability to walk, watching their mothers, sisters and aunts. At my friend Sayed's house, the three-year-old could already do fluid hip drops and scissor steps. Sayed's sisters tried their best with me, but it was hard for them to teach something that they had never actually learned.

"You need a *maalimah*," they said. The *awalim* were the

learned women of Egyptian arts, who danced, sang, played instruments and passed on the traditions to their apprentices. Finding a maalimah would have been easy enough a few decades ago. For centuries, clans of entertainers from the Nile villages handed the purest form of Egypt's ancient dance from generation to generation. When these families settled in Cairo, they clustered in an artists' quarter. Their remnants are still there, along Mohamed Ali Street, in little shops pungent with the glue and wood shavings of lute carvers and the stinky, drying fishskins of drum makers. From the open doorways, the wail of flutes or the thump-tap-tap of drums signaled a craftsman testing his wares.

But the dancers had gone. "They became tired of the police bothering them," an elderly craftsman explained. "The police treated them like prostitutes, always busting into their apartments to see if there were men there." Right now, he said, no one was encouraging a daughter to seek a career in dance. "The pressure is too much. But it will pass. They'll be back one day." The old man looked almost ancient enough to have been around when it all happened before. When Gustave Flaubert visited Cairo in 1850, he found that all the famous dancers had been banned from the city because the governor thought they encouraged prostitution. He had to travel up the Nile to find the performers. His diaries record dancers so erotic that the accompanying musicians had to cover their eyes with a fold of their turbans so they wouldn't become too aroused to play.

With a hand that seemed too palsied for his trade, the old man scribbled an address in Arabic on the edge of a torn piece of newsprint. "Go to this place," he said, handing it to me. "Tell her that the lute stringer sent you."

The taxi drove for almost an hour through Cairo's dense jumble of apartment buildings. Just before the city ended abruptly in desert, the driver stopped to ask directions. As always in Egypt, the two men he asked each pointed a different way. Eventually we found the place: a neat house surrounded by oleander. Music drifted faintly over the low brick wall. The door was open, and I wandered in. Inside, half a dozen women and girls were dancing, balancing canes on their heads as their hips shook vigorously. The women signaled that I could join in. I tried as best I could to follow their movements, but their speed and suppleness were way beyond me. An hour later I gave up, exhausted. Flopping in a corner, I watched as the others continued. One woman, clearly the most graceful and skilled, led the dance. But if she were teaching, it was only by example. She said nothing to the others to correct their stance or movement.

Finally one of the other women stopped, sweating, and went out to get some water. I followed, asking who the teacher was. The woman sipped her water slowly. We were, she said, in the home of one of Cairo's best-loved performers. But for her own reasons she never appeared in public anymore. If I wanted to learn, she said, I would find them there in the afternoons, every Tuesday and Thursday.

I had found my maalimah. From then on I went to the house whenever I could. Gradually I learned how to isolate each muscle group so that the cane stayed on my head. I learned to listen to the music and to follow it with my body. Watching the other women, I learned to move without the crass, bump-and-grind exaggerations that Westerners instinctively associate with oriental dance. In its pure form, less is more, and the most powerful movements are often the tiniest and most controlled twitches.

I began to wish there was some way to counter the fundamentalists' campaign against this artful dance. Finally I decided that, as a small act of solidarity with the dancers who refused to be pushed behind the veil by fundamentalists, I would take to the stage, somewhere in Cairo, for an unlicensed performance. I confided my plans to my friend Ian, the Australian ambassador. He buried his head in his hands in mock despair. "I can see it now: I'll be hauled out of bed at 2 A.M. one morning to answer a 'distressed Australian' call, and it'll be you—busted for belly dancing."

The more immediate problem was finding a venue modest enough to match my talents. I went back to Mohamed Ali Street for advice. I'd become friendly with a young drum maker there, who played in the band of a famous dancer named Lucy. He immediately ruled out the fancy hotels and the clubs along the Pyramids Road. "They range from first class to fifth class," Khalid mused. "What you need is something really tenth class."

He suggested the New Arizona Nightclub, admission ninety

cents. With Tony in tow, I cased the joint. There were women as well as men in the audience, the performers' standards weren't very high, and the management seemed laissez-faire enough about risking an unlicensed dancer, so long as my act appeared to be the impulse of the moment. If the politeness police showed up, I was to pretend I'd been propelled to my feet by the irresistible power of the music.

As I sat waiting for my cue a few nights later, I doubted I'd be able to sustain a defense of unpremeditated belly dancing. Under my coat I was wearing a black and gold costume with enough beading to buy a small Pacific atoll.

I was to go on in the middle of the bill, after the third dancer, Ashgan. Like most of the performers, she was a middle-aged woman with a figure well beyond Rubenesque. Her dancing was indifferent, but the audience didn't seem to mind. Judging from their turbans, mostly askew at this late hour, the bulk of the clients were Saydis, Egyptian country folk, in town for a big night out. Dotted among them, I could see one or two tables of Gulf Arabs in their distinctive red-checkered headcloths. The place seemed way too down market for wealthy Gulfies: either they'd drunk so much earlier in the night that they could no longer tell the difference, or the oil-price slump was more serious than I thought.

Finally Ashgan took her bow, then led me onto the stage. I looked down on a sea of turbans and felt a wave of panic. But with an insistent boom-tap-tap from the drummer, the music took off, and I went with it, losing myself in its circles and switchbacks. Oriental dance is improvisational, and demands an intuitive understanding between musicians and dancer. As the drumming gained speed and intensity, I had to match the rhythm with a buildup to a frantic, isolated hip shimmy that sent the thousands of gold beads in my belt shivering. Later the pace slowed until I was almost stationary: just a few muscles twitching to the long-drawn-out notes of the rebaba.

It seemed as though I'd been onstage for a thousand and one nights. Finally I heard the shift in the music that allows the dancer to bring the dance to an end with a graceful salaam. I made my bow and turned to leave the stage. A Saudi leapt up, waving an Egyptian ten-pound note, demanding an encore. To my astonishment, the rest of the audience banged the tables for more. Ashgan, in her most graceful arabesque of the night, reached for the ten pounds with one hand and grasped my wrist with the other, propelling me back under the spotlight. We did the encore together. Halfway through, she leaned over and peered down the front of my costume, then turned to the audience. "*Mafish!*" she cried in Arabic. "Nothing there!" We left the stage together to thunderous applause.

Later the manager, Samy Sallam, gave my performance a more hard-nosed review. "Your dancing," he said, "it is technically quite good. But you don't have enough feeling. You must learn the emotion as well as the steps." He gave me his business card and remarked, rather ambiguously, that I should give him a call. I knew I wouldn't. I'd made my little protest about a woman's right to dance.

I walked out of the steamy club into the wintry night air. Although it was after 3 A.M., the streets and cafés were still full of people, laughing together, enjoying themselves. In Egypt it seemed unlikely that a dour, fun-denying fundamentalism could ever really take hold for very long. The Egyptians seemed too much like the Italians: they'd listen politely to the Pope, but they'd still manage to put a porn star into Parliament.

Most Egyptians were too intensely pious to accept the extremists' wanton gunning down of tourists or writers or people who happened to be standing in the wrong place when they launched an attack in the streets of Assuit and Cairo. Despite lives of hardship and frustration with a sluggish, corruption-riddled government, it was hard to imagine Egyptians turning their backs on the tolerance and good humor that made their crowded cities and muddy villages so pleasant and livable.

The old lute stringer in Mohamed Ali Street was right. It might take awhile, but the dancers would be back.

Conclusion: Beware of the Dogma

> "Say: O unbelievers! I will not
> worship that which ye worship,
> nor will ye worship that which I
> worship. . . . Ye have your religion,
> and I have my religion."
>
> THE KORAN
> THE CHAPTER OF THE UNBELIEVERS

I have learned to live by the rhythm of other people's prayers. In Cairo, I woke at sunrise to the voices of muezzins and timed my lunch break by the midday call to prayer. There are no muezzins where I live now, on a lane of old London houses built two hundred years ago by refugees from France. The refugees, all Catholics, also built a small church by their cottages and so, these days, it is the Angelus bell that wakes me in the morning and sends me to the kitchen at noon in search of food.

One day in the summer of 1992 there was a guest for lunch. A detective arrived first, to search my closets and poke his head into the attic. A filament of dust clung to his hair as he gave the all clear over a walkie-talkie. The cars roared into the lane, fast. "Leave the door open now," the detective said. The guest couldn't risk lingering on the doorstep. He entered, suddenly, at the center of a flying wedge of bodyguards. A floppy brown fedora fell low across his face. Sunglasses hid the distinctive droop of his eyelids and the improbable circumflex of his brows. After four years in hiding, Salman Rushdie's skin had the fishlike translucence of a man who never sees the sun. His posture had eased into the self-effacing slouch of an adolescent who desperately doesn't want to be noticed.

I was living in Cairo when the storm broke over *The Satanic Verses*. Just after Khomeini condemned Salman Rushdie to death, I took my copy of the novel to Naguib Mahfouz, Egypt's Nobel laureate, whose own novels had been censored on religious grounds. I hoped he might write a defense of Rushdie: a plea for tolerance, for the freedom of ideas. Mahfouz took the book from my hands and pushed it to the far side of his desk, where he wouldn't have to look at it. He was tired, he said: worn out from his own battles with fundamentalism. He did not think he would enter this engagement.

Perhaps he was wise. On the day Salman Rushdie came to lunch at my house, we talked together for an article I was writing on the chilling effect the fatwa was having on all writers dealing with Islam. I had felt the chill myself, sitting on a sunny terrace in southern Lebanon with a leading cleric of Hezbollah. By then, I was used to the averted gaze of devout Muslim men, and it seemed normal to me to be conversing with someone whose eyes were focused on a floor tile an inch in front of my shoe. He was considering whether to let me meet his wife. He found it troubling that my book would mention the prophet Muhammad's wives and daughters. "You will have to be very careful," he said. Suddenly, he raised his turbaned head and shot me a single, penetrating glare. "Be sure you do not make any mistakes."

Rushdie and I didn't know, as we sat talking of these things, that the Egyptian writer Farag Foda lay dying, that same day, of gunshot wounds inflicted by Islamic Jihad in reprisal for his eloquent and often scathing critiques of religious extremism.

In the progressive Shiite magazine *Dialogue*, Ali Allawi writes of the difficulties of potential European converts to Islam in seeing the faith standing separate from "the prejudices and social baggage of Islamic lands." Once Westerners "are able to dissociate Islam from this background noise," he writes, "they are able to quickly appreciate its veracity."

But these days the background noise is very loud. And every day's news seemed to raise the decibels. The World Trade Center explodes on the apparent say-so of a militant Islamic preacher. A United Nations human rights report finds Sudan's Koran-based punishments in conflict with the international human rights agreements the country has signed. In response, the government of Sudan threatens the report's Romanian-born author with death. In Egypt a militant cleric named Ali Yehya commands his followers to tear down the Pyramids and all other pharaonic monuments because civilizations that existed before Islam were base and idolatrous. In Algeria two women are gunned down at a bus stop because they are not veiled. In Saudi Arabia a newspaper editor goes to jail because his English-language newspaper runs a cartoon strip, "BC", that the Saudi government deems heretical. The offending cartoon was a two-frame piece in which a Stone Age man stands on a hill and asks, "God, if you're up there, give me a sign." In the second frame, the man is deluged with a sudden rain shower. "Well," he says, "we know two things: He's up there, and He's got a sense of humor." The Saudis jailed the editor, a Hindu, for running a cartoon strip that questioned the existence of God.

Like the Rushdie fatwa, these incidents come at us from so deep in left field that we, as Westerners, have no coherent way to think about them. We shrug. Weird foreigners. Who understands them? Who needs to?

And yet, as I made my home in London, gradually shaking the last few fine crumbs of Cairo dust from the pages of my books, I found that the background noise of Islam remained always there, in the distance, like a neighbor hammering. And eventually I accepted that it was neither possible nor right to ignore it.

That summer, not long after Salman Rushdie came to lunch, I answered the phone to a distraught friend whose neighbor had just been knifed to death. The dead woman was an imam's daughter from the Sudan. She had been stabbed by her husband, also a Sudanese.

It was winter by the time the case came to trial. Every day for five days I walked through a cold London drizzle to a small court in the Old Bailey. To the great machine of British justice, it was a routine case. The press benches were empty. A simple "domestic" between middle-aged marrieds from a middle-class suburb was too ordinary to be of interest.

The facts of the killing weren't in dispute. Just before dinner-time, in the kitchen of his handsome Victorian house, Omar stabbed his wife, Afaf. With the dripping knife still in his hand, he walked to the phone and called his closest friend to tell him what he had done, and then called the police.

In the small public gallery I sat between the man's brothers and the woman's neighbors. The brothers, who had flown from the Sudan for the trial, shivered in their summer-weight suits. The neighbors, well-groomed young mothers who knew the victim from parent-teacher nights and weekday excursions to garden-supply centers, seemed uneasy with the Old Bailey's hard-bitten police procedures. In the gallery they scribbled in notebooks perched on their knees, as if their meticulous records would somehow help them make sense of the thing that had happened on their tranquil, tree-lined street. Just once in the five days, when the barrister for the prosecution held up the weapon—a good-quality Sabatier cook's knife—and questioned a pathologist as to the exact wounds it made when it plunged five times into the victim's chest and abdomen, one of the women put down her pen and sobbed uncontrollably.

At issue in the court was whether the act was a premeditated murder or, as the defense claimed, manslaughter that took place when the accused was temporarily out of his mind as the result of "reaction depression" brought on by the knowledge that his wife had had an affair, and that she had, on the morning of the stabbing, obtained a court order restraining him from taking their children out of Britain to live with his family in the Sudan.

As I listened to the facts of the case, I could interpret them two ways. The Western way, as the jury was interpreting them, led to a description of something we all understood: a crime of passion in a spur-of-the-moment insane frenzy. The other way, the way I'd learned living among the women of Islam, described something very different: a cleansing of family honor, a premeditated killing that would, under British law, draw a sentence of life imprisonment.

From where they sat in their jury box, the men and women of the jury couldn't see Omar as he stood each morning beside his police guard, waiting to be escorted into the court. But from the elevation of the public gallery I could see him, and so could his brothers. Each morning he looked up at them and raised a clenched fist in a defiant victory salute. His step, as he entered the dock, was almost jaunty.

Afaf, thirty-eight years old when she died, was a kinswoman who had been married to him by arrangement. She was barely fifteen; he was already thirty. That Omar was her relative, as well as her husband, mattered perhaps more than any other single fact in the court case. It was as a relation, a male of her blood kin, that tradition deemed him most dishonored by her adultery.

Afaf had made the most of a life that had offered her few choices. She had had no choice when they scraped away her clitoris, married her to a man she barely knew and sent her thousands of miles from home, to a city whose language she didn't speak.

Afaf lived in London with Omar while he studied for his doctorate. In 1985, unable to find an academic post in Britain, he began work in Saudi Arabia. For ten months of every year Afaf raised her four children alone. While working in clerical jobs, she managed to finish high school and a computer course and to begin a degree in social science. A heavy-set woman with a wide smile and an open manner, she managed to break through British reserve and make friends. For Omar, returning only once a year from Saudi Arabia's austere religious atmosphere, it wasn't so easy. He was hostile to some of Afaf's closest friends, especially an unmarried couple who lived across the street. He felt such neighbors created an "atheistic atmosphere" for his children.

Gradually, the long separations and Afaf's change from docile young wife to an independent, accomplished woman began to fray the marriage's fragile bonds. In 1987, Afaf and Omar stopped sharing a bedroom. But Afaf was afraid to ask for a divorce, fearing that Omar would spirit the children back to the Sudan, where Islamic law would give her no right to their custody.

Then one of her work mates, Andrew, a tall, sandy-haired divorcé, fell in love with her. At first she kept her distance, but slowly his support at the office extended to help at the house, where the years of Omar's absence had left odd jobs undone and rooms dilapidated. It was Andrew who explained to Afaf that British law would protect her rights to her children. In January 1991 she wrote to her husband asking for a divorce.

Omar agreed. But then, on his next trip home, he learned that Andrew had been to his house and even spent the night there once when he'd worked late painting the sunroom. Omar was outraged that the neighbors might have noticed. His main concern was to keep the visits secret, because, he told the court, he was concerned for his family honor if Afaf's relationship with another man became public. According to Andrew's testimony at the trial, Omar told him he had no objections to his meeting Afaf, so long as it happened away from her home and the prying gaze of the neighbors.

Afaf may well have lived to divorce Omar and marry the man of her choice if it hadn't been for one long, stressful day of arguments over Omar's right to go out alone with the two younger children, whom Afaf feared he might try to abduct. Omar, frustrated and furious, went to visit his one Sudanese friend, broke down, and confided his suspicions of his wife's infidelity.

That friend, called as a witness in court, described how he'd burst into tears as Omar spoke. Those tears—straight from the heart of a fellow Sudanese who knew the depths of Omar's dishonor—may well have caused Afaf's death. Omar's Western-trained intellect might have been able to win the war with his social baggage if, as he'd intended, his wife's relationship had remained secret. But once his friend knew, the dishonor was an accomplished fact that could be wiped away only in the ancient, bloody way. That Omar's first call after the killing was to this friend—not a doctor, not an ambulance, not the police—seemed to me the strongest evidence of motive presented in the court. Yet the prosecution never made this connection.

At the end of the week the jury reached a manslaughter verdict on the grounds of "diminished responsibility." For ending his wife's life, Omar received a prison sentence of six years. Taking off the time he'd already served since the killing and a likely two-year remission for good behavior, he will probably be free by July 1996.

From the facts presented in that small courtroom, there was little chance of any other verdict. What was missing wasn't evidence but understanding of the prejudices and social baggage of Islamic lands that Omar had carried with him from the Sudan, his country of upbringing, and from Saudi Arabia, the country in which he worked ten months of every year.

Nothing in their own culture or experience equipped this jury of very ordinary-looking English people to comprehend that what had been described in court was an honor killing, one of the hundreds that every year claim Muslim women's lives.

This was not an isolated case; it simply happened to be the one I heard about. In a British study of family violence completed not long after Afaf's death, the researchers found that women married to men of Muslim background were eight times more likely to be killed by their spouses than any other women in Britain. Yet British barristers, judges and juries continue to assess these crimes by a yardstick that's completely inadequate to measure what is really going on.

Presented with statistics on violence toward women, or facing the furor over the Rushdie fatwa, progressive Muslims such as Ali Allawi, Rana Kabbani and others ask us to blame a wide range of villains: colonial history, the bitterness of immigrant experience, Bedouin tradition, pre-Islamic African culture. Yet when the Koran sanctions wife beating and the execution of apostates, it can't be entirely exonerated for an epidemic of wife slayings and death sentences on authors.

In the end, what Rana Kabbani and Ali Allawi are proposing is as artificial an exercise as that proposed by the Marxists who used to argue that socialism in its pure form should not be maligned and rejected because of the deficiencies of "actually existing socialism." At some point every religion, especially one that purports to encompass a complete way of life and system of government, has to be called to account for the kind of life it offers the people in the lands where it predominates.

It becomes insufficient to look at Islam on paper, or Islam in history, and dwell on the inarguable improvements it brought to women's lives in the seventh century. Today, the much more urgent and relevant task is to examine the way the faith has proved such fertile ground for almost every antiwomen custom it encountered in its great march out of Arabia. When it found veils and seclusion in Persia, it absorbed them; when it found genital mutilations in Egypt, it absorbed them; when it found societies in which women had never had a voice in public affairs, its own traditions of lively women's participation withered.

Yet there are exceptions. When the armies of Islam swept into India, Muslims were appalled by the practice of *sati*, in which widows, on a husband's death, would burn themselves alive on his funeral pyre. In 1650 the traveler Jean-Baptiste Tavernier wrote of Hindu widows, banned by their faith from remarriage and reduced by their husbands' deaths to penury and contempt, choosing instead to end their lives through sati. "But it should be remarked," he wrote, "that a woman cannot burn herself without having received permission from the governor of the place where she dwells, and those governors who are Musalmans [Muslims] hold this dreadful custom of self-destruction in horror, and do not readily give permission." For those women's saved lives, at least, Islam can take the credit. But why did such a powerful and resilient faith not stand its ground more often in the face of "dreadful customs"?

Once I began working on this book, I looked everywhere for examples of women trying to reclaim Islam's positive messages, trying to carry forward into the twentieth century the reformist zeal with which Muhammad had remade the lives of many women (other than his own wives and the Muslim army's war captives) in the first Muslim community at Medina. It turned out to be a frustrating search. In most places the direction of the debate seemed to be exactly the reverse. Palestinian, Egyptian, Algerian and Afghani women were seeing a curtain come down on decades of women's liberation as Islamic leaders in their countries turned to the most exclusionary and inequitable interpretations. For those women who struggled against the tide, the results were a discouraging trio of marginalization, harassment and exile.

In Morocco, Fatima Mernissi's Koranic scholarship has made a formidable case for Islam as a religion of equality and human dignity, whose message has simply been buried over time by self-serving misogynists in positions of power. Yet her work is read in Western universities much more than it is in Moroccan mosques. No matter how precise her research into the hadith, the male-dominated Islamic establishment doesn't seem willing to open its ears to the scholarship of a Muslim woman who doesn't veil or otherwise flaunt her piety.

Perhaps that is why I found the brightest hope for positive change camouflaged among the black chadors of devout Iranian women. Even the most narrow-minded fundamentalists can't criticize the Islamic credentials of women such as Khomeini's daughter Zahra Mostafavi or Rafsanjani's daughter Faezeh Hashemi. Their conspicuous adherence to religious rules gives them a high ground from which to make their case for women's rights. So far, they have used that position sparingly, to get women a greater political voice, more equal job opportunities and the right to participate in sport. To be sure, these women will never tear down the walls of tradition. They will never make the arguments that *can* be made within Islamic reasoning against veiling or polygamy. But within those traditional walls they can make a much safer haven for women at risk of abuse and exploitation in the name of Islam.

To Western women, that mightn't look like much. It is easy to see these grim figures in their heavy shrouds as symbols of what's wrong rather than what's right with women and Islam. But to Muslim women elsewhere in the strictest parts of the Islamic world, the Iranian woman riding to work on her motorbike, even with her billowing chador gripped firmly in her teeth, looks like a figure to envy.

"They are our Superwomen," said Iman Fadlallah, the shy twenty-four-year-old wife of the Hezbollah sheik in southern Lebanon who had sat on his terrace and warned me about this book. Iman's father, the most prominent Hezbollah cleric in Beirut, had abruptly ended her schooling when she was fourteen years old, choosing a husband for her whom she didn't meet until the wedding. Now she stayed mainly in her house raising her children. In Iran, where she had lived with her husband while he continued his clerical studies, she had glimpsed a much wider world, even for the most devout of women. She spoke wistfully of Iranian women's opportunities to study and work. "We have to struggle to be as strong as they are," she said.

Everyone has her own way of remembering her travels. Some keep journals. Others take photographs. I go into the bedroom and open my closet. There are memories hanging there, semaphores from six years and twenty countries. There is the homespun scarf in red and black, still faintly scented with wood smoke from the cooking fire of the Kurdish woman who untied it from her own hair to wrap around mine. There is the long Palestinian dress Raed's mother Rahme made for me so that I would feel comfortable sitting on the floor among them. I still have the Italian pin-striped "king suit," a discreet little mend hiding the rip from the day I toured with Hussein in the Jordanian desert. I threw out my wedding shoes—the ones with the tide line of camel blood. And I keep meaning to give away the pair of black acrylic socks I had to buy in a hurry when the Islamic dress inspector at a Tehran bank objected to the inch of too sheer stocking peeking between the top of my shoes and the hem of my chador.

Limp on a hanger is the chador itself, the big black square of silk and synthetic that I used to despise. But that well-worn black rag, stained on the hem and torn on the shoulder, has become an old friend. Like a 1980s dress-for-success suit, it has been the camouflage that helped me do my job in a world where I wasn't quite welcome.

When I look at that chador I no longer get the little shudder of fear or the gust of outrage that I used to feel when I saw the most extreme forms of Islamic dress. These days my feelings are much more complex. Chadors are linked in my mind to women I've felt close to, in spite of the abyss of belief that divided us.

When I lived among the women of Islam, I became part of a world that is still, in the last decade of the twentieth century, an intensely private one. In public, most women move like shadows, constrained physically by their hijab or mentally by codes of conduct that inhibit them. It is only behind the high walls and the closed doors that women are ever really free.

For me, entering that world touched emotions that had been a long time dormant. From the time I'd taken my first job, as a cub reporter on the sports desk of *The Sydney Morning Herald,* my career had pushed me into a man's world. When I became a foreign correspondent, most of my colleagues were men. It wasn't until I went to Cairo and started seeking out Muslim women that I realized I hadn't made a close female friend since I left school.

I'd forgotten how much I liked to be with women. And yet there was always a sourness lurking at the edge of even the sweetest encounters. Squatting on the floor of a Kurdish friend's kitchen, helping the women with their bread making, I realized what an agreeable thing it was to be completely surrounded by women, to have a task that was ours alone. As the women's deft fingers flung balls of dough under my rolling pin and the fire roared beneath a baking sheet of blackened metal, I felt contentment in shared work well done.

But an hour into the labor, as my shoulders ached and scalding sweat dribbled down my back, I began to resent the boy toddler who kept ambling up to the steaming pile of fresh bread and breaking off tasty morsels in his fat little fists. His sister, not much older, was already part of our bread-making assembly line. Why should he learn so young that her role was to toil for his pleasure?

The nunlike clothes, pushed to the back of my closet, remind me of all those mixed feelings. Every time my hand brushes the smooth fabric of the chador, I think of Nahid Aghtaie, the Iranian medical student who gave up an easy life in London to go home and work at low-paying jobs to advance the goals of her revolution. I remember her, in Qum, drifting toward me over the marble-floored mosque to tell me that she'd prayed for me "to have nice children." And then I think of her beautiful face—the small visible triangle between brow and lip—radiant on the morning of the murder of Rushdie's Japanese translator in July 1991. "This," she said triumphantly, "shows the power of Islam." I told her that, to me, it no more showed the power of Islam than an Israeli soldier's shooting of a Palestinian child showed the power of Judaism. Why not, I asked her, cite the "power of Islam" in the humanitarian work that Iran was doing for the flood of Iraqi refugees that was then pouring over its borders? "Because nobody notices when we do such things," she said. "But every news report in the world will note this execution."

Eventually I became worn out by such conversations. Friendships with women like Nahid were an emotional whipsaw: how was it possible to admire her for the courage of her convictions, when her convictions led to such hateful reasoning?

Just after that trip to Iran, tired from months of covering the war with Iraq and its aftermath, I went home to Australia for a brief vacation. My plane landed in Sydney just ahead of a flight from Jakarta. As I waited for my luggage, the doors to the arrival hall swished open on a crowd of Indonesian-Australians, waiting to greet their relatives. Almost all of the women were veiled. A swift, mean-spirited thought shot through my jet-lagged brain: "Oh, please. Not here too."

I wasn't raised to be a bigot. My parents considered religious intolerance a sin. My mother had seen too much of it in her child-hood, among rural Irish Catholic immigrants. Her mother's marriage to a non-Catholic had been an act of courage. Hers was a typically Australian story: within two generations she had kicked the dirt of the old country's prejudices from her shoes and adopted Australia's own "religion"—a passionately tolerant secularism. It happened to almost everybody. One of the most revealing statistics I ever learned about my country concerned the twelve members of the Board of Management of Sydney's main synagogue. In 1890 those twelve men were among the city's most observant Jews. Less than a hundred years later, none of the twelve had a single identifiably Jewish descen-dant. Mixed marriages and the siren song of secularism had claimed them all.

I wondered if that would happen to the new wave of Muslim immigrants. Would their children, too, learn to doubt the Koran's doubt-free prescription for how to live? Would they see that Austra-lia, where atheists routinely got elected prime minister, was a much fairer, gentler society than the religious regimes of places like Saudi Arabia and the Sudan? Or would they, as their numbers increased, seek to impose their values on my culture? During the Rushdie out-cry, Australian Muslims had demonstrated, as was their right. But pictures of their toddlers holding placards saying "Rushdie Must Die" had sent a shudder through the society.

An Iranian-born friend who lives in London, a gentle, middle-aged woman who practices family medicine, says the only war she would willingly fight would be one to stop Islamic fundamentalism telling her how to live her life. She is a Zoroastrian, a member of the ancient Persian faith in which dark and light, good and evil are for-ever locked in a struggle for supremacy.

Should we also struggle to stop Islamic extremists telling others how to live their lives? As Westerners, we profess to believe that human rights are an immutable international currency, independent of cultural mores and political circumstances. At a Geneva conference on the International Declaration of Human Rights in 1993, Iran was among a handful of countries that argued otherwise. Cloaking their argument in fashionable dress such as cultural relativism, delegates from Iran and Cuba, China and Indonesia argued that the West had imposed its human rights ideology on nations whose very different religious and political histories gave them the right to choose their own. To me, their argument boiled down to this ghastly and untenable proposition: a human right is what the local despot says it is.

The concept of the universality of human rights prevailed at the conference, and the charter was not amended. And yet the charter has done little so far for the genitally mutilated, the forcibly secluded, the disenfranchised women of the world.

Is it even our fight? As a mental test, I always try to reverse the gender. If some ninety million little boys were having their penises amputated, would the world have acted to prevent it by now? You bet.

Sometimes substituting race for gender also is an interesting exercise. Say a country, a close Western ally and trading partner, had a population half white, half black. The whites had complete control of the blacks. They could beat them if they disobeyed. They deprived them of the right to leave the house without permission; to walk unmolested without wearing the official segregating dress; to hold any decent job in the government, or to work at all without the permission of the white in control of them. Would there have been uproar in our countries by now? Would we have imposed trade sanctions and subjected this country to international opprobrium? You bet. Yet countries such as Saudi Arabia, which deprive half their population of these most basic rights, have been subjected to none of these things.

It is, I suppose, possible to argue that outside pressure is counterproductive when it comes to traditions that are seen to be religious, even if in fact they aren't. Early attempts to ban genital mutilation by colonial-government fiat were dismal failures. But, even if we decline to act on what goes on inside others' borders, there is no excuse for not acting inside our own.

In an era of cultural sensitivity, we need to say that certain cultural baggage is contraband in our countries and will not be admitted. We already draw a line at polygamy; we don't recognize divorce by saying, "I divorce you." We have banned these things even though the Koran approves them. It should be easier to take a stand against practices that don't even carry the sanction of the Koran. "Honor" killings need to be identified in court and punished as the premeditated murders they are. Young women need to be protected against marriages arranged during hasty "vacations" abroad for teenagers too young to give informed consent. And, most urgent of all, clitoridectomy needs to be made illegal.

In 1994 the United States still had no laws whatever banning migrants from countries such as Somalia and the Sudan from mutilating the genitals of their daughters, and the operation was taking place in migrant communities throughout the country. The first ever bill on the issue had just been introduced to Congress by Colorado Democrat Patricia Schroeder. While it addressed education of migrants and laws against carrying out mutilations within the United States, it didn't propose any means of protecting girls taken out of the country for the procedure.

There is something else we can do: advance the right to asylum on the grounds of "well-founded fear of persecution" to women from any country where fathers, husbands and brothers claim a religious right to inhibit women's freedom. In January 1993 the Canadian government, after almost two years of consideration, granted asylum to a Saudi student who had requested it on the grounds of gender persecution. It was, they said, "an exception." Why should it be? "Nada," as she asks to be called, experienced the same violent harassment that any woman is subject to from her country's authorities for the "crime" of walking outside her home with uncovered hair. If Nada had remained in Saudi Arabia, and continued to disobey, she might have found herself imprisoned and even tortured, without formal charges ever having been laid.

There is, unfortunately, no chance that granting of automatic asylum to women suffering such gender persecution would lead to a flood of refugees. Only a minority have the means to leave their country, or even their house, when men control the keys to doors and the car, and must sign their approval for the shortest of journeys. But such a step would send a signal to regimes whose restrictions have nothing to do with the religion they claim to uphold. And that signal would be that we, too, have certain things we hold sacred: among them are liberty, equality, the pursuit of happiness and the right to doubt.

It is a long time since I stood under Rafsanjani's gaze at a press conference in Iran and told him I was wearing a chador "in a spirit of mutual respect." At that moment, standing in my black shroud under the hot TV lights, I had a mental image of myself, as I liked to be in summer, bare-skinned on the beach near my parents' home. The "mutual respect" I had in mind demanded that he, and those like him, acknowledge my right to sunbake on those Australian sands and, if I chose, to take *The Satanic Verses* along as my beach reading.

Last year, when I was home in Sydney, I lay on that beach beside a Muslim family who seemed not the least bit troubled by the exposed flesh surrounding them. While the man splashed in the shallows with his toddlers, his wife sat on the sand, her long, loose dress arranged around her. It made me sad that the woman's tiny daughter, splashing so happily with her father and baby brother, would be, one day soon, required to forgo that pleasure. But that would be her fight, not mine. At least, in Australia, she would have a choice. She would choose between her family's values and what she saw elsewhere.

Every now and then the little girl's mother fiddled with her headscarf as it billowed in the sea breeze. That woman had made her choice: it was different from mine. But sitting there, sharing the warm sand and the soft air, we accepted each other. When she raised her face to the sun, she was smiling.

GLOSSARY

Abaya: A black cloak with arm slits that falls from the top of the head to the ankles. Generally worn in Persian Gulf countries.

Abu: Father

Allah: The core of the Islamic faith is its monotheism. *Al Lah* is simply the arabic for the God.

Andarun: In traditional Persian homes, the inner, or private, quarter where women live, barred from contact with the outside world.

Anfal: Literally, the spoils of war. The name of a chapter of the Koran and the code name given by Saddam Hussein to his terror campaign against the Kurds.

Aqd: A wedding contract.

Ayatollah: Literally, reflection of God. In Shiite Islam, the most learned of religious teachers and law interpreters receive this title.

Burka: The face mask, made of leather or stiff fabric, worn by women of the Gulf countries. Covers the entire face except for the eyes.

Caliph: Literally, one who comes after. Muhammad's successors as leaders of the early Muslim nation.

Chador: A square of fabric that falls from the top of the head to the ankles and is held or pinned closed under the chin. Worn in Iran and among Lebanese Shiite women.

Dhow: A boat commonplace in the Persian Gulf.

Esma: A clause in a wedding contract giving a woman the right to divorce.

Farsi: The official language of Iran.

Fatwa: A formal legal opinion or decision by a religious leader on a matter of religious law.

Feast of the Sacrifice: The last day of the Hajj. All pilgrims, and other Muslims who can afford to, slaughter a sheep and distribute its meat to the poor.

Fitna: Chaos, civil war. In some Arab countries, fitna is also a slang term for a beautiful woman.

Hadith: A saying of the Prophet Muhammad or a saying about him or his teachings by contemporaneous sources.

Hajj: The pilgrimage to Mecca that all Muslims are obliged to make at least once in their lives, if they can afford it. Also, the month of the Islamic calendar in which the pilgrimage takes place.

Halal: Religiously lawful, fit, permitted.

Hanafi: One of the main schools of Sunni religious thought.

Hanbali: The strictest of the four main schools of Islamic thought.

Haram: Religiously forbidden. It is necessary to abstain from that which is haram. If one performs a haram act, one will be punished by the Islamic court, or in the hereafter, or both.

Harem: The private quarters of a house, or the women's rooms. Also the women of a family.

Hezbollah: Literally, the Party of God. The political/religious group associated with Khomeini. Influential among Lebanese Shiites.

Hijab: Literally, a curtain. Generally, any women's dress that follows Islamic principles.

Hijrah: The flight of Muhammad and his followers from Mecca to Medina on July 16, in the year 622 of the Christian calendar. The date from which the Muslim calendar begins.

Husseiniya: A Shiite center for study and prayer.

Imam: Leader of community prayers. Also, among Shiites, the first twelve leaders of their community were given the title. Many Iranians revived the title for Khomeini.

Jalabiyya: A button-through, neck-to-ankle coat worn by women, or a loose-fitting robe worn by men.

Jihad: Holy effort, or struggle, or war to defend Islam. The closest English equivalent is crusade.

Kaffiyah: A checked headdress, black-and-white or red-and-white, widely worn by men in parts of the Arab world but particularly associated with Palestinians, for whom it has become something of a nationalist symbol.

Kunya: The practice of naming a man or woman after a first-born son. A woman known as Umm Walid (mother of Walid) has an eldest son named Walid.

Kurd: A non-Arabic, mostly Muslim people who inhabit the mountainous region between Iraq, Iran, Syria, Turkey and the former Soviet Union.

Maalimah: In Egypt, a woman skilled in folk music and dance who passes her knowledge to others.

Madrassa: School.

Magneh: A cowl-like head covering worn, mostly in Iran, by women.

Majlis: Gathering or council. Majlis-as-shura is a consultative council, the closest concept to parliament in Islamic teachings.

Makruh: Religiously discouraged, disliked. If one does a makruh act, one won't be punished as for a haram act; but if one refrains from it, one will be rewarded.

Maliki: One of the major schools of Islamic thought.

Meuzzin: One who sings or chants the call to prayer.

Minaret: The spire of a mosque from which the meuzzin traditionally calls the faithful to prayer. In modern times, loudspeakers often broadcast record-ings instead.

Minbar: The pulpit in a mosque.

Mosque: In Arabic, *masjid*. A place of Muslim worship. It may be a simple room or a magnificent marble edifice.

Mujtahid: A religious scholar who is an authority on Islamic law and may advise others.

Mullah: A clergyman or religious leader.

Muslim: Literally, one who submits to God's will and laws.

Mutawain: Saudi Arabia's religious police.

Muwazzaf: A government bureaucrat.

Niqab: A veil worn by women that completely covers the face.

Roosarie: An Iranian name for a head scarf.

Salwar Kameez: A calf-length tunic worn over pants.

Sharia: Islamic law. Literally, the road to the water hole.

Shayla: An Arabic word for head scarf.

Shehada: The first pillar of the Islamic religion. Literally, profession of faith: "I testify there is no God but God and Muhammad is the messenger of God."

Shiite: Adherent to the Islamic faction that arose in the seventh century in a split over who should be caliph, or successor, to Muhammad. The Shiat, or partisans, of Ali ibn Abu Taleb, Muhammad's cousin and son-in-law, believed that Ali was the legitimate successor and that the leadership should stay with Muhammad's descendants. The number of Shiites worldwide is estimated at around ninety million, or some 9 percent of all Muslims. They are the overwhelming majority in Iran and a slight majority in Iraq, Dubai and Bahrain. Elsewhere, such as Lebanon and Saudi Arabia, they have traditionally been a disadvantaged minority.

Sigheh: A temporary marriage recognized by Shiites.

Sunnah: The traditions of the Prophet Muhammad. Those things he did himself, or approved of by him, or that were done in his presence without earning his disapproval.

Sunnat: Recommended, desirable, in keeping with Muhammad's traditions. One will not be punished for neglecting to do sunnat acts, but will be rewarded for doing them.

Sunni: An orthodox Muslim. Literally, one who follows Muhammad's tradition.

Talaq: Divorce by repudiation. The husband merely repeats the words "I divorce you" three times.

Thobe: The long robe, usually made of white cotton, worn by the men of the Arabian peninsula.

Ulema: A body of religious scholars who interpret Islamic law for the community.

Umm: Mother.

Ummah: The worldwide Islamic community.

Wahabi: Puritanical, ultraconservative movement founded in the 1740s in what is now Saudi Arabia by a preacher named Muhammad ibn Abdul Wahab. Women under Wahabism are denied many rights considered due to them according to more orthodox readings of the Koran and hadith. Backed by Saudi oil wealth, Wahabi teachings are increasingly influential throughout the Islamic world.

Wajib: A religiously obligatory act. One will be punished in the afterlife for neglecting a wajib act such as daily prayer or annual alms-giving.

Zakkat: Compulsory giving of charity to the poor. One of the five pillars of the Islamic faith, all Muslims are required to give a percentage of their wealth each year, usually calculated on net worth rather than annual income.

Select Bibliography

Abbott, Nabia. *Aishah the Beloved of Mohammed*. London: Al Saqi Books, 1985.

Ahmed, Leila. *Women and Gender in Islam: Historical Roots of a Modern Debate*. New Haven: Yale University Press, 1992.

Akhtar, Shabbir. *Be Careful with Muhammad! The Salman Rushdie Affair*. London: Bellew Publishing, 1989.

Alireza, Marianne. *At the Drop of a Veil: The True Story of a California Girl's Years in an Arabian Harem*. Boston: Houghton Mifflin Co., 1971.

Aloskooee, M. H. A. Alehghaghi. *Letter from the Shiites*. San Rafael: Islamic Foundation, 1983.

Amini, Ibrahim. *Principles of Marriage and Family Ethics*. Tehran: Islamic Propagation Organization, 1988.

Amos, Deborah. *Lines in the Sand: Desert Storm and the Remaking of the Arab World*. New York: Simon & Schuster, 1992.

Armstrong, Karen. *Muhammad: A Western Attempt to Understand Islam*. London: Victor Gollancz Ltd., 1991.

Badran, Margot, and Miriam Cooke, eds. *Opening the Gates: A Century of Arab Feminist Writing*. London: Virago, 1990.

Bani-Sadr, Abol Hassan. *My Turn to Speak: Iran, the Revolution & Secret Deals with the U.S.* Washington, D.C.: Brassey's, 1991.

Bashier, Zakaria. *Sunshine at Medina: Studies in the Life of the Prophet Muhammad.* Leicester: The Islamic Foundation, 1990.

Campbell, Dugald. *On the Trail of the Veiled Tuareg.* London: Seeley, Service & Co., 1928.

Connolly, Clara. "Washing Our Linen: One Year of Women Against Fundamentalism." *Feminist Review* 37 (Spring 1991).

Esposito, John L. *Islam: The Straight Path.* Oxford: Oxford University Press, 1988.

Farmaian, Sattareh Farman. *Daughter of Persia: A Woman's Journey from Her Father's Harem Through the Islamic Revolution.* New York: Crown, 1992.

Fernea, Elizabeth Warnock, and Basima Qattan Bezirgan, eds. *Middle Eastern Muslim Women Speak.* Austin: University of Texas Press, 1990.

French, Marilyn. *The War Against Women.* London: Hamish Hamilton, 1992.

Givechian, Fatemeh. "Cultural Changes in Male-Female Relations." *The Iranian Journal of International Affairs.* 3, no. 3 (Fall 1991).

Holton, Patricia. *Mother Without a Mask: A Westerner's Story of Her Arab Family.* London: Kyle Cathie Ltd., 1991.

Kabbani, Rana. *Letter to Christendom.* London: Virago, 1989.

Lacey, Robert. *The Kingdom.* London: Fontana, 1982.

Lewis, Bernard. *The Political Language of Islam.* Chicago: University of Chicago Press, 1988.

Mabro, Judy, ed. *Veiled Half-Truths: Western Travellers' Perceptions of Middle Eastern Women.* London: I.B. Tauris & Co., 1991.

Macleod, Arlene Elowe. *Accommodating Protest: Working Women, the New Veiling, and Change in Cairo.* New York: Columbia University Press, 1991.

Mahfouz, Naguib. *Palace Walk.* London: Doubleday, 1991.

Mahmoody, Betty. *Not Without My Daughter.* London: Corgi, 1987.

Mernissi, Fatima. *Beyond the Veil: Male-Female Dynamics in Muslim Society.* London: Al Saqi Books, 1985.

———. *Women and Islam: An Historical and Theological Enquiry.* Oxford: Blackwell Publishers, 1992.

Minai, Naila. *Women in Islam: Tradition and Transition in the Middle East.* London: John Murray, 1981.

Minnesota Lawyers International Human Rights Committee. "Shame in the House of Saud: Contempt for Human Rights in the Kingdom of Saudi Arabia." Minneapolis, 1992.

Mohammad, Abdel Ghany A. *Wives of Mohammad the Prophet and Wisdom of Polygamy.* Cairo: Madbuli Bookshop, 1984.

Muhawesh, Odeh A. *Fatima the Gracious.* Qum: Anssarian Publications, 1990.

Mutahhari, Murtada. *The Rights of Women in Islam.* Tehran: World Organization for Islamic Services, 1981.

Naipaul, V. S. *Among the Believers: An Islamic Journey.* London: Penguin, 1981.

Pickthall, Mohammed Marmaduke. *The Meaning of the Glorious Koran.* New York: New American Library Mentor Books, 1953.

Rahnavard, Zahra. *The Message of Hijab.* London: Al Hoda Publishers, 1990.

Rizvi, Sayyid Muhammad. *Marriage & Morals in Islam.* Vancouver: Vancouver Islamic Educational Foundation, 1990.

Sadat, Jihan. *A Woman of Egypt.* New York: Simon & Schuster, 1987.

Sahebjani, Freidoune. *The Stoning of Soraya M.* New York: Arcade, 1994.

Sale, George, trans. *The Koran.* London: Frederick Warne.

Shaarawi, Huda. *Harem Years: The Memoirs of an Egyptian Feminist (1879–1924).* New York: The Feminist Press, 1987.

al-Shaykh, Hanan. *The Story of Zahra.* London: Quartet, 1986.

Steegmuller, Francis, trans. and ed. *Flaubert in Egypt: A Sensibility on Tour.* London: Michael Haag Ltd., 1983.

Tucker, Judith E., ed. *Arab Women: Old Boundaries, New Frontiers.* Bloomington: Indiana University Press, 1993.

Women's Society of the Islamic Republic of Iran. Articles and Speeches Delivered at the First International Congress on Woman and World Islamic Revolution. February 1989.

INDEX